EVOLUTION: R.I.P.

John Thomas

Evolution: R.I.P.

Published in Great Britain by Thomas Winter Associates Ltd
www.twa-uk.com

Cover image iStockphoto.com
Illustrations by Bob Cooke

PREFACE

FACT AND FICTION In this devastating expose of the shocking facts that destroy the fiction of evolution that has hoodwinked the intellectual elite of the western world for over a century, Random House author John Thomas shows that Charles Darwin's theory is, on close inspection, found to be a complete tissue of half-truths, unwarranted assumption, deliberately vague verbosity and wishful thinking. It is in fact little more than an atheistic faith whereby "all things are possible" for the true believer - as with the deluded Darwin himself.

PREPOSTEROUS NONSENSE No wonder it is reported that biologists and mathematicians brave enought to risk their careers by querying the revered dogma, now see it for the preposterous nonsense it is -- totally unfit to explain the incredible "complexity within complexity" of the "simplest" living organism. Let alone sex, male and female forms, instinct, mind or emotion, etc. So, on yer bike, Dr Dawkins, you have been rumbled! And step aside you cowering coprolites, for the game is up, and the word is out, on the streets - Evolution is bunk and should now be quietly layed to rest with Darwin and the Dodo.

THE CRISIS IN CREATIONISM The report is must reading for any Christian person looking for a simple but technically accurate explanation of the pros and cons of the evolution/creation debate - and why it is, despite the glaring errors of evolution, that creationists frequently find themselves regarded by the media, school boards, law courts, and the scientific community as superstitious peasants. Sadly, although creationism is in crisis, it is also in stubborn denial of the facts - once again bringing the Bible into scientific disrepute, as in the days of Galileo.

THE LITERAL TRUTH OF GENESIS By revisiting and updating the oddly neglected old-earth, gap- or G-Theory teachings of Thomas Chalmers and Rev. William Buckland, Oxford University's very first professor of geology, our author discovers new insights that confirm the scientific accuracy of the Genesis account of creation.

AN OLD EARTH Although young-earth creationists vehemently reject the possibility of an old earth, using specious scriptural arguments, equally devout but professionally qualified believers, such as the members of the Affiliation of Christian Geologists and the Society of Ordained Scientists know better, but do little to publicize their position at the present time. Hopefully, the time for change has come.

CONTENTS

PART 1

G-THEORY
(THE REAL ORIGIN OF SPECIES)

1.1

THE GENESIS ALTERNATIVE

Although Charles Darwin's seductive theory of the origin of species by means of evolution has beguiled the intellectual elite of the western world for over a century, many people, even Nobel scientists, still cannot conceive that the incredible complexity and elegant design now revealed by the electron microscope in the simplest living organism, or even a single cell, could possibly have originated from the accumulation of random DNA copying errors when some primitive common ancestor somehow learned to reproduce. Let alone discover sex, with independent male and female forms, or mind, instinct and emotion, or even assemble the DNA itself from individual, inert atoms.

In fact, many readers may be surprised to learn that, despite the massive media hype, and evolution's pervasive influence in every university science course and biology textbook,   Darwin's theory still continues to fail two simple scientific tests he set for it himself, and still lacks a credible mechanism, as honest insiders will admit. A truly astonishing state of affairs.

Despite irresponsible claims by the BBC that "evolution is a fact", it remains at best, a half truth -- for although the limit-*ed* variation now called "micro-evolution" that shaped Darwin's thinking is a fact of life, as exploited by plant and cattle breeders for thousands of years to produce new varieties, its   limit-*less* extrapolation to try to account for the creation of totally new organisms by the myth of "macro-evolution" is still unjustified by the findings of geology and the fossil record, as we shall see.   Evolution is in fact a gargantuan fraud, perpetrated by a desperate and disillusioned man, as every Christian person should understand and help expose.

A FAITH

Nevertheless, as we shall see, evolution persists because for many intellectuals, and atheists in particular, it is a self-evident Truth, a seductive concept they eagerly embrace as a "faith", no real proof actually needed, ever confident the elusive missing mechanism will one day be discovered. They want to believe it. And like the tragic Darwin himself, they seemingly have to believe it.

Meanwhile, on the other hand, as evolutionists await that elusive epiphany, well-meaning creationists, desperate to deny Darwin the "deep time" his theory demands, also continue to stretch our credibility to the limit by insisting that the earth is only six thousand years old, and that the bulk of its vast rock strata, extinct fossil beds, and useful oil and gas and mineral deposits were formed in a matter of months by Noah's Flood. So, what can be done? Can two wrongs finally make a right?

MOONSHINE!
To young-earth "creationists" I would pose one simple question. If the earth and universe are only six thousand years old, when did the moon (and also every planet NASA surveys) reach it present devastated condition? Did God create it like that, and if not, then where in human history is that catastrophic event recorded? Surely it would be found in the ancient writings of many peoples. The best answer one leading creationist could offer me was that "It had something to do with Noah's Flood". Why must educated Christian people insist on bringing the Bible into scientific disrepute like that?

Although young-earth creationists reject the possibility of an old earth, equally devout and professionally qualified believers, such as the members of the "Affiliation of Christian Geologists" (http://www.wheaton.edu/ACG) and the "Society of Ordained Scientists", happily subscribe to Buckland's view, but do little to publicize their position.

THE GENESIS ALTERNATIVE
Perhaps the time has come to reconsider a third, more credible possibility -- the Genesis alternative to evolution, or "G-Theory", a new and closer look at the oddly-neglected old-earth teachings of Oxford University's very first professor of geology, Rev. William Buckland. A simple literal reading of the Genesis account of creation that accommodates the latest facts of modern science and offers easier answers to the criticisms of evolutionists as it does so.

Since accurate Science and a right reading of the Bible, as the inspired word of God, should not be in conflict, G-Theory aims to harmonize the two and propose a simple new model for further study.

AN ECCENTRIC CLERGYMAN
William Buckland, as already mentioned, was a devout, if highly eccentric, clergyman who became the first professor of geology at Oxford University in 1818. As a Christian and a geologist, and fully awareof evolutionary ideas already extant at the time, he struggled to reconcile the avalanche of new

and bizarre fossil discoveries in the rock strata of southern England with what he had always assumed to be the truth of the Genesis account of Creation. Could Noah's Flood, for example, possibly be responsible for depositing all the thousands of feet depth of highly consolidated and often topsy-turvy and metamorphosed rock strata - whose fossils also revealed a very different world to ours, one populated by a wide range of now-extinct and often gigantic, repulsive and ferocious reptiles?

SATAN'S CREATURES
Fragments of undigested food that Buckland found in the fossilized intestinal remains of those fearsome creatures, including large lumps of faecal matter called coprolites, showed beyond doubt that their world had been one of horrific carnage, one inhabited by cannibalistic monsters that devoured even their own kind. No wonder they became known as "Satan's Creatures".

The discoveries and events that led Buckland to his new understanding are beautifully described by Deborah Cadbury in her superb book: "The Dinosaur Hunters".

MIND THE GAP
Forced to study Genesis anew, Buckland finally concluded: "Nowhere is it asserted that God created the heaven and the earth in the first day, but 'in the beginning'; this 'beginning' may be an epoch of unmeasured distance . . . during which all the physical operations disclosed by geology were going on . . . millions upon millions of years may have occupied the *indefinite interval* between the beginning in which God created heaven and earth, and the evening or the commencement of the first day of the Mosaic narrative". That interval came to be called "the Gap".

As we shall see later, Buckland's view of the antiquity of the earth seems to agree with that of geologist James Hutton who believed that God had used a previous age to prepare the earth for man's later occupation, so creating valuable mineral deposits and building materials such as clay, sand, gravel, limestone and marble.

However, the "Gap Theory" did not originate with Buckland, and has been traced by writers such as the late Arthur Custance as far back as the Early Christian Church Fathers. G-Theory attempts to harmonize this ancient belief with the findings of modern science -- as a more credible and scriptural alternative to young-earth creationism.

WAS OR BECAME?

Buckland's reading of Genesis 1:1 is supported by the King James Bible translation of this verse which suggest in the marginal rendering that the phrase "the world *was* without form and void" could equally well be translated as "the world *became* without form and void", suggesting again that something important happened to the original earth.

The Hebrew verb in question is the same one that appears later in the phrase: "the man *became* a living soul" (Genesis 2:7). Although some modern commentators reject this marginal rendering, it should be borne in mind that the language scholars commissioned to make the historic translation were of astonishing intellectual calibre, some of them having been able to read Greek and Hebrew as children at the age of five or six years old -- and not the victims of modern scholarly misconceptions.

THE GAP THEORY – RE-CREATION

In his detailed paper which discusses the much-misrepresented and exaggerated conflict between Christianity and the infant science of geology, "Genesis and Geology Unearthed", Rev. Michael Roberts says: "Chalmers is remembered for the Gap Theory on Genesis One, though he did not invent it. Under this theory, a 'gap' is postulated between the initial creation and the first day, during which all the geological strata were laid down."

He continues: "The work of the Six Days are in fact the Re-creating of the world from the original Chaotic creation. This exegesis . . . was *the dominant interpretation until the 1850s.*" Notice, however, that, contrary to what Roberts says, G-Theory does not suggest that the original creation was a *Chaotic* one.

To understand why this interpretation of Genesis, which has the "ring of truth", came to fall out of favour, I would direct readers to "The Creationists", by Ronald Numbers, which seems to lay the blame on an impressively detailed but erroneous book entitled "The Genesis Flood" by John Whitcomb and Henry Morris.

THE ANTIQUITY OF THE GLOBE

It may well be that Buckland was assisted, or influenced, in reaching his conclusions by a contemporary, Thomas Chalmers, a Scottish clergyman and university lecturer with a keen interest in science and a prolific writer on Biblical matters.

Chalmers also presented this theory during lectures on chemistry given at the University of St. Andrews during the winter of 1803-4, commenting: "By referring the origin of the globe to a higher antiquity than is [commonly assumed to have been] assigned to it by the writings of Moses, it has been said that geology undermines our faith in the inspiration of the Bible . . . This is a false alarm. The writings of Moses *do not fix the antiquity of the globe.* If they fix anything at all, it is only *the antiquity of the species*". Please note that key point – because we are often told that "The Bible says that the earth is only six thousand years old". Not so, as we shall see in detail later.

In fact, what Chalmers and Buckland realized was that Moses' statement in Exodus 20, that in six days God made heaven and earth and the sea and all that is in them, refers to the reformed heaven and earth of creation week, not the original ones created "In the beginning" -- as will become clear when we also take "a closer look" at the meticulous wording of the Genesis account.

1.2

AN OVERVIEW OF G-THEORY

KEY CONCEPTS

On the basis of these two key insights, namely that Genesis allows for the earth itself to very old, and that a prehistoric age seems to have preceded the present one, the following very simple alternative scenario suggests itself, rendering Darwin's theory of evolution redundant as it does so. Each point will be examined in more detail later:

1) There was pre-historic age prior to man, possibly lasting millions of years, during which the earth was inhabited by now-extinct creatures such dinosaurs - as evidenced by the fossil record.

2) Much or all of the flora and fauna of that pre-historic world were destroyed in one or a series of catastrophic mass extinctions, as geologists have discovered, leaving the earth in the empty and formless state described in the first verse of Genesis, possibly as the result of the same meteorite bombardment that destroyed the surface of the moon and planets.

3) Those extinct pre-historic organisms belonged to a separate, previous divine creation and were not ancestors of the flora and fauna of our present age - making Darwin's evolutionary "tree of life" a myth.

4) The record of that pre-historic world is written primarily in the fossil record and rock strata of the Paleozoic and Mesozoic eras, with the Genesis transition to our present age taking place somewhere in the Cenozoic era, probably as marked out by the more recently discovered K-T boundary.

5) Most rock strata, mineral beds, coal and oil deposits were formed in the pre-historic age, the impact of Noah's flood on the earth's topography probably being minimal, since that was not its purpose.

6) All organisms, in both the present and the pre-historic age were genetically engineered by God to mutate and vary in constructive manner "after their kind" - the limit-*ed* process of micro-evolution, as envisioned by evolutionist Derek Hough's "Self-developing Genome", and foreshadowed by the teachings of Lamarck.

7) Mutational changes, as exploited by plant and animal breeders for thousands of years, are constructive, not accidental, and take place within their basic bauplan or "kind". This creative process may be the function of the mass of non-coding DNA found in all organisms that scientists were too quick to dismiss as "junk DNA".

8) Gene expression is not the whole story of inheritance, and factors such as animal instinct , emotion and intelligence may be controlled, at least in some organisms, by a non-physical component or spirit, similar to the morphic field postulated by evolutionist Rupert Sheldrake.

9) Man has not descended from apes or any other organism. Although similarity in gene structures in various organisms is often cited as proof of descent from a common ancestor, based on the principle of "cladistics", it equally suggests a common designer.

10) Although the earth itself and the universe may be many millions of years old, as geologists and cosmologists suspect, man was only created approximately six thousand years ago.

11) Although G-Theory accepts radio-metric measurements in the millions of years for the age of the earth, it questions any measurement dating human remains in excess of the six thousand years suggested by the Bible. The dates allocated to various prehistoric rock strata and fossils by radiometric techniques are basically irrelevant, anyway, to an understanding of the origins and development of the earth's present organisms.

12) All radiometric methods involve assumptions, and are open to misapplication in complex situations. The assumptions and limitations of Carbon-14 dating are now known, and it may be that other techniques have as-yet-unsuspected technical weaknesses that render them equally unreliable.

13) The natural environment is metaphorical by design, and at the "fall

of man", when the first human beings rejected divine guidance in their affairs, the ecology changed to depict the evil end results of their chosen path - competition and greed, disease, violence and death.

14) The ecology created with and for man, as described in the Genesis account, was originally benign, and free from violence and killing, a condition that the Hebrew prophets tell us will one day be restored.

With this alternative scenario in mind, in Part 2 we shall examine, the supposed proofs of Charles Darwin's theory of evolution, the motivation behind it, and its real impact on our lives -- and in Part 3 we shall take a much closer look at the meticulously worded Genesis account of creation to find out what it really does say, and where scholars have misrepresented it.

PART 2

WHERE DARWIN WENT WRONG

2.1

THE DARWIN DELUSION

WHAT WAS DARWIN'S THEORY ANYWAY?

According to the "Oxford Dictionary of Biology": "Present day species *evolved* from *simpler* ancestral types by the process of *natural selection* acting on the *variability* found in populations . . ."

Thus the incredible diversity of life on earth is supposed to have developed, tiny variation by tiny variation, from a microscopic bundle of atoms that somehow organized themselves into "life" in a prehistoric pool of slime. That embryonic creation then discovered how to reproduce and diversify over billions of years. With Natural Selection discarding the "unfit" forms onto the compost pile of paleontology, so that only the "fittest" survived.

Darwin himself described this mythical process as follows: "If, then, animals and plants do vary, let it be ever so slightly, why should not variations or individual *differences*, which are in any way beneficial, be preserved and *accumulated* through natural selection?"

THE DELUSION

Notice, right here at the outset, the Darwin delusion. The fatal flaw in his theory. The school-boy error of insisting that since limit-*ed* variation in the offspring of organisms is an observed fact of life, as exploited by plant and animal breeders for thousands of years, then limit-*less* variation must also be possible. So that, given enough time, sufficient small variations could be sifted by Natural Selection and accumulated to turn a worm or a fish, for example, into a dog or a man, or even vice versa. And in so doing, generate a limitless range of "transitional forms", each one a tiny bit different to those before and after.

As Darwin himself was quick to point out, one obvious implication of this theory is that the overwhelmingly vast majority of fossils found in the earth's rock strata should be those of the zillions of unfit, imperfect transitional forms to which Natural Selection gave the thumbs down. For example, fish without proper scales or fins, sea creatures trying to grow legs, land animals trying to sprout wings, giraffe trying to elongate their short necks, etc., and ditto ad infinitum for any and every detail of their physiology.

Of course, they did not "try" to do anything, because all this imagined evolution, as now explained, supposedly resulted from the fortuitous accumulation of zillions of random accidental DNA copying errors when the organisms reproduced. That is the modern scientific theory as embraced by the ubiquitous Richard Dawkins and his followers.

GETTING ON THE RIGHT WAVELENGTH
However, according to another devout evolutionist, Derek Hough: "The idea that *innumerable random changes* in the genome can *accumulate* over time to eventually construct an organism as complex as the *human being is inconceivable on the grounds of improbability*". Inconceivable! Need we go any further? And is a human being nothing more than atoms and molecules anyway?

Speaking of biologists who blindly believe such infantile nonsense, Hough adds: "I find it very difficult to get onto their wavelength". So that, in promoting his new own-brand evolution theory that we shall discuss later, the honest Hough is happy to expose the errors and utter impossibility of the old. So according to Hough, Darwinism doesn't work! The cat is well and truly out of the bag already, and what page are we on?

MOVING ON FROM THAT DIFFICULTY
Darwin himself was forced to make the crucial admission that the fossil record in his day did not show the transitional forms his theory demanded, but just fully formed complex organisms. As is still the case today, a hundred and fifty years later, despite the desperate digging of armies of paleontologists all over the globe. Ah, well. "Moving on from that difficulty", as Darwin was fond of saying.

I SEE NO SHIPS!
Darwin insisted that even the tiny variation, as in a litter of kittens, for example, might be accumulated, generation by generation, and extrapolated ad infinitum in order to finally turn a cat into a totally new and different kind of creature. As Hough clearly understands, that assumption is as infantile and unscientific as extending a graph of the growth of a new puppy over its first few weeks of life to "prove" that in five years' time it will be the size of an elephant. Darwin's fundamental claim is that childish - an elementary "schoolboy" error. Not surprisingly, as we shall see, despite his genius, basic mathematics was

not his strong suit.

Darwin was, I suspect, fully aware of this fatal flaw. This leap from the known into the unknown. In fact he boldly added: "What *limit* can be put to this power, acting during long ages . . . favouring the good and rejecting the bad? *I can see no limit*". That reminds me of the admiral who put the telescope to his blind eye, and remarked: "Ships? What ships? I see no ships!"

DARWIN'S DESPERATION
Accordingly, in blissful ignorance of the complexities of genetics, cell structure, genes, jumping genes, master genes, slave genes, DNA, RNA and all the rest, Darwin deluded himself that evolution had simply happened - as the desperate hidden agenda we shall discuss later required. That desperation, incidentally, may have manifested itself in the severe psychosomatic illness he experienced -- emotional breakdowns and episodes of boils, vomiting, elephantiasis, rashes and heart palpitations.

Again, I suspect, the tormented Darwin knew he was talking nonsense, which helps explain why he delayed the publication of his book for 20 years. And was fortunate when he did publish it that nobody yet knew enough about the "complexity within complexity" of the natural world, or the content of the fossil record, to refute his deceptive claims. And why he himself was also led to comment: "The more important objections relate to questions on which we are confessedly ignorant - *nor do we know how ignorant we are*". Amen to that.

G-THEORY
Notice again in the Oxford Dictionary definition of evolution, the phrase that runs: "Present day species evolved from *simpler ancestral types* . . ." Readers may be surprised to realize that if we equate those "ancestral types" to the unspecified number of organisms, such as horses and cows and cats and dogs, whose creation is described in the Genesis account, then this definition of evolution would actually be in total harmony with the Bible. However, as we shall see, Darwin was not happy with that possibility at all.

Science allows, for example, that all the dog breeds we now have could have originated from one original pair, a fact also implied in Genesis when it says that God commanded creatures to reproduce "after their kind". That carefully constructed phrase allows dogs to vary massively in shape, color, size, hair length, etc. and even assume giant proportions. But they still remain "dogs", rather than turning into some other "kind" of animal such as sheep or horses.

That in fact is a key element of G-Theory teaching, a common sense interpretation of Genesis that was promoted decades before Darwin by Oxford University's very first professor of geology and an ordained minister, William Buckland. It was in fact Buckland who analyzed the fossilized faeces called "coprolites" that he discovered at Lyme Regis to prove that some extinct creatures had been carnivores, even eating their own kind like cannibals.

Whereas the claims of young-earth creationists are seen as bringing the Bible into scientific disrepute, G-Theory accommodates the facts of science and offers easy answers to evolutionist claims -- suggesting that the meticulously worded Genesis account of creation is scientifically accurate and literally true.

A PRE-HISTORIC WORLD?
As a result of his massive practical experience as a fossil hunter, Buckland rejected the early evolutionary ideas extant at the time, and maintained that the extinct organisms whose fossils he discovered had existed on earth long before man, in a pre-Adamic or pre-historic age. Genesis, he claimed, clearly allowed for that possibility, a previous and separate creation.

His ideas, which we shall discuss in more detail later, were set out in a two-volume work "Geology and Mineralogy", commissioned as part of "The Bridgewater Treatises on the Power, Wisdom and Goodness of God as Manifested in Creation". Incidentally, it was also Buckland who discovered and named the Megalosaurus, that being the first scientifically valid name given to a dinosaur. He believed it to be a giant, extinct lizard.

MICRO-EVOLUTION OR VARIABILITY
The process of limit-*ed* change, within the bounds of the original Genesis "kinds", as demonstrated by dogs and cats and pigeons, the *variability* observed and exploited by breeders for thousands of years before Darwin came on the scene, has more recently come to be called "*micro-evolution*". So Darwin's elementary and crucial mistake was to extrapolate the limit-*ed* "*micro-evolution*" (fact) observed by breeders ad infinitum, way beyond the evidence of the available data, into the mythical limit-*less* process of "*macro-evolution*" (fiction).

Confusing micro-evolution fact and macro-evolution fiction, the BBC, for example still insist that "evolution is a measurable, *indisputable fact*". They are forced to admit, however, that the "*debate*" about the "*precise mechanisms that drive evolution*" continues to "*engage them*", with "*academic niceties being batted to and fro at conferences and symposia*". The simple fact of the matter is that the sophisticated mechanism of micro-evolution was designed into the Genesis kinds at their creation, but no mechanism beyond random DNA copying errors has ever been found to justify the mythical concept of macro-evolution. Note well how the BBC insists that evolution is a "fact", when it is actually no more than a dodgy theory with no credible mechanism -- a scandalous attempt to hoodwink the public.

But more of that later, when we discover that evolutionists increasingly cling to Darwin's theory as a matter of "faith" as they still desperately search for that mythical mechanism. The more honest among them admit that it continues to fail to be validated by two simple scientific tests Darwin himself devised for it.

Just as the variation of micro-evolution occurs in this age, as demonstrated by animal and plant breeds and varieties, there is no doubt it also occurred, perhaps even more prolifically, in the extinct organisms of the pre-Adamic age. As a result, all kinds of dinosaurs and varieties of strange aquatic and amphibious creatures existed, all diversifying within their original "kinds".

DESCENT WITH MODIFICATION
Darwin was correct in claiming that there has been "descent with modification" of both ancestral plant and animal forms over the millennia. This is why, for example, the cattle shown in old paintings look somewhat different to modern breeds, as he observed. However, the crucial truth of G-Theory is that such *descent*, in this age, has been from the set of organisms created in Genesis, and their *modification* within their Genesis "kinds" or "bauplans".

As a result, dogs have remained dogs, and cows have remained cows, and roses have remained roses, and always will do. The consequence is that present day organisms have not descended from extinct "prehistoric" forms, as evolutionists fondly imagine - organisms which, according to G-theory, belonged to a pre-Adamic age anyway. A separate creation

However, Darwin was not happy with Genesis because he wanted those "ancestral types" to number very few indeed. Preferably just one - thereby envisioning them as something far different and more "primitive" than the cats and dogs and cows and other kinds of creatures we are now familiar with.

LAMARCK AND THE SELF-DEVELOPING GENOME
As we shall see later, the earlier evolutionary theory of Jean Baptiste de Lamarck, which soon fell out of favour when Darwin came on the scene, actually provided a more accurate description of the workings of nature than that proposed by Darwin, even though it still could not explain it.

What Lamarck had theorized, but could not explain, was that rather than populations of organisms being sifted and sorted by a process of Natural Selection in order to fit them to their ecological niches, they seemed to actually sense the needs of their chosen environment and vary or mutate accordingly, but in a constructive manner. As a result, as Darwin himself later concluded, organisms appear to possess some kind of sophisticated "feedback" mechanism designed to bring out useful mutant forms, the genetic patterns of which may have been dormant within them since their original creation.

Such a store of potentially useful mutant forms - such as longer hair for cattle in colder climates, or earlier and later fruiting trees, etc. - Darwin once alluded to as "being written in invisible ink", and might be regarded as a kind of "genetic wardrobe". This may well prove to be the function of the mass of supposedly surplus, non-coding DNA in organisms that science currently dismisses so lightly as "junk".

Some biologists, such as avowed evolutionist Derek Hough, are now beginning to suspect that organisms may contain a "Self-developing Genome", an incredibly sophisticated mechanism with the power to respond in creative and meaningful ways to perceived needs and environmental pressures, but still within the bounds of their "kind".

NO NEED FOR MISSING LINK
It seems significant therefore that Lamarck's understanding, like Hough's, of how organisms adapt to ecological niches did not require the trial-and-error creation of the myriad "unfit" forms that Darwin's theory required - the elusive "missing links" that, according to Darwin, should comprise the vast majority of fossil forms ever found in any and all strata. As a result of a growing disillusionment with Darwinism, Lamarckism may be experiencing a revival. The creative mechanism involved, however, requires a sophisticated inner complexity that cannot begin to be explained as the result of the accumulation of random DNA copying errors, as Hough admits.

COMPLEXITY WITHIN COMPLEXITY

So, although evolution has hoodwinked the intellectual elite of the Western world for more than a century, insiders increasingly admit that Darwin's theory has now proved unfit to explain the complexity-within-complexity revealed by the scanning electron microscope and new genomic techniques in even the "simplest" living organisms.

As a result, the theory is now increasingly regarded by thoughtful biologists and mathematicians as simplistic nonsense, and devoid of credible proof. As already mentioned, however, many still cling to it as a matter of hopeful faith.

EVO-DEVO

However, devotees of the new Darwinian deity "Evo-Devo", have a more fundamentalist sort of faith - "the science of Evolutionary Development". Evo-Devo supposedly does not need Darwin's "innumerable random changes". In fact, according to the New York Times: "Evo-Devo researchers are finding that the evolution of complex new forms, rather than requiring *many* new mutations or many new genes *as had long been thought*, can instead be accomplished by a *much simpler process requiring no more than tweaks to already existing genes*".

The point they play down however, is that since Evo-Devo deals with the mysteries of "embryonic development", those *already existing genes* are indeed already existing in the complex organisms they study - and in an amazingly highly structured form, whose sophistication science is only just beginning to appreciate.

Up-and-coming Evo-Devo evangelist Professor Sean B. Carroll enlightens us: "The development of an organism - how one end gets designated as the head or the tail, how feet are *enticed* to grow at the end of a leg rather than at the wrist - is controlled by *a hierarchy of genes, with master genes at the top controlling a next tier of genes, controlling a next and so on*." By my count that makes at least four tiers of interacting genes! And all that complexity packed inside every single cell in our bodies! Gadzooks!

UPWARDLY MOBILE ERRORS!

And where did those hierarchies of "already existing" master genes, slave genes, or even one single gene, come from? The only answer evolution has is, by the fortuitous accumulation of ambitious and evidently upwardly mobile random and accidental DNA copying errors when their supposed ancestral "organisms" reproduced. When quizzed about such fundamental matters, top Cambridge University Professor of Evolutionary Paleobiology, Simon Conway Morris simply replies that such matters are "below the Darwinian horizon".

ABIOGENESIS

The phrase "below the Darwinian horizon" is not an admission of the failure of evolution, but meant to inform us that the pesky problem of explaining how any kind of life actually got started in the first place has a special theory all to itself – namely "Abiogenesis". And, we are assured, already, "several hypotheses about early life have been proposed". Darwin himself, however, simply assumed it. No problem! Don't confuse me with the facts!

Like evolution, Abiogenesis is still just another ambitious but unproven belief. However, the true believers kid themselves that because they keep making up elaborate theories and molecular models that then fail the tests of experimentation, they are actually practising true science.

As they admit, although much scientific work has been done in testing different hypotheses relating to abiogenesis, even the sequence of chemical events that led to the first nucleic acids is not known. However, "Several hypotheses about early life have been proposed." Sounds good, so please keep the funding coming folks! We know we can do it!

SEEING THE LIGHT

His eyes tightly wide shut against reality, Carroll then enthuses: "This is the illumination of the utterly dark". Kidding himself that he is explaining the origins of life, he is simply prodding and probing at the incredible genomic structures that God designed into all organisms at their creation. Yes, the good professor can tweak the "toolbox genes" of fruit flies that control their body morphology and cause them to grow extra eyes and legs in the wrong places, but so what?

Sadly, since the clever Carroll has total faith in the Truth of evolution, he takes the very existence of such incredible genetic complexity as absolute proof that evolution works – a classic display of circular reasoning.

BLOODLESS FISH

In "The Making of the Fittest", Dr. Carroll does in fact provide the perfect illustration of Hough's Self-developing genome at work in enabling an organism to adapt to its environment. Although the boastful Dr. Carroll promises to "vaporize" the arguments of Darwin's detractors, his book actually does a superb job of revealing yet more of the incredible complexity-within-complexity of God's creation, and the utter impossibility of macro-evolution.

For example, although the textbooks assert that all vertebrates must have red blood because of the hemoglobin required to transport oxygen around their bodies, the icefish found in Antarctic seas have transparent blood that looks like water, and virtually is water. DNA techniques can now reveal that the two genes that normally "code" for the creation of hemoglobin in fish have somehow "gone extinct" in this case. In his book, Carroll has much to say about such "fossilized genes" that organisms may still possess but apparently never use, because they have been "switched off", perhaps not being needed in their present environment.

COORDINATED INVENTIONS
In explaining how the icefish survive in freezing temperatures without red blood cells and the hemoglobin that normally acts as an antifreeze, Carroll lists the following design changes from normal fish: larger gills, scaleless skin with unusually large capillaries, large heart and bigger blood volumes. In fact, he says, the fish has "many cardiovascular adaptations" that somehow get the vital oxygen to its muscles. Survival has even required that the micro-structure of the "tubules" in its cells be modified for freezing conditions.

Carroll comments that a number of other *coordinated* "inventions" were also needed – such as special "antifreeze proteins" in its blood plasma, without which the fish would turn into a block of ice. He then attempts to describe in terms of amino acids how "many more genes" must have been modified to make these adaptations possible. And again I say "Gadzooks!"

The adaptations he describes are truly amazing, but the fish still remains a fish. However, evolutionists seriously expect us to believe that all these "inventions" resulted ultimately from the fortuitous coordination of zillions of random accidental DNA copying errors over gazillions of years, with Natural Selection tossing to one side all those that did not work properly. As evolutionist Derek Hough would admit, such claims are utter impossibility, irrational childish nonsense and an affront to any sound-minded person who has not yet nibbled the magic mushroom of Darwinism.

A FREUDIAN SLIP
Then, in a Freudian slip that contradicts the whole concept of Natural Selection, Carroll comments that the creative power of evolution "tinkers with the materials available" and that "I have to admire the icefishes' grit and ingenuity". No, Dr. Carroll, it is the ingenuity of God that you need to admire – the creative genius that engineered the Self-developing Genome that Derek Hough has postulated into every organism on the planet.

Incidentally, one of the elegant features of the divine design process involved here is a classic creative reversal, exploiting the fact that since oxygen is actually more soluble and therefore more readily available in cold arctic waters than in warm, the required amounts can be absorbed directly through the fish's scaleless skin, rather than by the more obvious approach of refining the gill structure. That is real science at work, Dr. Carroll, not the pseudo-science of evolutionary superstition.

A LESS AMBITIOUS THEORY
Notice that Darwin's own theory, as described previously, was a whole lot less ambitious than that popularly portrayed and promoted in the media by the likes of Oxford academic Richard Dawkins and his sidekick, co-defender of the faith, Prof. Steve Jones.

Darwin made no claims, for example, that his theory could explain the ultimate origin of life, or mind, or consciousness, or emotion or instinct. Nor did he exclude God from the equation, but acknowledged Him as the original creator of "life" - although in the form of only one or a handful of prototype organisms.

That said however, Darwin did later write in a private notebook that he thought reverence for God was just a chemical reaction in the brain, and that it was arrogant to think otherwise. Naturally, he kept such radical ideas under his hat, so we don't hear much about them. How odd therefore, that befuddled officials of the Church of England have recently seen fit to issue a grovelling apology to this sad critic of Christianity for ever having doubted his infantile theory in the first place.

EVERY WHICH WAY BUT UP!
Perhaps the Church of England officials who issued a posthumous apology to Darwin for ever having doubted him should have saved their praise for maverick physicist and Nobel Prize contender, Carl Woese, who claims that "early" organisms did not evolve *vertically*, a la Darwin, by the magical

acquisition of new genetic units from parents and ancestors -- but *horizontally* by the donation of useful bits and pieces from other denizens of the microbial morass, even other species.

So impressed is the New Scientist magazine by this bit of lateral thinking that they assure readers: "Woese has done more for biology writ large than any biologist in history, including Darwin." Wow!

THE MOST IMPORTANT PROBLEM IN SCIENCE NEGLECTED

Well aware of the scientific sham and utter confusion in conventional evolutionary circles, Woese himself comments: "It is a case of scientific *complacency* . . . biologists were seduced by their own success into *thinking they had found the final truth.*" As a result , he adds, they: "*neglected to study the most important problem in science -- the nature of the evolutionary process* . . . Most biologists, following Francis Crick, simply *supposed* . . . "

What Woese is admitting is the shocking fact that Darwin's theory has *no credible mechanism* for the evolution of any living organism at all. They simply "supposed" it happened, then opened up their thesaurus of vague verbs to paper over the gaps in the fossil record without actually explaining anything in cause-and-effect detail -- e.g. evolved, developed, acquired, learned, invented, etc. They just know it happened, so let's not get too bothered about the details. Be creative! Use your imagination! As the honest among them will admit, evolution is simply a wishful atheistic belief, a "faith".

SIMPLY CANNOT EXPLAIN THE GENETIC CODE!

Speaking of the "exquisitely tuned" genetic DNA code that people like prolific professor Sean Carroll are busy investigating, Woese continues: "Darwinian evolution *simply cannot explain* how such a code could arise."

If that's not plain enough, he adds: "*Nothing in the modern synthesis explains* the most fundamental steps in early life", such as "how evolution could have produced the genetic code and the basic genetic machinery used by all organisms".

THE WRONG KIND OF EVOLUTION!

Having exposed the bankrupt state of the evolution movement for all to see, Woese then claims that his new own-brand of evolution with added vitamins can explain these miracles -- or will do once he gets the bones out of it. Just so we know that he is right, he assures us that: "Everyone has been thinking in terms of the wrong kind of evolution" -- i.e. vertical rather then horizontal..

With one of his biological buddies adding: "The process of evolution just isn't what most evolutionary biologists think it is." Ah well, moving on from that difficulty, as Chas used to say . . .

KNOCK KNOCK

Very important mistakes can be made by blindly trusting logic and supposed fact over intuition. The reason is that the most convincing argument is frequently limited by ignorance of the full facts, and is often based on unwarranted and unquestioned assumptions. This is why it is well known in political circles that governmental quick-fix solutions to particular problems frequently end up making bad situations worse. Beeching, for example, in the 1960s, persuaded the government of the day to rip up half of Britain's railway tracks. Then everyone wondered why the roads got bottle-necked and polluted by big trucks and the unforeseen growth in car ownership.

If someone comes knocking on your door carrying a big Bible and is allowed to engage you in a discussion of the purpose of life, the chances are they will have far more technical knowledge of the good book than you do, and be easily able to tie you up in proverbial knots and prove you "wrong". Hopefully however, your intuition will warn you that despite their impressive knowledge, seemingly logical arguments, and their confident quoting of scriptures, they are actually talking sinister nonsense, and looking to lure you into some kind of fanatical sect intent on taking control of your thinking and your life.

Perhaps you are now ahead of me, in perceiving the parallel between false religion and the modern myth of macro-evolution, with its confident and smooth Dawkinesque arguments, and glossed-over assumptions that actually reflect a quite superficial understanding of the miraculous complexities of any and all living organisms. As already noted, for example, despite regular pronouncements in the press regarding the "human genome project", science does not actually understand the function of the bulk of the DNA found in living organisms, blithely dismissing it as "junk".

For anybody who has ever watched puppies at play, or a bumble bee at work, or a robin perched on the handle of a fork in the garden on a cold frosty morning, intuition alone, without resort to any kind of scientific reasoning, should be sufficient to assure them that evolution is bunk.

PERSISTENT PONTIFICATION

Perhaps this explains why, despite the persistent pontification of evolutionary egg-heads such as Dawkins and Carroll, a recent opinion poll conducted for the

BBC found that less than half of Britons accept the theory of evolution as the best description for the origins of life. And more than 40% of those questioned believe that creationism or intelligent design (ID) should be formally taught in school science lessons, as do a third of school teachers.

People are, of course, rightly impressed by the achievements of science, but compared to the complexity-within complexity of the living cell, our cars, computers and TV sets are on the technical level of a child's mud pie.

Nevertheless, let us now take a very close look at the supposed "facts" and "proofs" of evolution - and the marketing of the Darwin delusion that has hoodwinked the intellectual elite and the mass media of most of the Western world for the past hundred and fifty years.

As we do so, be on the lookout for glib and unfounded assertions of evolutionary faith that actually explain and prove nothing, such as one infantile explanation of the Cambrian Explosion, the sudden appearance in the fossil record of more than a hundred different kinds of amazingly complex creatures out of nowhere - Quote: "They must have invented toolbox genes". Easy when you know how!

2.2

EVOLUTION FAILS FOSSIL TEST 1

Despite intense efforts by paleontologists, evolution has failed, and continues to fail, on two counts out of two to be validated by the practical requirements of the Scientific Method. Darwin himself was fully aware of this fact, as he admits in his book. But "moving on from that difficulty", as he puts it, he goes on to expound his theory anyway. These misgivings clearly help explain why he delayed so long in submitting his manuscript for publication, and only did so when fellow British naturalist Alfred Russel Wallace came up with the same idea and threatened to pip him to the post and grab the glory.

THE SCIENTIFIC METHOD

The scientific method requires a theory to do two things:

1) Give a plausible explanation of an important phenomenon.
2) Provide the basis for logical predictions, sometimes called "hypotheses", that can then be tested by experiment to find out if the theory is correct in its implications.

Scientific hypotheses normally concern the future - suggesting, for example, that if the theory is correct and we were to do *this*, then *that* should happen as a result. Formulating an hypothesis makes it possible to design experiments that can be carried out to validate the theory.

Such experiments could be devised for the theory of evolution, if only we had the time to see them through. If the human lifespan were several million years or more, we could wait and see if one kind of organism could really evolve into a totally different kind. Unfortunately we don't live that long, so what we have to do instead is look in the opposite direction, backwards into the past. So that if evolution is true, an examination of the fossil record should show that simpler organisms have evolved into more complex ones, leaving behind a vast graveyard of the failed misfits that Darwin requires.

VARIABLES

However, experimental success in validating any hypothesis requires complex situations to be simplified, so that key variables can be identified, controlled and then tweaked one by one to test their effect.

Nature and living things however, are vastly more complex than the copper wires, electrons and lumps of silicon found in a physics lab, and the interplay of variables often unfathomable. Which is why it was once observed that putting a man on the moon was far easier than educating rebellious children. Electrons obey laws. Children make their own choices.

Hence the hopelessness of Charles Darwin's heroic but now discredited attempt to create a unifying theory of biology on the basis of the scant knowledge available to him at the time. And conversely, the difficulty, even now, of our tracing out cause-and-effect chains and accumulating sufficient detailed knowledge of nature to put that naïve but seductive theory to a reliable and conclusive experimental test - which explains why the delusion has managed to survive for so long. Hence, also, the need for G-Theory which re-directs us to the only truly reliable source of fundamental scientific information regarding the origins of man, the universe and life on earth – firm foundational knowledge on which science can safely build.

DARWIN'S FIRST FAILURE

After cheerfully admitting in "The Origin of Species" that his theory requires "*infinitely numerous organisms*" and that "*innumerable transitional forms must have existed*", Darwin asks: "Why then is not *every geological formation* and *every stratum full* of such intermediate links?" Why not indeed! Evolutionists are still struggling to answer those questions.

Darwin even admits this error, adding: "Geology assuredly *does not* reveal any such *finely-graduated* organic chain; and this, perhaps, is the most *obvious* and *serious* objection to my theory".

However, in defiance of his own logic, Darwin then predicts that the transitionals would somehow be found in the future, as more strata were explored. He was so bold as to say that people should "*rightly reject*" his theory if the fossils did not appear as the result of further geological investigation. We are still waiting!

EVERY STRATUM FULL!

As already explained, Darwin saw evolution as the accumulation of minute variations, like those found in a litter of puppies, for example. A pup having legs a tiny bit longer and stronger than the rest, would supposedly be a bit more "fit" to survive and reproduce than others. As a result, given enough time, Natural Selection working on zillions of such finely graduated and random variations over gazillions of generations, supposedly has the power to change a fin into a leg, a scale into a feather, a fish into a frog, and a worm into a mammal, even a human being.

Darwin's intermediate forms, then, were not the kind evolutionists claim to have discovered in recent decades - fully functioning and unique creatures such as Archeopteryx, which had some fully developed features of a bird and some of a reptile. Or Acanthostega, a fish-like creature with fully developed little legs and webbed hands and feet and lots of fingers and toes. Darwin's imaginary extinct intermediates were not perfectly formed half-way houses in between the grouping of modern classification systems. And there needed to be zillions of them anyway for each organism, forming "*finely-graduated organic chains*" – and with "*every stratum*" required to be "*full of such intermediate links*".

That then, is what any and *every* fossil bearing stratum should look like. Packed with unfit intermediate forms. As a result, the evidence of evolution should be very clear and obvious, but it is not. Because that is not what the fossil record looks like. Even with only a tiny percentage of the fossil record examined, as in Darwin's day, that is what it should have looked like even then. But it did not! I suspect, therefore, that the desperate Darwin knew his theory was nonsense from the beginning. But he brazenly refused to accept the facts. He could not accept the facts.

AD NAUSEAM

Just in case we have not made the point clear enough, Darwin also said: "According to the theory of natural selection, an interminable number of intermediate forms must have existed . . . why do we not see these linking forms all around us?" Why indeed? And: "Why does not every collection of fossil remains afford plain evidence of the gradation and mutation of the forms of life?" There is a very simple answer to that question, Chas. Your theory is coprolitic in the extreme!

As already noted, I believe that in his heart the tormented Darwin know his theory was nonsense from the start, which is why he also admits: "I have felt these difficulties far too heavily during many years to doubt their weight".

Little wonder then that in 1979, and fully aware of Darwin's precise statements, University of Chicago paleontologist David Raup felt obliged to admit that even some 120 years after Darwin, with our knowledge of the fossil record greatly expanded: "We now have a quarter of a million fossil species but *the situation hasn't changed much.* The record of evolution is still surprisingly jerky and, ironically, we have *even fewer* examples of evolutionary transitions than we had in Darwin's time." Thank you, Dr. Raup. Next witness, please,

CRIPES! IT MUST BE THE THEORY!
And just a few years ago the British "Manchester Guardian" newspaper cited the following significant admission from another grand master of evolution: "If life had evolved into its wondrous profusion of creatures little by little, Dr. Eldredge argues, then *one would expect to find fossils of transitional creatures* which were a bit like what went before them and a bit like what came after. But *no one has yet found any evidence of such transitional creatures.* This oddity has been attributed to gaps in the fossil record which gradualists expected to fill when rock strata of the proper age had been found. In the last decade, however, geologists have found rock layers of all divisions of the last 500 million years and *no transitional forms were contained in them.* If it is not the fossil record which is incomplete then *it must be the theory."* Oh dear!

More recently, in his book "Evolution: A Case of Stating the Obvious", forthright evolutionist Derek Hough laments that the situation has not improved, saying: "The continuing search has not helped." Oh dear, dear!

FEELING HIS PAIN
Hough's expert opinion is confirmed in the recently published "Evolution for Dummies" which says of Darwin's distress at the clear lack of intermediate fossils: "Today's scientists *feel his pain*", adding that although they know better where to look and have more people out there doing the looking "*they still struggle to find them*". They are, in effect, looking for the end of the evolutionary rainbow.

Perhaps we should give the final word here to the prolific evolutionary writer, Professor Steve Jones, who says in his book "*Almost Like a Whale*": "The fossil record - *in defiance of Darwin's whole idea* of gradual change - often makes *great leaps from one form to the next.* Far from the display of intermediates to be expected from slow advance through natural selection *many species appear without warning,* persist in fixed form and disappear, leaving no descendants." And your point is, Prof?

He continues: "Geology *assuredly does not reveal* any finely graduated organic chain, and this is the most obvious and *gravest objection* which can be urged against the theory of evolution." Note the words "assuredly does not reveal"! So the objection is not merely "grave", Steve, it is crushing and fatal.

FITTER FOSSILS?
At this point, evolutionists will of course accuse me of "quote mining", even lying, if I fail to mention that Steve Jones then goes on to try to explain away the lack of fossil evidence by pointing out that most dead organisms do not get preserved. How odd, however, that all that do get preserved are the fully functioning ones, not the plethora of failed misfits and imaginary intermediates. Not quite what Darwin had in mind, I think, when he spoke of the survival of the fittest!

A PUNCTURED THEORY
In an earlier attempt to explain away the painful the fact that the fossil record shows only fully formed and functioning creatures, that suddenly appear then disappear, without zillions of unfit forms in between, evolution superstars Stephen Gould and Niles Eldredge devised their modified theory of "punctuated equilibrium". According to this theory, evolution supposedly occurs in explosive but inexplicable abrupt leaps from one complex form to another totally different one. This is usually followed by a mysterious extinction, rather than in the tiny steps Darwin required.

What Gould actually believed was that any changes in a mainstream population would get absorbed and diluted. But somewhere tucked away in isolated populations on the fringes, the supposed changes could be preserved and accumulated, and be less likely to be found in the fossil record. But when they were, the change would look abrupt, not gradual.

It was in fact Gould who once admitted, to his eternal regret, that: "The *extreme rarity of transitional forms* in the fossil record persists as the *trade secret* of paleontology", and that "The evolutionary trees that adorn our textbooks have data only at the tips and nodes of their branches; *the rest is inference,* however reasonable, *not the evidence of fossils.*" What an astonishing admission! But more about those textbooks in a moment.

DON'T BELIEVE ALL YOU READ IN SCIENCE TEXTBOOKS!
In seeking acceptance from the scientific establishment for their revolutionary new theory of punctuated equilibrium - which actually postulated gaps in

the fossil record - Eldredge and Gould lamented "the impact of textbooks in molding the thought of new professionals", and the sad fact that, intake by intake, a few classic college tomes dispensed "normal science" i.e. orthodox views sometimes quite unfounded by fact, in particular the claim that the fossil record showed gradual and continuous evolution.

One of the cited texts ran: "*Weighty evidence* for the *progressive evolution* of organisms is afforded by *fossil transitional series* . . .*" As Eldredge and Gould point out, that confident assertion was completely untrue – it was false, scandalous and contrary to the facts, as their own punctuated equilibrium data showed.

Nevertheless, the textbook continued: "*. . . a considerable number are known to us*, not withstanding the imperfection of the fossil record". Again, that "weighty evidence" being foisted onto gullible students was completely false, and unfounded by the facts of the fossil record.

However, in keeping with comments still found in modern encyclopedias, the text then asserted that these transitional forms provided "*. . . a practically unbroken morphic chain*", thereby giving us "*documentary evidence of gradual evolution*". In a kind of literary cannibalism, such false claims get repeated over and over again as lazy textbook writers trust the expertise of others and uncritically purloin and repeat falsified information from the books of the old.

SORRY, CHAPS! – YOU'VE PROVED THE WRONG THING!
Commenting on the subjective nature of the scientific enterprise and the desperate distortions of evolutionists bent on validating Darwin's demented theory of gradual development at all costs, the exasperated Eldredge and Gould comment: "All observation is colored by theory and *expectation*" – which is perhaps why Peter Medawar once commented: "Innocent, unbiased observation is a *myth*".

Then, in a comment that seems relevant to the science of Cladistics which has revitalized the search for the end of the evolutionary rainbow in the last ten years or so, Eldredge and Gould themselves continue: "That *theory dictates what one sees*, cannot be stated too strongly". In other words, they see what they want to see! They make the facts fit the theory! It cannot be stated too strongly! But more about Cladistic analysis in a moment.

Meanwhile, Eldredge and Gould continue: "Paleontologists should recognize that *much of their thought is conditioned* by a peculiar perspective that they must bring to the study of life". Our thoughts become "conditioned" when we act on the basis of unquestioned assumption and blind prejudice.

Astonishingly, what Eldredge and Gould are pointing out is that these evolutionists were so keen to prove Darwin right that they actually *falsified the facts* of the fossil record, proving black is white, blinded by their belief into seeing only what they wanted to see – i.e. a gradual evolution of organisms, when what the record really showed were gaps! They "proved" the wrong thing! Would you buy a used dinosaur from these men?

And in a comment pertinent to the work of Charles Darwin himself, and his hidden agenda, the philosophical Hanson says: "In any observation statement, *the cloven hoof* of theory can readily be detected". Clip, clop.

DOGGED DISSENTERS

However, despite these expert testimonies, which evolutionists scornfully dismiss as "quote mining", YouTube carries video clips of condescending professors of evolution confidently assuring the faithful that "numerous" intermediate forms have been discovered in the last couple of decades since those admissions were made. The on-line encyclopedia Wikipedia even has charts showing the latest efforts at shuffling fossils into imagined sequences of evolutionary development. This is based of course on the assumption that evolution must be true and that any similarities in structure absolutely prove common ancestry.

Although such arguments from analogy can be helpful in making creative breakthroughs, they can also be totally misleading. This is why, for example, prior to Harvey, science thought that by analogy with the tides of the oceans ebbing and flowing (false analogy), the blood flowed to and fro from the heart along the same vessels. This convincing analogy from nature made a lot of sense. However, Harvey was able to demonstrate that the blood actually circulated, like the moon around the earth (true analogy). Just as Harvey was able to demonstrate that orthodox theory of blood flow was wrong, so the fossil record shows Darwin's seductive theory to be wrong.

Incidentally, Harvey's original papers show that he was so excited by this breakthrough that although he started recording it in scientific Latin, his impatience got the better of him and he completed the notes in English.

VAGUE VERBS
Because they share the Darwin delusion that the micro-evolution we can see at work in our world can be extrapolated into macro-evolution, evolutionists happily make glib claims, such as "genes were *tweaked*", "fins *developed* into legs", or "scales *evolved* into feathers". Because they believe it, they see no need to prove it. Best not ask difficult questions, or you might get blackballed and lose your research grant!.

The technique is well illustrated by dogged dissenter geologist Donald Prothero, author of: "Evolution: What the fossils say and why it matters". Claiming in the "New Scientist" that "reports of huge gaps in the fossil record have been greatly exaggerated", he cites our perfectly formed old friend Archeopteryx as a classic intermediate form, then dredges up a clutch of other "missing links" that are apparently "not missing" at all. The Synapsids for example - key players in the imagined macro evolution of mammals from reptiles.

"Part of their lower jaw", he seriously informs us, "*migrated* into the ear to *become* the hammer and anvil" of the middle ear. Or as Steve Jones puts it in his more folksy manner "As the ancestors of mammals appeared, the ear began to *hijack* other structures." I suppose "migrated" and "hijacked" make a change from "evolved", "developed" or "acquired". Such is the paleozoic piffle being foisted on young school and college students as serious scientific fact by these Darwinian desperadoes.

Although such vague generalities facilitate concise communication, there comes a time for specifics and concrete detail. Florence Nightingale, like today's NLP psychology practitioners, for example, understood such matters, and always demanded specific symptoms rather than being fobbed off with vague observations about a patient's welfare, such as "He had a bad night."

HOW? HOW? HOW?
Civil servant Reg Jones, personal assistant to Winston Churchill in World War II, likewise had a love of specifics. In fact, he made a habit of challenging the assertions of military experts wheeled in to advise his boss with a series of simple questions – "How?" and "How?" and again "How?"

Jones discovered that just three or four such simple challenges could often reduce high powered "experts" to abject frustration and the admission that much or most of what they were claiming was mere assumption and opinion, supported by little, if any, real fact. I understand that Bill Gates took a similar tough line with his advisors at Microsoft.

The glib assertions of evolutionists merit the same treatment: "The fins *evolved* into legs and then wings?" Oh really? *How* did that happen? ...and *how* does that work? ...and *how* does the DNA do that? And . . . Please give us a detailed, assumption-free, cause-and-effect chain of explanation from first principles.

Incredible transformations in extant organisms can and do occur of course, such as tadpoles growing tiny legs and turning into frogs. Or the metamorphosis of a caterpillar into a butterfly, or a maggot into a fly. Let alone the process of growth of a mammal from ovum to adult. The vital difference is that these miraculous phenomena cannot be explained by the nonsense of accumulating random accidental DNA copying errors – but by the infinite genius of divine design.

TIKTAALIK

It is instructive to apply the Jones technique to Tiktaalik, a prized fossil discovered in Northern Canada in 2006 after several years' intensive searching. Tiktaalik, like Acanthostega, is held up as a model transitional form – claimed to be to tetrapods what Archeopteryx is to birds. If this unique creature did "evolve" in Darwinian manner, it would be nice to know how Natural Selection operating on random accidental DNA copying errors, even toolbox gene gyrations, somehow created its incredibly complex features:

According to Wikipedia, Tiktaalik *acquired* fins/legs with basic *wrist bones and simple fingers,* showing that they were weight bearing, but probably not used for walking. The bones of the fore fins show large muscle facets, suggesting that the fin was both *muscular* and had the *ability to flex like a wrist joint.*

Question*: How* did those several connected and coordinated finger and wrist bones, with their ability to flex, along with muscles and tendons, ligaments, cartilage, nerves and skin covering arise from fins by accidental DNA copying errors, or cleverly coordinated mutations? And if they did, where are the zillions of unfit and uncoordinated forms with malformed parts? *How* did the various tendons take shape and attach themselves to the bones, and at just the right positions? *How* was the tendon material synthesized anyway? Ditto for the ligaments and cartilage. Ditto for the bone morphology and material. And *how* can any intelligent person believe such infantile nonsense?

Wikipedia continues: Tiktaalik had front fins featuring arm-like skeletal structures more akin to a crocodile . . . It had rows of *sharp teeth of a predator fish,* and its *neck was able to move independently of its body, which is not possible in other fish.* This makes *Tiktaalik* the earliest known fish to have *a neck*. This would give the creature *more freedom in hunting prey* either on land or in the shallows.

Question: Please explain how the accumulation of random DNA copying errors created the specialized array of "teeth" of a predator fish, upper and lower, and aligned them and attached them to the jaws, and also formed a "neck" with the coordinated musculature to manipulate it in hunting prey. And why in this sole survivor?

Notice here the infantile attempt to justify these miraculous developments by suggesting that the would give the creature *more freedom in hunting prey* -- a typical Darwinian argument that explains absolutely nothing at all. The answer, of course, would be that this particular model was the most fit. But if so, where are the zillions of *un*-fit forms, both ancestors and descendants?

Wikipedia adds: Also notable are the spiracles on the top of the head, which suggest the creature had primitive *lungs* as well as gills. The animal also had a flat skull resembling a crocodile's; *eyes on top of its head*, suggesting it spent a lot of time looking up.

Question: How and why did random accidental DNA copying errors, in addition to creating gills, also create lungs with all their complex architecture and membranes, plus the necessary connections to the blood circulation system? Oh, sorry – they were just "primitive" lungs were they not?

And there is more: A small *gill slit* called a spiracle that, in more derived animals, *became* an *ear*.

Question: So a small gill slit turned itself into an ear and also acquired the acoustic morphology and the nerve connections and sensors needed to detect sound waves, generate electrical impulses and lead them to the brain for interpretation. How? How? How?

With regard to such impossible antics, it is interesting that even one of Darwin's strongest early supporters, Thomas "Bulldog" Huxley, unlike Dawkins today, would not accept that evolution could advance by a series of complementary "chance" events, but felt there must be a "law" at work. However, so beguiled was he by Darwin's basic concept, that he said he was "prepared to go to the Stake" for him if need be.

WAS IT JUST A CROCODILE?
Tiktaalik is discussed at the Devonian Times web site (www.devoniantimes. org/Order/re-tiktaalik.html), which describes a wide variety of such creatures, with the following comments suggesting that they all might simply have been varieties of prehistoric crocodile. Another case, perhaps, of micro-evolution at work creating diversity in the prehistoric world, rather than evolutionary descent.

THE LITERAL TRUTH OF GENESIS
Jesus evidently accepted the Genesis account of creation as literal truth, as all Christian people should, not as myth and superstition to be dissected and shredded by moronic scholars. Regarding the origins of human beings, for example, he reminded his disciples that "in the beginning, God made them male and female" (Matthew 19:4). How could the physical bodies of man and woman possibly have evolved anyway – as two separate yet complementary and incredibley complex organisms?

Consider any detail of their separate physiologies and ask how it could possibly have made itself by the accumulation of DNA copying errors? How did sperm and ova independently evolve in separate organisms, even if in possession of complex structures of master and slave genes – and how did man acquire the penis and erection, and woman the vagina and womb to bring them together for the miracle of reproduction? Think about it and wonder. Then you will understand why Dr. Dawkins shies away from the subject! Sadly, even some Christian people, evidently delirious from nibbling Darwin's magic mushroom in school or college, will spout nonsense such as "Yes, but Jesus didn't know the things we know!" In other words, the executive Creator of the universe was more stupid than they are! "A man of his time", is the phrase, I believe.

WHY EVOLUTION IS NOT TRUE
In one sentence, Jesus has nailed the lie of evolution. So let us be very clear. Evolution CANNOT explain male and female – whether it be in man, or cats and dogs, cows, sheep, horses, elephants, mice . . . . . That is the big picture.

The usual Darwinian approach in dealing with what any rational person would regard as irreducible complexity, such as the human eye, is to line up series of increasingly complex specimens, claiming they demonstrate gradual evolutionary development over billions of years. However, they cannot do that with sex, because the miraculous but perfectly complementary male and female organs have to have evolved separately in totally independent organisms.

No wonder the desperate Jerry A. Coyne is forced to write yet another book, "Why Evolution is True", lamenting the fact that lay people increasingly refuse to be bamboozled by what their intuition tells them is evolutionary claptrap and microbiological mumbo-jumbo. To Coyne's chagrin, the game is up, with one Chicago businessman attending his lecture telling him afterwards: "I found your evidence for evolution very convincing - but I still don't believe it". For evolutionists, however, "incredulity is not a scientific argument". You just have to believe it, brother.

Coyne prefers to focus on peripheral twiggy matters such as why if God made us did he give us a supposedly functionless appendix, or why are some children born with an "atavistic" tail-like spinal deformity, evidently caused by a failure of master genes to switch of the appropriate hox genes at the right time.

He is, however, forced to admit that evolution really cannot explain miraculous structures such as the bacterial flagellum or propeller, "an ion-powered rotary motor, anchored in the membranes surrounding the bacterial cell". His simple cop out is that although evolution is supposedly a self-evident fact of life, evolutionists cannot be expected to understand and explain every detail or how it worked its miracles. Oh, go on Jerry, just for me!

I would urge everyone to read Kenneth R. Miller's tortuous attempt to explain the imagined evolution of the flagellum, and judge for themselves (www. millerandlevine.com/km/evol/design2/article.html).

A NON-RUNNER
Typical of the search for mythical transitional forms is the shuffling of fossils in order to fabricate the supposed evolutionary history of the horse. The magic wand of natural selection, no doubt accompanied by the mantra "Darwin woz right!", then being waved to perform miracles such as these: "Over geologic time and within several lineages, the *skull became much deeper*, the *eyes moved back*, and the *brain became larger*. The *incisors were widened*, premolars were altered to molars, and the *molars became very high-crowned with a highly complex folding of the enamel*".

And Voila! We have a horse! Jus' like that! Jus' like that! Plus zillions of unfit forms, of course, to get conveniently lost in the compost pile of paleontology and never be seen again. Abracadabra!

Admitting the impossibility of such contortions being the fortuitous accumulation of zillions of accidental DNA copying errors, devout evolutionist Derek Hough now postulates the existence in all organisms of a "Self-developing Genome" -- a sophisticated creative mechanism capable of sensing and responding to its environment in a constructive rather then random fashion.

EOHIPPUS

Wikipedia informs us that "The first trace of the first horse was found by a brick maker in Suffolk, England, 1838. While digging in his backyard, he found a small tooth. Later, he found a piece of a jaw with a tooth attached."

However, scientists from the London Geological Society thought the creature he had found was a monkey. In typical Darwinian fashion, this resulted in many theories, from "England was long ago a jungle with monkeys chattering and screaming in the trees" to "some gypsies traveling through England years before had lost one of their monkeys". A few months later, the monkey idea was discarded and the creature was given the name Hyracotherium or Eohippus.

In a determined search for intermediate forms it was then decided that the "modern" horse, Equus, was descended from a dog-sized, five-toed creature that lived about 75 million years ago, and stood about twelve to fourteen inches at the shoulder and weighed about twelve pounds.

Although this imagined ancestor "*looked nothing like a horse*" and "had an arched back, short neck, short snout, short legs, and a long tail", flow charts showing the required evolutionary tree of the horse were drawn up and have more recently been updated.

DON'T CONFUSE US WITH THE FACTS!

Although such nonsense is still funneled into the receptive minds of school and college students, leading evolutionist Dr. Niles Eldredge, curator at the American Museum of Natural History, was moved to comment: "*I admit* that an awful lot of that has gotten into the textbooks *as though it were true.* For instance, the most famous example still on exhibit downstairs (in the American Museum) is the exhibit of *horse evolution* prepared perhaps 50 years ago." Clip, clop.

He continurs: "That has been *presented as literal truth in textbook after textbook.* Now I think that is lamentable, particularly because the people who propose these kinds of stories themselves may be aware of *the speculative nature* of some of the stuff. But by the time it filters down to the textbooks, we've got *science as truth* and we've got a problem." What a scandalous deception! What sinister lies!

CLADISTICS

Realizing, I suspect, that the fossil record would never "prove" his theory, the desperate Darwin latched onto the infantile and ancient assumption that similarities in the physiology of organisms proves descent from a common ancestor, especially with regard to man, the real target of his machinations. This concept has more recently "evolved" into the science of "Cladistics", a term derived from the Greek word for "branch". Henry Gee's book "Deep Time" is an ode to the wonders of Cladistics - and also to the achievement of Charles Darwin, whose intellectual stature he eulogizes as being eternal and beyond need of physical memorial. How tragic.

On the assumption that evolution is Truth, Cladistic exponents draw branching tree diagrams supposedly relating different organisms to their common ancestors. Since I and my dog Ollie, for example, both have backbones, it is assumed that we must share a common ancestor, "X", an assumption which is demonstrated by drawing a diagram with a line from each of us in a V-formation linking us both to "X". If we then want to include my cat Tiddles, whose backbone clearly proves that she also descended from "X", then I have to decide whether she is a lateral off my branch of the V or Ollie's.

Tiddles' black fur coat would probably put her on Ollie's branch. In this way, very complex diagrams can be created as we add in more organisms, such as the mouse that Tiddles chewed up last week and moles that have been ravaging my back lawn. Furrry interesting.

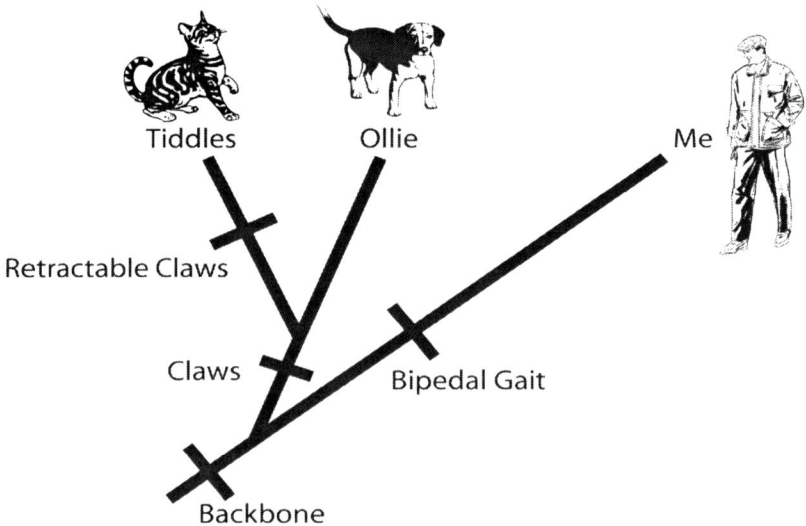

MAN AND KANGAROO

The goal of Cladistics is to "prove" evolution, to create a diagram or family tree where all members of the analysis are descended from a single common ancestral species. Features considered in Cladistic analysis might include the number of legs, possession of a tail, fins, or fur.

Bipedalism, for example - the habit of walking upright - would relate man to apes, but also to kangaroos! Oh dear! And whales are mammals, but have no fur. Oh dear again! In such cases the results are dismissed as being "anomalous", or manipulated further by the inclusion of more and more features until the desired result is obtained, one that accords with "intuition" – i.e. the requirements of evolution.

As one "Cladist" confesses: "Although Cladistics is touted as the greatest thing since sliced bread and a totally objective method, it is still no better than the researcher who decides what characters to use in the analysis." And your point is?

Another Cladist concurs, saying: "Depending on which characteristics we use, we have a *different common ancestor.*" Oh dear again! But he continues: "If *metabolism* is used, birds and mammals are close cousins and crocodiles unrelated to each. If *skull and heart structure* is used, birds and crocodiles are close cousins, and mammals unrelated to each. This proves that despite being an attempt to construct a more 'objective' system than the Linnean one, Cladistics still has to fall back on the same subjectivity." Would you buy a plastic fossil from these people?

A WHALE OF A TALE

Typical of Cladistic claptrap camouflaged with scientific jargon is the claim made by the University of California Museum of Paleontology web site regarding the imagined evolution of the grey whale from an extinct land creature named *Pakicetus* which apparently existed 50 million years ago.

Pakicetus is described as an early ancestor to modern whales. "*Although they were land mammals*", with a fearsome array of teeth like a crocodile, it is clear to evolutionists at Berkely that "they were related to whales and dolphins *based on a number of specializations of the ear, relating to hearing*" – i.e. on the basis of the Cladistic assumption that since evolution must be true, similarities in ear structure actually prove common ancestry, rather than a common designer. Of course, other evolutionists would simply assume that the miracle of evolution had struck twice in different times and places, and so the commonality or "convergence" would not prove common origins.

NO PROOF
After stressing that paleontologists have no proof to support the conventional evolutionary speculations found in books, Henry Gee claims that by devising several alternative Cladistic diagrams and then choosing the one he deems the simplest, he is actually "testing" and "proving" his ideas in a kosher scientific fashion – since, according to the ancient test known as "Occam's Razor", the simplest possible explanation of a phenomenon must invariably be the correct one. As a result, the buzz word amongst Cladistic fans now appears to be "parsimony" or simplicity.

In attempting to promote Cladistics as the only truly scientific approach to understanding the deep past, Gee describes the evolutionary assertions commonly found in books as "Just So stories". Paleontologists, he informs us, "*invent* these stories" according to their "*prejudices*", working from "*assumptions*" that are "*baseless*". You mean they make it up? But these guys have white coats!

As he points out, fossils do not "carry labels" or "certificates of authenticity" so we cannot possibly know what really happened long ago in "deep time" and so link cause to effect. To illustrate his point, he informs us that more than 50 explanations have so far been offered for the demise of the dinosaurs. Cladistics is not concerned with events, he says, but with theoretical relationships based on similarities in structure. All based, of course, on the *assumption* that evolution is Truth.

VIRTUALLY EVERYTHING WAS WRONG!
Having taken a long hard look at his former field of expertise through his newly-opened eyes, Gee comments: "We are forced to accept that *virtually everything* we thought we knew about evolution is *wrong*". You cannot be serious, man!

Having been so disarmingly honest and scrupulously logical, Gee then steps into a very deep pool of unwarranted assumption himself, when he says: "If it is fair to *assume* that all life on earth shares a *common evolutionary origin* – it follows that every organism that ever existed *must* be related to every other. *We are all cousins*". That said, Gee apparently feels that yes it is fair to make that massive assumption, because the rest of his book is based on it. As a result, in a classic example of circular reasoning, all known organisms can be tightly woven together in order to "prove" evolution and generate vast numbers of supposed "transitional forms".

The complexity and extent of the speculative relationships generated by Cladistic analysis, now aided by powerful computer programmes, is limited only by the fertility of the human imagination that devises them - with not a few disagreements along the way as to which particular diagram of descent is the most "parsimonious". Cladistic analysis may be based on visible characteristics, such as the possession of wings by birds, beetles and bats, or even on similarities in the DNA of such organisms.

Contemplating the incredible amount of time and effort that has been invested in the futile pursuit of Cladistics, I am reminded of the scripture which says: "Where is the wise man? Where is the scholar? Where is the philosopher of this age? Has not God made foolish the wisdom of the world?" (Romans 1:20).

THE SCIENTIFIC METHOD AT WORK
In the famous incident of the apple falling from a tree in a Cambridge college garden, scientific genius Isaac Newton was inspired to theorize not that gravity existed, but that its effect did not stop at the earth's surface, or even the top of the apple tree. Gravity's pull, he realized, must reach out into space, even as far as the moon. We can only imagine what an exciting Eureka! moment that must have been.

This insight proved very useful to Newton because it helped him explain the fact that the moon revolves around the earth rather than shooting off into space – since according to his newly formulated first law of motion, a moving object should carry moving in a straight line, at a constant speed, unless an unbalanced force makes it do otherwise. An applied force was therefore required to keep the moon orbiting the earth – and the earth's gravity was that force, he realized.

This was a massive breakthrough in our understanding of astronomy, because up to that time, people had believed that circular motion, as demonstrated by "the heavenly bodies", was the natural or perfect form of motion.

On the basis of his new theory, Newton hypothesized that the moon moved in a circle, or "ellipse" to be technically correct, because the gravitational force from the earth was continually pulling it sideways, stopping it flying off in a straight line into space – as it would do if gravity could be switched off. He also theorized, conversely, that the moon must also exert a gravitation pull on the earth and, in particular, its oceans – an insight that helped him explain the tidal movements of the sea. Some people thought that was a lunatic idea!

On the basis of this theory, Newton was even able to calculate the "escape velocity" of a rocket, the speed it needs to attain in order to go into orbit around the earth, a figure familiar to NASA engineers. Or in Newton's case, the speed required for a cannonball fired from the top of a very high mountain, where there would be no air and hence no friction, to move so fast that as it fell towards the ground, the curvature of the earth would drop away beneath it at the same rate, so it would never ever land.

I wonder how long it took for Newton to realize that the sun's gravity must also reach out into space, thereby holding the earth and the other planets in their orbits? Magic stuff!

HEAVENLY SPHERES & DISAPPEARING FOSSILS
However, prior to Isaac Newton's time, it was commonly believed that a moving object, such as the moon, required a force to actually keep it moving, otherwise it would slow down and stop. This, after all, was the common-sense experience of people shooting arrows or playing bowls. Newton realized, however, that in a friction-free environment, an object would never slow down, but would just keep on moving at a constant speed, with no need for a force to keep it going – the principal of inertia, as he explained in his famous "Principia Mathematica" with his three laws of motion.

Consequently, prior to Newton, people believed that the moon and the planets needed applied forces pushing them to keep them moving. They theorized as a result that they must be affixed to invisible "crystal spheres" that carried them along – a prediction they had no means of putting to a scientific test. Then, of course, the spheres themselves also would need something to keep them moving, perhaps a gigantic set of invisible crystal gear wheels and levers, all energized perhaps by some angels on a treadmill.

No doubt, in their time, the spheres could have been the subject of fascinating and heated debate: How thick was the crystal? What was it made of? How were the moon and planets attached to their spheres? Was it by means of large screws or nails, or simply some form of celestial glue? People probably wrote books about the finer points of their design.

In one stroke, however, in one little book, Newton rendered the spheres totally obsolete, extinct and unnecessary. The inertia of the moon and planets simply kept them moving. No spheres were needed. The spheres did not exist. They never had existed. Eureka!

And now we know, after a century and a half of searching, that the same thing is true of Darwin's famous fossils, the missing links and the failed intermediate forms which have proved as elusive as the spheres. And for the very same reason. They do not exist. They never did exist! All gone! Abracadabra! Pouf! All gone.

Both spheres and fossils were constructs of misconceived theories – the difference being that whereas Newton displaced error, Darwin displaced Truth.

THE MEGA EXPLOSION

As we shall see later, on the basis of the fossils found in them, the earth's rock strata have been sorted into three major groups – the Paleozoic (meaning ancient life), the Mesozoic (middle life) and the Cenozoic (recent life). The Cambrian rocks already mentioned are supposedly the lowest and therefore the oldest of the Paleozoic era.

Notice that even these important geological terms are evolutionary in origin, being based on the assumption that life on earth developed and diversified through various stages, from primitive ancient forms, through a middle era, and finally a modern or recent era.

G-Theory challenges this Darwinian assumption, however, and suggests that the organisms found in the strata of the Paleozoic and Mesozoic eras in particular may actually constitute the entire flora and fauna of a Pre-Adamic or Pre-historic age which was catastrophically destroyed, perhaps in one massive extinction.

As already noted, any search for transitional forms would of course be complicated by the fact that G-Theory would predict evidence of mutation and variation among extinct creatures, such as dinosaurs, as with dogs and cattle in the present creation.

Conversely, in direct contradiction to evolution, G-Theory also suggests that those extinct organisms of the Paleozoic and Mesozoic eras were all created

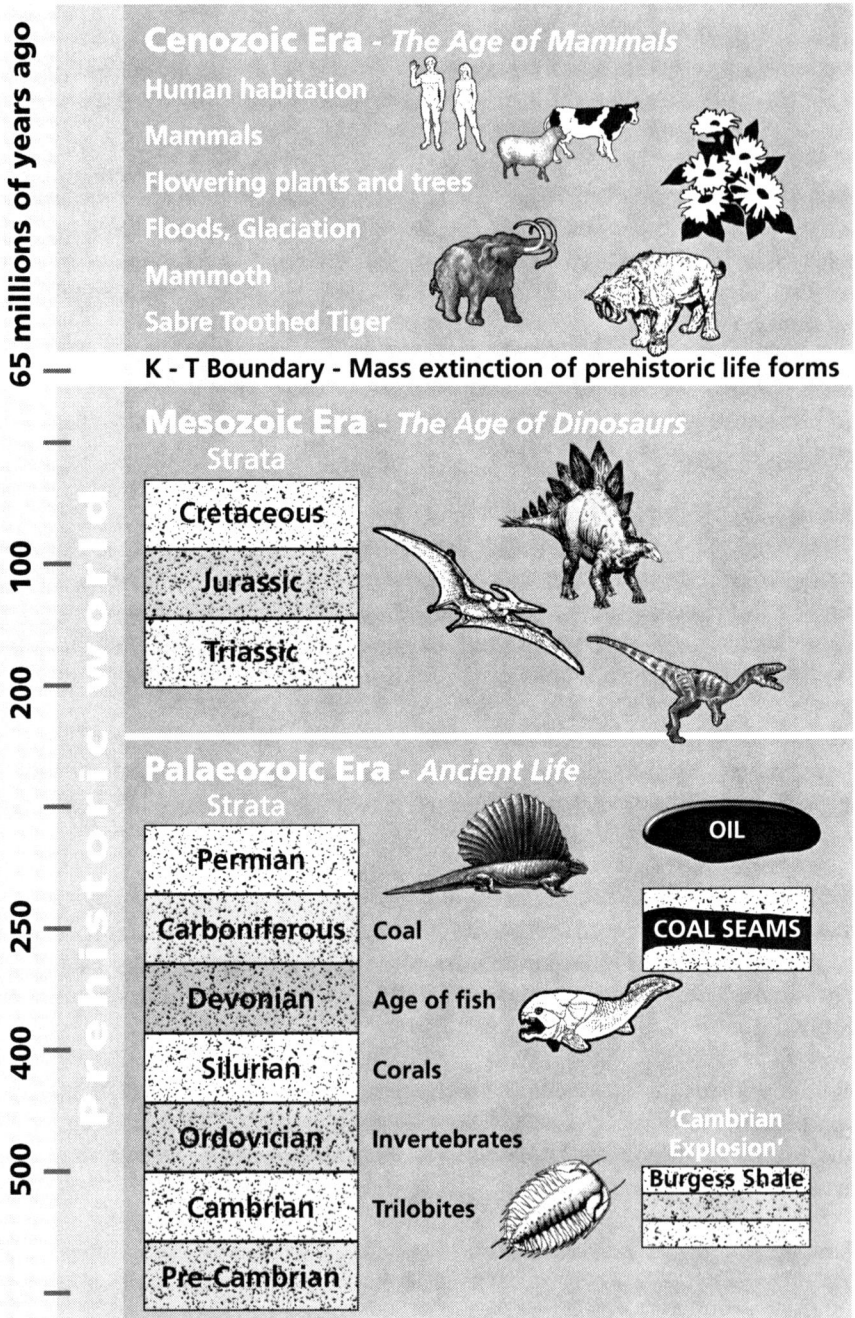

65 millions of years ago

Cenozoic Era - *The Age of Mammals*

Human habitation
Mammals
Flowering plants and trees
Floods, Glaciation
Mammoth
Sabre Toothed Tiger

K - T Boundary - Mass extinction of prehistoric life forms

Mesozoic Era - *The Age of Dinosaurs*
Strata

Cretaceous
Jurassic
Triassic

Palaeozoic Era - *Ancient Life*
Strata

Permian
Carboniferous   Coal
Devonian   Age of fish
Silurian   Corals
Ordovician   Invertebrates
Cambrian   Trilobites
Pre-Cambrian

OIL

COAL SEAMS

'Cambrian Explosion'
Burgess Shale

Prehistoric world

The rock strata of the Geological Column clearly offer important insights into the history of our planet. Although the idealised column was first constructed by early geologists with no evolutionary axe to grind, its fossil record constitutes the strongest "proof" of evolution, their sequence supposedly demonstrating the development of living things, from primitive marine organisms, up to fish, amphibians, and then land animals such as reptiles, birds and mammals.

According to creationists, however, the column simply shows the sequence of burial of organisms destroyed by Noah's flood and the sedimentary rock strata created by it. And that all those organisms were created in the six days of the Genesis account

The G-Theory view would be that the Mesozoic and Paleozoic fossil records show the flora and fauna of a prehistoric age, which were destroyed and buried in one or a series of mass extinction catastrophies.
Observations conflicting with the idealized evolutionary model are deemed "anomalous" and are either ignored or manipulated to conform. Fossils being found in the wrong sequence, for example, is simply explained by formations having been turned upside down.

On a much larger scale, the famous Lewis Overthrust, in which Precambrian rock strata several miles thick and hundred of miles long lie on top of Cretaceous rocks supposedly over 1,400 million years younger is also easily sorted. This glaring anomaly is explained by one tectonic plate having been lifted up and "thrust" over another one.

Putting aside all arguments, the major facts of geology demonstrated by the fossil record are that:
> *A) Prior to our present Cenozoic world, the "age of mammals", there existed a horrifying "age of reptiles", a prehistoric world populated by grotesque and often gigantic organisms, such as the dinosaurs. Even the smaller creatures, such as the trilobites, appear to have been violent predators.*
> *B.) Those "Satan's creatures" were wiped out, buried and sometimes fossilized, in one of more "mass extinctions" – in particular at the end of the Mesozoic era and the start of the Cenozoic era. The recently discovered K-T boundary layer illustrates the break between the two and points to meteorite bombardment as the cause.*
> *C) In direct contradiction to evolutionary theory, it follows that the familiar flowers, fruit trees, mammals and other organisms of our world, as descried in the Genesis account of creation, did not evolve from prehistoric ancestors.*

Since the vast ages assigned to the geological column are absolutely essential for Darwin's theory of gradual evolution, creationists have been keen to support the concept of a very young earth. This has required them to assign the formation of most rock strata, mineral, oil and coal deposits to the action of Noah's flood – a time scale of about one year. G-Theory solves those problems.

The ages assigned by radiometric techniques to Mesozoic and Paleozoic strata are basically irrelevant in G-Theory.

at the same time, rather than being the outcome of repeated evolutions and extinctions, and that they existed contemporaneously.

In other words, the Cambrian Explosion, the appearance of more than a hundred "phyla" or types of organism at the start of the Paleozoic era, may simply have been just a small part of a vastly greater mega "explosion", i.e. the divine creation of all the whole flora and fauna of the pre-Adamic world, none of which therefore had any kind of evolutionary ancestors. But more about the Cambrian Explosion in a moment.

A DRAMATIC TRANSITION
The final section of the Mesozoic era, the Cretaceous period, has been described as the *"transition between the very different earlier Earth and the Cenozoic, a world relatively similar to that of the present day"*.

This evidence of a dramatic transition from an alien prehistoric world to our present age, one designed for human habitation, is one of the key discoveries of geology – the implication of which is that the array of bizarre and grotesque creatures evidenced by Paleozoic and Mesozoic fossils were not the ancestors of the earth's present flora and fauna, and were, in any case, all fully-formed complex organisms in their own right, not the unfit, primitive transitional forms Darwin's theory required.

In fact, George Gaylord Simpson, described as the most influential paleontologist of the twentieth century, once commented that "The *most puzzling event in the history of life on the earth is the change from the Mesozoic Age of Reptiles, to the Age of Mammals*. It is as if the curtain came down suddenly on a stage where all the leading roles were taken by reptiles - especially dinosaurs - in great numbers and bewildering variety, and rose again immediately to reveal the same setting but an *entirely new cast*, a cast in which the dinosaurs do not appear at all. Other reptiles are supernumeraries and the leading parts are all played by mammals of sorts barely hinted at in the previous acts" (*Life Before Man*, 1972, page 42).

Ah well, there's no business like show business!

2.3

EVOLUTION FAILS FOSSIL TEST 2

The second scientific test proposed by Darwin was the prediction that the fossils found in the lowest and oldest rock strata, the Pre-Cambrian and Cambrian, would be the "simplest" and "most primitive".

Unfortunately for his theory again, although some very tiny and microscopic fossils have been found in the most ancient Pre-Cambrian strata, in the next strata up, the Cambrian, all manner of highly complex organisms suddenly make their appearance, storming or "exploding" onto the geological scene in vast numbers. In particular, the famous "Trilobites", the most diverse group of extinct animals preserved in the fossil record. Ten orders of Trilobites are recognized, encompassing more then 20,000 species.

This magical appearance out of nowhere of such highly complex organisms is known as the "Cambrian Explosion", or, according to Michael Behe, in his book "Darwin's Black Box" - the "Biological Big Bang", apparently by parallel with the equally inexplicable cosmological "Big Bang", another event in which "nothing" suddenly turned into "something" – i.e. the universe, which then set it off expanding out towards infinity. The mystery of the Cambrian explosion was in fact a major factor in the development of Gould and Eldredge's punctuated equilibrium theory.

Unable to explain the sudden appearance of swarms of highly complex life forms at what is supposed to be the dawn of life, Gould was moved to comment: "The Cambrian explosion was *the most remarkable and puzzling event in the history of life*". G-Theory solves that puzzle.

SCUTTLING SCAVENGERS

As the name implies, the body of the Trilobite, which was sometimes 30cm or more in diameter, was in three segments, and was equipped with two sets of appendages along its body, one set apparently for walking and one for swimming. In some varieties the double row of legs had quite large feet equipped with claw-like spikes that were apparently used for shredding food and passing it along, conveyor-belt fashion to the mouth, like a miniature combine harvester. The rock strata where such organisms are found seem to represent just thin slices of ecosystems, and we can only wonder what they found for food before somebody invented photosynthesis and food chains.

These highly complex creatures, we are asked to believe, were among the world's first and most "primitive" products of evolution. Despite his awareness of this massive impossible problem for his theory, Darwin dreamed on anyway - and the world applauded. But as every con man knows, people believe what they want to believe. And Darwin desperately wanted to believe it.

TRILOBITE TECHNOLOGY
In his fascinating book "Trilobite! Eyewitness to Evolution", Richard Fortey describes the amazing optical design of the creature's eyes. Unique in nature, the compound eye of the most common Trilobite was composed of several thousand tiny crystals of calcite, a pure and hard form of calcium carbonate, packed together like the spines on the back of a hedgehog. Each of these tiny elongate crystals, with its hexagonal cross section, focussed light onto an array of tiny light receptors – each of which was connected to an optic nerve fibre leading to a brain, thereby enabling the Trilobite to sense its environment and "think" and make appropriate decisions. Some Trilobites have even been found with scars, evidence of surviving wounding by predators - because the wounds had healed. How's that for complexity?

In true Darwinian manner, Fortey speculates that the process of evolution that supposedly created this technological marvel must have been "encouraged" by the discovery of vision as a new and useful tool for exploring the environment. Such is the power of positive thinking. Apparently, many creatures acquired the power of flight in the same way, because they just knew it would be useful - and would help them stop getting their feet so wet and dirty in those pools of primordial slime we hear about.

Fortey then informs us that the Trilobite also had electrical sense organs, antennae designed to sweep the water in front of its mouth in order to "sniff" and "taste" any chemical hints of the presence of food or an enemy.

Furthermore, Fortey explains, it has been discovered that as the Trilobite repeatedly outgrew and shed its exoskeleton, the outer layers of the compound eyes were also shed and replaced. Add to this their inner architecture and specialized cells, and you have mind-boggling complexity.

PHACOPS!

Nevertheless, Fortey then goes on to describe another kind of Trilobite, Phacops, that had an even more incredible optical system. This time the compound eye was composed of an array of tiny calcite spheres – the effectiveness of which was demonstrated by a researcher who used one as a camera lens to take a passable photograph of the FBI's Hoover Building.

If you focus a beam of light, such as that from the sun, using a sphere, the image formed will be very distorted because the rays passing through the outer regions will be refracted more than those passing through the centre. This distortion, called "spherical aberration", was first recognized just a couple of centuries ago by physicists such as Christiaan Huygens, who was working to improve the lenses used in microscopes and telescopes. The solution to the distortion problem, Huygens discovered, was to combine two lenses, a more powerful convex and a less powerful concave, made of different kinds of glass, having what is technically described as different refractive indexes or optical densities - an arrangement called a "doublet".

Perhaps you are again ahead of me – in guessing that the tiny spheres in the Phacob's eyes had a similar but even more sophisticated design, the variation in refractive index in different parts of the lens being caused by an appropriate admixture of magnesium in place of some of the calcium in the calcite.

The revered evolutionist S. J. Gould is on record as stating that the existence of this unique optical system in this "ancient" and "primitive" organism is "the most puzzling fact of the fossil record". Gould seems to have spotted several "most puzzling" events.

Although the Trilobites were so numerous in Cambrian times, they are, as far as we know, now extinct. Fortey makes the technical reason for this very clear, saying: "Trilobites did not cut the evolutionary mustard". So there you have it.

Extensive information about Trilobites, including superb detailed diagrams of their body structures, and eye design in particular, can be at found at http://www.Trilobites.info/eyes.htm. The authors of the site attempt to explain how one kind of eye magically evolved into other forms, saying: "All early

Trilobite Eye Design

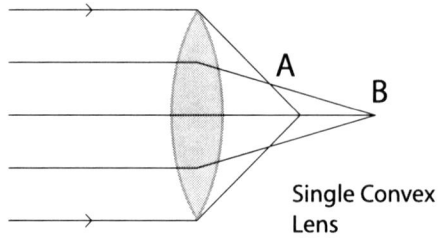

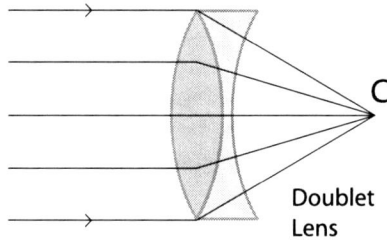

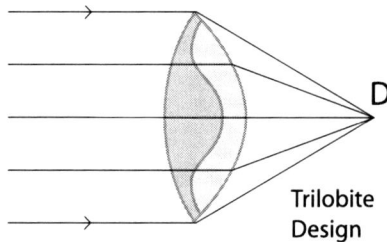

A

B

Single Convex
Lens

C

Doublet
Lens

D

Trilobite
Design

Spherical aberration: With a simple convex lens, the image is distorted because outer rays are bent more than inner rays, as shown.

In the 1600s Christiaan Huygens and his friend Renee Descartes found that spherical aberration could be corrected with a doublet lens, made of two different kinds of glass. The aberration caused by the concave lens cancels that due to the convex lens.

This astonishing design of Trilobite eye uses a doublet lens in which the differential distribution of minerals creates two lenses in one.

Dr. Carroll please note this example of Intelligent Design genius, which incinerates the insane idea of evolution of organisms by the fortuitous accumulation of accident DNA copying errors.

Trilobites (Cambrian), had holochroal eyes and it would seem hard to evolve the distinctive phacopid schizochroal eye from this form. The answer is thought to lie in ontogenetic (developmental) processes on an evolutionary time scale." The phrase "clear as mud" comes to mind!

The blind faith of evolutionists in the face of such clear disproof of Darwin's theory is illustrated by Richard Dawkins' comment in "*The Blind Watchmaker*" regarding the Cambrian fossils: "And we find many of them already in an *advanced state of evolution, the very first time they appear.* It is as though they were just planted there, *without any evolutionary history.* Needless to say, this appearance of sudden planting has delighted creationists." Could the good professor be wandering down the Road to Damascus, given enough time of course?

THE BURGESS SHALE

The Trilobite is just one of thousands of complex organisms that suddenly appear out of nowhere in the ancient Cambrian formations of the Paleozoic era. Legend has it that in 1909 when Charles Walcott was prospecting for fossils in the Burgess shale deposits of Canada's Rocky Mountains, his horse suddenly pulled up by a large rock, as if by divine command. When Walcott attacked the rock with his geologists' hammer, it burst open to reveal some very bizarre fossils. Walcott basically spent the rest of his life exploring the formation, collecting and attempting to classify some 65,000 specimens.

A tiny few of those amazing extinct but incredibly complex organisms are shown below. The amazing *Opabina* that had 5 eyes and a flexible snout like a vacuum cleaner hose. The *Marella* or "lace crab" which resembles a crawfish. The astonishing *Hallucigenia* and the bizarre *Anomalocaris.*

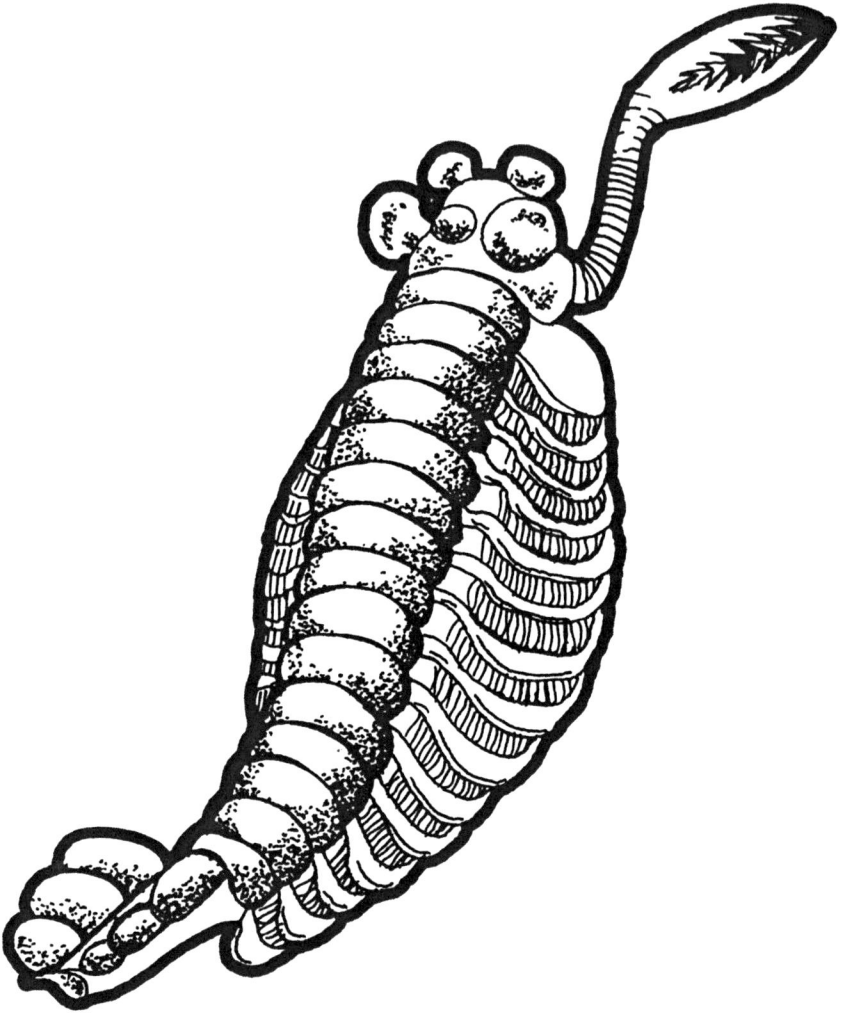

Opabinia

Opabinia is a soft-bodied fossil animal of modest size found the Middle Cambrian Burgess Shale. Its segmented body had lobes along the sides and a fan-shaped tail. The head shows unusual features: five compound eyes, a mouth under the head and facing backwards, and a proboscis that probably passed food to the mouth. Opabinia probably lived on the sea floor, using the proboscis to seek out small, soft food.

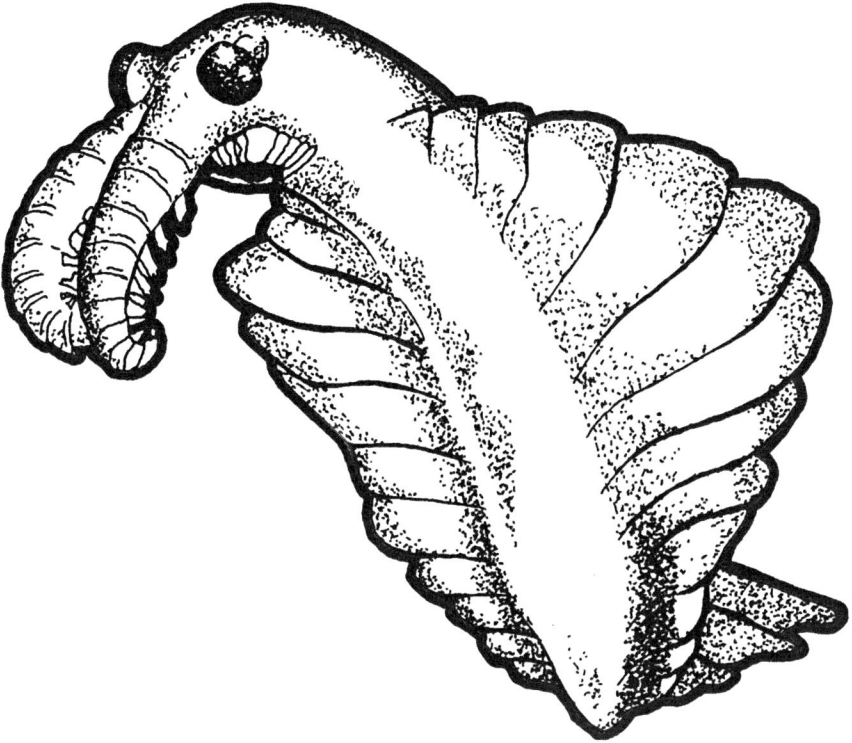

Anomalocaris

Anomalocaris is thought to have been a carnivorous predator, propelling itself through the water by undulating the flexible lobes on the sides of its body. Anomalocaris had a large head, a single pair of large, possibly compound eyes, and an unusual, disk-like mouth. The mouth was composed of 32 overlapping plates, four large and 28 small, resembling a pineapple ring with the center replaced by a series of serrated prongs. The mouth could constrict to crush prey, but never completely close, and the tooth-like prongs continued down the walls of the gullet. Two large 'arms' (up to seven inches in length when extended) with barb-like spikes were positioned in front of the mouth, and were probably used to grab prey and bring it to its mouth.

For the time in which it lived Anomalocaris was a truly gigantic creature, reaching lengths of up to one meter.

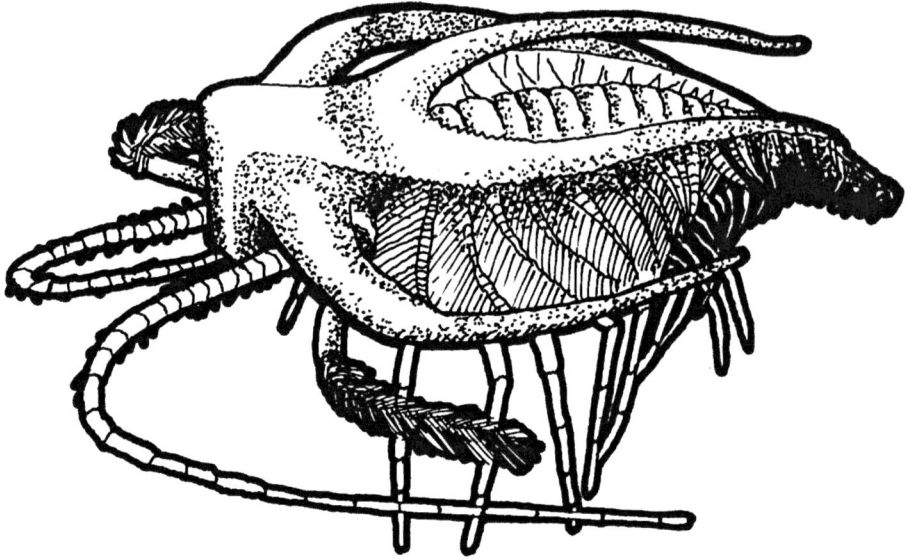

Marella

The most common fossil in the Burgess Shale. The first fossil collected by Charles Walcott from the Burgess Shale. Walcott described Marrella informally as a "lace crab". Marrella itself is a small animal, 2 cm or less in length. The head shield has two pairs of long rearward directed spikes. On the underside of the head are two pairs of antennae, one long and sweeping, the second shorter and stouter. Marrella has a body composed of 24–26 body segments, each with a pair of branched appendages. The lower branch of each appendage is a leg for walking, while the upper branch is a long, feathery gill. It also contains eyes under its head. The identification of a diffraction grating pattern on well-preserved Marrella specimens proves that it would have harboured an iridescent sheen — and thus would have appeared colorful.

Marrella has demonstrated that the soft bodied Burgess fauna were much more complex and diverse than anyone had previously suspected.

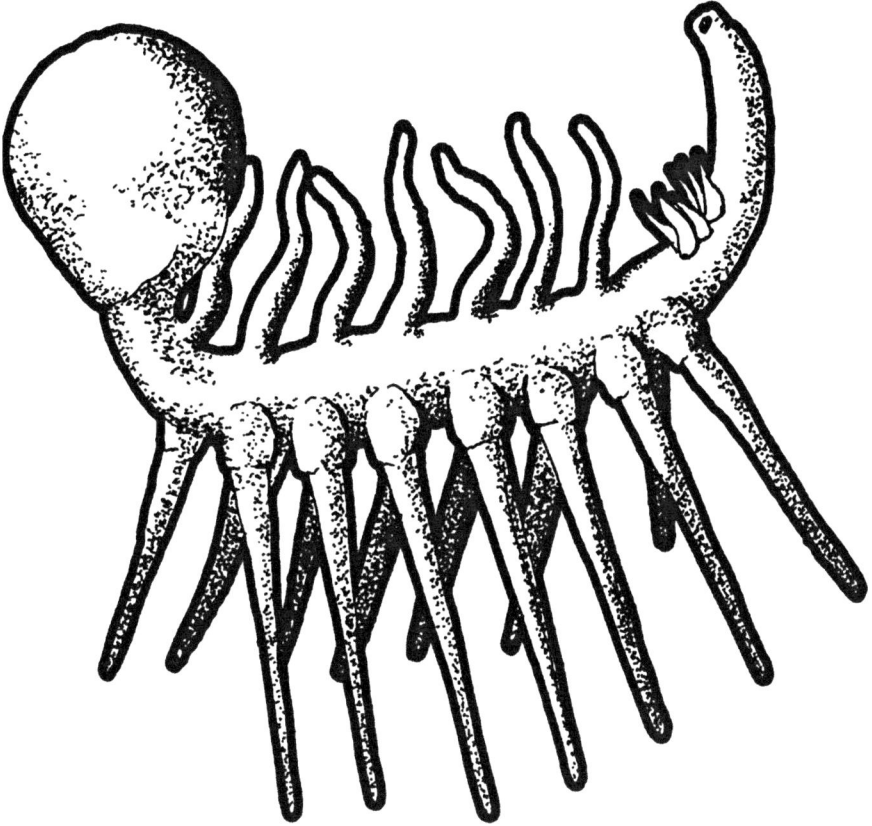

Hallucigenia

The 0.5 to 3 cm-long animal is wormlike — that is, long and narrow — with a poorly defined blob, or stain, on one end. This "blob" was arbitrarily designated the 'head'. The animal has seven pincer-tipped tentacles lined up on one side and seven pairs of jointed spines on the other. Six of the tentacles are paired with spines, while one is in front of the spines. There are also six smaller. In addition, there is a flexible, tube-like, tail-like body extension behind the tentacles.

Faced with an animal that had no obvious head and two types of appendages, neither of which seemed appropriate for any reasonable form of locomotion, Morris assigned the blob as the head and hypothesized that the spines were legs and that the tentacles were feeding appendages. Morris was able to demonstrate a workable, if improbable, method of walking on the spines. Only the forward tentacles can easily reach to the 'head,' meaning that a mouth on the head would have to be fed by passing food along the line of tentacles. Morris suggested that a hollow tube within each of the tentacles might be a mouth.

Further information: Animations and details of such "Cambrian critters" can be found at: http://evolution.berkeley.edu/evolibrary/article/_0_0/arthropods_toc_01
A Google image search for specific organisms brings up a vast amount of information.

Keep in mind that the invisible inner complexity of these creatures was even more massive than that of their bizarre external morphology. That must have included nerve and brain cells along with the constituent DNA, with tiers of master genes and slave genes, toolbox genes, and the ability to reproduce. Plus the mind-boggling detail now revealed by the electron microscope in any and all cells.

In the words of a Cambridge professor of evolutionary paleobiology, Simon Conway Morris, who is not normally a fan of ID, the intricate design of such organisms is not just good, it is "staggeringly good".

Adding to this evolutionary headache, comes the discovery that the Cambrian strata now also contain the fossils of fish, with all their complexity.

LAGERSTATTEN
The Burgess Shale is an example of a Lagerstatte, a German word meaning "place of storage". A Lagerstatte is rock formation that contains an extraordinary quantity and variety of fossil forms, as if they were buried in a mass grave as the result of some kind of catastrophe.

The Burgess Shale is in fact a "Konservat" Lagerstatte, a special formation where the dead organisms decayed extremely slowly due to oxygen being excluded by mud. Because the decay was so slow, even the fine tissues of the internal organs had time to petrify before rotting away, revealing even more inner complexity. Normally, decay would be quite rapid, leaving only hard parts such as shells and bones.

The more recent Chengjiang find in China is similarly rich in complex fossils. Extensive information about both formations is available on the internet.

INVISIBLE ANCESTORS

Evolutionists do not easily forsake their pseudo-scientific superstition, however. So how do they explain the Cambrian Explosion which spewed out these incredibly complex creatures from nowhere and actually blows Darwin's theory of gradual evolution to smithereens?

The explosion, so they claim, is simply an illusion created by the loss of "invisible ancestors". According to Darwin's theory, the Trilobites and all the other denizens of the Burgess Shale must have had oodles of ancestors that "evolved". Random accidental DNA copying error by copying error, over gazillions of years, to create structures such as bones, shells, arms, legs, mouths, stomachs, digestive tracts, nervous systems and brains. But what became of them? The evolutionist answer is that they were not fortunate enough to die in Konservat Lagerstatten and so perished without trace because they had not yet evolved hard body parts – they were "non-calcified". How convenient!

Supposedly, however, the Trilobites are found because they did suddenly decide to acquire some hard body parts, an example perhaps of the inexplicable "explosive" evolution required by Gould's "punctuated equilibrium" theory. And so, once again, the theory generates the need for zillions of invisible "crystal sphere" intermediates, so to speak. Where none actually ever existed. And the cloven hoof is firmly imprinted on the observations. Clip, clop.

Mindful, perhaps, that this desperate attempt to salvage Darwin is just so much wishful thinking, one professional evolutionist cautiously commented to me that this "invisible ancestor" idea "somewhat ameliorates" the problem situation. And so evolutionists live in hope that Darwin's messianic predictions will one day come true, and the zillions of invisible transitional forms he enthusiastically envisaged will be magically resurrected from their phantom Lagerstatten – no doubt crying "vote Konservat!"

Darwin himself realized that there should be "strata rich in fossils beneath the Cambrian formation", but there are not. Did that lead him to forsake his false theory? Far from it. Instead he speculated that "formations much older than any now known may buried beneath the great oceans".

I WON'T GO TO REHAB – I SAID NO! NO! NO!

Evolutionists, like their idol, find it hard to forsake their addiction to error, always hopeful that one more fossiliferous fix will explain away the facts of the Cambrian Explosion, for example.

In struggling to explain the sudden appearance of fully formed complex creatures such as Trilobites in the Cambrian rocks, Keith B. Miller of Kansas State University is ever optimistic, enthusing: "Our understanding of the early history of life is presently in an exciting stage of rapid change and revision." Revision being the key word.

Attempting to explain away the lack of intermediate fossils in general, he continues: "The recognition of transitional forms is as much a question of taxonomy as it is a statement about the nature of the fossil record . . . it is thus important to recognize that names do much more than describe nature. *They also interpret it*. There is considerable ferment now within the field of taxonomy because of conflicting philosophies of classification". Clip, clop.

IS THIS A TRANSITIONAL FORM I SEE BEFORE ME?
What Miller seems to be saying here is that by modifying the definition of what constitutes a "transitional form", evolutionists once again twist the facts to fit the theory, see what they want to see, and so create oodles of intermediates out of thin air – a not-uncommon procedure apparently in the mucky bog of evolutionary biology. Clip, clop.

CLADISTIC CLAPTRAP
This in fact is the thrust of "Cladistics". As we have seen, Cladistic analysis is based on the fundamental assumption that since evolution is True, then all organisms must necessarily be related to one another anyway, and must have descended from a single common ancestor. No proof needed. It is apparently self-evident, axiomatic, as it was to Darwin and some of the ancient atheistic Greek philosophers.

As a result, any similarity between organisms can be taken as absolute "scientific proof" that they are cousins sharing a common ancestor, and belong on the same branch or twig of an evolutionary tree - as shown opposite for mammals, reptiles, amphibians and fish. Notice how birds are supposed to be descended from reptiles. Transitional forms, such as "fishibians", would exist where the chart branches.

Cladistics supposedly demonstrates, for example, that birds evolved from dinosaurs, and that human beings had worms as ancestors, an intellectual affront to any right thinking person who has not yet nibbled the magic mushroom of Darwinism.

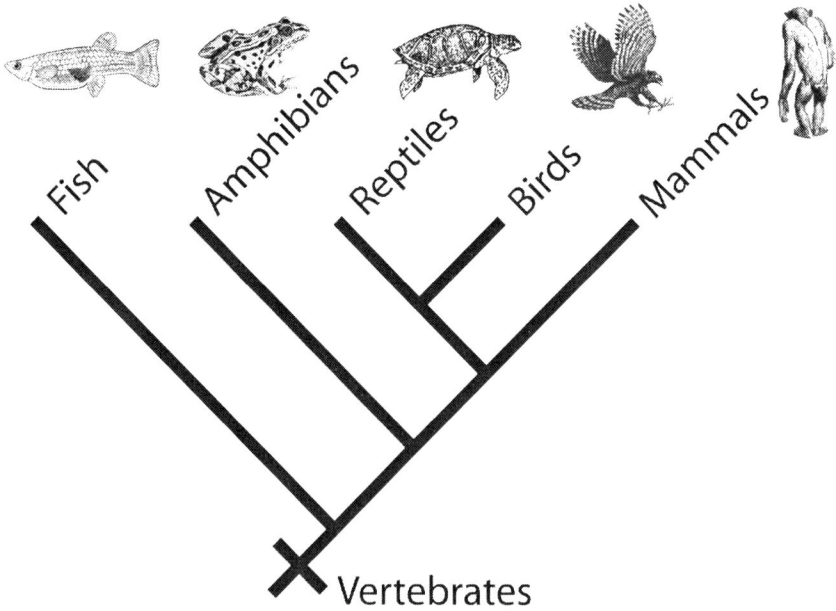

Vertebrates

That said, however, some evolutionists do reject such nonsense and even question the sacred technique itself, claiming that "Cladistics has become dogma" - a fact lamented at length by Kevin Padian of the University of California, Berkeley. So disturbing is the refusal of such heretics to bend the knee to Cladistics, that more faithful brethren have been known to grumble to Padian: "So what is it with these anti-theropod people? It sounds like you are arguing with creationists."

Perhaps Kevin's students should heed to the following comment on the cladistic method from top Cambridge professor, Simon Conway Morris: Quote: "It doesn't work!" The reason being "convergence", the common phenomenon of virtually identical features existing in clearly unrelated organisms that even the cladistics computer cannot link together, such as the identical eyes of human beings and squid. Ah well, moving on from that difficulty.

I should point out that Conway Morris has a refreshing attitude, as well as keen sense of humor -- being more interested in examining and investigating the unexplained, rather than sitting back and assuming evolution has solved all mysteries. Although a confirmed evolutionist, he is not blind to the problems that lesser disciples prefer to close their eyes and minds to.

HISTORY REPEATS ITSELF

We have already seen, as Eldredge and Gould discovered, how evolutionists have a talent for seeing what they want to see in the fossil record. Now, with Cladistics, they can actually create what they want to see by the use of computers, tweaking the variables and re-running the program until the outcome is acceptable.

As explained previously, Cladistics works on the assumption that evolution is an absolute Truth. So wings were "invented" more recently than legs, and legs more recently than fins, and feathers more recently than scales, and lungs more recently than gills, and so on. Then, on the basis of such assumptions, even minute features of organisms' morphologies are analyzed to sift and sort them into detailed branching family trees of descent. As thousands of new fossils are found, they are slotted into the scheme. That chart does of course include existing as well as extinct organisms, although G-Theory regards them as separate creations.

Since modern evolution simply regards all organisms as being "transitional" anyway, vast numbers of supposed intermediate forms are instantly created where none existed before. Abracadabra! It's just a matter of squeezing the gaps, by finding some kind of common feature. Little wonder, as we saw earlier, that over recent decades many evolutionists regard Cladistics as the best thing since sliced bread.

So prolific has computerised Cladistics been in generating such mythical family trees, that the esteemed "New Scientist" magazine now claims that: "In fact, there are *too many fossils with intermediate features to count* - trillions if you include micro fossils. These fossils show the transitions between major groups, from fish to amphibians for instance, as well as from one species to another. New discoveries are continually made."

Of anybody who still doubts the contrived claims of Cladistics, "New Scientist" comments: "There isn't a nice way of saying this", they are "either appallingly ignorant or an *outright liar.*"

WHEN IS A TRIANGLE NOT A TRIANGLE?

The following quote from Keith Miller illustrates the convenient flexibility of Cladistic thinking as applied to simple geometric shapes: "Triangles and quadrilaterals . . . are easily separated into two classes of geometric shapes. Now, if one side of the quadrilateral were reduced in length by infinitesimal amounts until it was only two geometric points wide, it would still be a quadrilateral by definition, although absolutely indistinguishable from a triangle." Clip, clop.

Darwin would be delighted! "Yes sir, this does look like a triangle, but if you really want a quadrilateral, we can give it an infinitely short and invisible fourth side! See? Of course, you could have a pentagon, if you prefer, but we do charge a bit more that." And so the "cloven hoof" imposes its sinister imprint – as "gaps" in the fossil record suddenly close up and become "transitions". As with the heavenly crystal spheres mentioned earlier, the whole Cladistic construct is imaginary and unnecessary nonsense that is swept away by G-Theory.

G-THEORY

G-Theory, the literal and accurate reading of the Genesis account of creation, as promoted by William Buckland, requires no missing links or imperfect transitional forms - but only perfectly formed micro-evolutionary varieties of the original "kinds" of organisms God created in Genesis -- with the bizarre and extinct organisms of the Paleozoic and Mesozoic rocks being consigned to a previous, pre-Adamic age. As a result, G-Theory is in complete accord with the fossil record and renders Darwin's theory of evolution redundant. Dare we say extinct!?

FUNNY PHYLA

Indeed, evolution, if true, appears to have worked backwards in the Cambrian Explosion. For although it would suggest that a few "simple" organisms would have arisen, and reproduced and diversified, over deep time, ready to be classified and grouped on the basis of similarities into species, genus, family, etc. , the fossil record shows the exact opposite.

To understand, note that Phyla are the broadest groupings of animals -- dogs and fish, for example, being "chordata" (having backbones), snails, slugs and squid being "mollusca" (soft, but sometimes with a shell), and bees, spiders and lobsters being "arthropods" (jointed feet). Note, however, that as with cladistics, the definitions of these terms is very fluid and confusing, and the whole classification system may well be a futile attempt to compartmentalize the creative genius of God.

That said, however, we are told that organisms from some 100 Phyla are found already existing in the Cambrian, compared with only 30 or so extant today. Perhaps this is another clue to the existence of Buckland's pre-historic world, one containing flora and fauna sometimes similar to those of our world and sometimes totally different. Those numbers can, of course, vary depending on definition.

As eager evolutionists Roger Lewin puzzles: "Why, if evolution has been so prolific, have no new animal Phyla or body plans appeared over the hundreds of millions of years that have elapsed since? How come it all happened at once?" . . . like an act of "Creation" perhaps! Ah well, moving on from that difficulty . . .

2.4

JEAN BAPTISTE PIERRE ANTOINE DE MONET LAMARCK

A few decades earlier than the arrival of "Origins", the French naturalist and evolutionist Jean Baptiste de Lamarck (1744-1829) had strongly promoted radical evolutionary ideas in a series of books claiming that all species, including man, had somehow descended, without divine intervention, from other, earlier species. And ultimately from lifeless matter.

Lamarck, who was described by Darwin as "the first man whose conclusions on the subject excited much attention", was the first person to present evolutionary ideas in a systematic form - supported by what was regarded at the time as convincing evidence, even proof.

Although Darwin's theory of evolution was totally different, as we saw earlier, few people seem to be aware that he did not reject Lamarck's ideas out of hand. He simply regarded Natural Selection as the major and more important mechanism at work.

LAMARCK'S SIGNATURE
However, although the scientific community did later totally reject Lamarck's ideas, Darwin having won the day, modern reference works show that his "dead" theory refuses to lie down. In fact, in their book "Lamarck's Signature", researchers Steele, Lindley and Blanden assure us that Lamarck's ideas work well in *describing* how animal populations acquire immunity to disease. Describing, of course, is not the same thing as *explaining*.

As a result, they strongly dispute the views of Darwin's modern disciple, Richard Dawkins, who seems to out-Darwin Darwin in maintaining that evolution occurs by Natural Selection exclusively. And that all the mind-boggling complexity of nature originally arose by the accidental accumulation of random blind-chance DNA copying errors that occur during reproduction.

Like Darwin, Lamarck had studied for the Christian ministry in his youth, but, on the death of his father, he left the Jesuit seminary at Amiens and joined the army. He later developed an interest in botany and biology – later still becoming the first person to distinguish "vertebrate" from "invertebrate" animals in classification, and one of the very first to apply the term "biology" to the study of living things.

AN ATHEISTIC THEORY
Unlike Darwin's theory, however, Lamarck's more elaborate and totally atheistic version sought to explain the ultimate origins of life itself, not just how variation might lead from one existing species to another.

Lamarck was said to have a vivid imagination. That talent, combined with an almost total ignorance of what he was talking about, led him to naively claim that "life" was created by "spontaneous generation - easily conceived as resulting from such agencies as heat and electricity causing in small gelatinous bodies a singular tension". Jus' like that, jus' like that!

Having so easily disposed of the minor problem of the origin of "life", Lamarck then went on to propose four laws by the agency of which, he claimed, modern organisms had arisen from those imaginary "small gelatinous bodies in singular tension":

1) Life naturally tends to increase the volume of any body possessing it.
2) The creation of a new organ in an animal body arises from a need.
3) Organs develop to the extent they are used.
4) All that has been acquired or changed in the organization of an individual is passed on to the next generation.

Although Lamarck could offer no explanation of how these magical mutational processes worked, his observations of the way nature actually operates are increasingly being found to be accurate. And, as such, more sensible than Darwin's speculations of evolutionary change by means of the steady accumulation of minute variations over thousands of millions of years, accompanied by a steady flow of unfit rejects onto the compost pile of paleontology.

Notice two key ideas:

A) The physiology of organisms can vary, generation by generation, in response to the *needs* or pressures of their environment, implying some kind of feedback mechanism as work – the famous "inheritance of acquired characteristics" theory, and B) Over generations, unused organs can atrophy and be lost, and new ones acquired according to need – the famous "use and disuse" theory.

Although the amazing mutational processes by which such real and observed micro-evolutionary variations occur are still not understood, it seems increasingly likely that such adaptive mechanisms have been engineered into all organisms. Thereby the original Genesis "kinds" were equipped with the ability, generation by generation, to colonize the corners of the planet and meet the needs of mankind.

Evolutionist Derek Hough's "Self-developing Genome" is just such a mechanism. Oddly, however, Hough claims that the first genome arrived ready made on earth on a comet from a parallel universe. I suspect he was misquoting the great Francis Crick, the chap who worked out the architecture of the DNA molecule, along with his co-worker, Dr. Watson.

HOW THE GIRAFFE GOT HIS LONG NECK
Thus, we are often told, although he apparently did not actually say it, that Lamarck claimed that the giraffe's neck became elongated by generations of stretching to reach high foliage on tall trees. And that the kangaroo's front legs, conversely, shrank from generations of disuse when it acquired the habit of sitting upright to carry its young in its pouch. Two classic examples of "acquired characteristics" being "inherited" and passed on from one generation to the next.

Lamarck's "Just So Story" kind of speculations were, of course, simplistic in the extreme. As evolutionist Gordon Rattray Taylor points out in "The Great Evolution Mystery", Lamarck's imaginary primitive giraffe with its newly extended neck would have immense problems breathing, needing to suck sufficient fresh air into the lungs via a narrow eight-foot tube and also discharge the carbon dioxide by the same route without suffocating in the process. Another problem would be that of dangerously high blood pressure developing in its head when bending down.

Taylor goes on to describe some of the astonishing and coordinated design features by which "evolution" supposedly solved these problems, one of which involves the presence of a special high-pressure fluid between the giraffe's body cells.

Taylor's point is that all this "evolutionary" change required multiple cunningly coordinated mutations to make it possible. Dismissing Lamarck's claim as inadequate nonsense, and in a neat reversal, Taylor suggests that the real reason a giraffe has or needs a long neck is because it has such long legs, and actually spends far more time grazing low down off the ground rather than off tall trees. And since the female's neck is some two feet shorter than the male's anyway, the suggestion that the long neck was crucial to survival was also nonsense.

THE EVOLUTIONARY SCRAP HEAP

Although Lamarck's theory was later discarded, partly because of the famous incident of research studies being foolishly falsified by a Soviet scientist who wanted to promote it for political reasons, it still refuses to go away, especially in the field of acquired immunity to disease, as already noted.

Notice, however, a crucial difference between the theories of Lamarck and Darwin. Although Darwin required Natural Selection to reject innumerable intermediate, unfit forms and "missing links" and chuck them on the evolutionary scrap heap, Lamarck postulated the emergence of only meaningful, holistic changes in response to the pressures of the environment.

Lamarck's concept of the way nature works therefore matched much better with the facts of the fossil record, and indeed the principles of G-Theory, which allows limited constructive variation, within the boundaries of the original Genesis "kinds". Since God evidently wanted dogs and cats and ducks, for example, to exist as separate creatures, he made no provision for one kind to "evolve" into another.

Notice, however, that Lamarck and Darwin did both share the same elementary and unscientific error of extrapolating observed, limit-*ed* variation to limit-*less* infinity, in order to make macro-evolution a possibility. Notice also that whereas G-Theory begins, in this age, with the Genesis "kinds", a discrete set of complex and familiar organisms, such as cows and sheep and bees and birds, Lamarck claimed that all extant organisms evolved from just one primitive organism.

Incidentally, the Russian scientist mentioned above, Trofim Denisovich Lysenko, rejected Darwin and embraced Lamarck, because he wanted to believe that just as organisms could actively adapt to the needs of their environment, so citizens could adapt themselves to the needs of the Soviet State. Incidentally, Lysenko was so scornful of genetic research being carried out on fruit flies by hopeful Darwinians that when he became director of the Moscow Genetic Institute, he had them all boiled to death - the fruit flies, that is, not the

Darwinians. A kind of purge, I suppose.

PANGENESIS

Some ten years after the publication of his original work, Darwin was forced to accept that Natural Selection simply could not credibly account for a whole range of complex phenomena, even the sexual and asexual reproduction of plants, let alone that of human beings. Another difficulty was the observed sudden reappearance in organisms of traits supposedly bred out of them generations earlier.

As a result, in a later publication he freely admitted that he had put too much stress on Natural Selection as a mechanism, and that an additional idea was needed. He called it "Pangenesis".

Pangenesis appears to have been Darwin's attempt to refine Lamarck's four laws into a formal theory. As it stood, Lamarck's so-called theory simply asserted, for example, that new characteristics acquired by organisms in response to their environment could somehow be assimilated into their "organization" and so passed on to their offspring. But no actual cause-and-effect mechanism by which that could occur was suggested. What the brilliant Darwin did was to devise a remarkably modern-sounding scheme by which such feedback could conceivably take place – given the help of a few vague verbs.

According to Pangenesis (the prefix "pan" means "everywhere" or "in all parts"), each and every part of an organism generates minute "gemmules" or "pangenes" of genetic information which flow around the body in the blood. Thus the pangenes would carry information, such as the disuse of the eyes by a mole living underground, back to sex cells. Those cells would then respond by creating in the next generation a few suitably modified offspring that Natural Selection could then get to work on - thereby generating a new population more suitably adapted to their working environment, i.e. blind moles in this case.

Notice, however, that although the moles become blind, the genetic potential to restore vision somehow lingers on. In fact, parallel experiments have been conducted with fast-breeding fruit flies, demonstrating that very "reversion effect". Perhaps I should mention here that "White Mice Day" occurs every April 1 – a time when white mice everywhere celebrate the fact that, due to a dramatically shorter gestation period, fruit flies are now the preferred victims of interesting scientific investigations rather than them. Cheese consumption usually doubles that day.

I suspect that part of the appeal of Pangenesis to Darwin was that it envisioned organisms actively responding to their environment – a much less passive, and potentially faster-acting mechanism than the accumulation of small random variations under the action of Natural Selection.

Of course, what Darwin was suggesting with Pangenesis implied even greater inner complexity in organism than ever before – and how the pangenes ever evolved in the fist place, he naturally had no idea. It's that power of positive thinking again.

A GENETIC CHASTITY BELT

In modern terminology, what both Lamarck and Darwin in his second theory postulated was that organisms contain a sophisticated *feedback mechanism* whereby their genetic structure can somehow respond creatively to the pressure and needs of the environment – which is precisely what G-Theory also suggests.

However, according to current evolutionary orthodoxy, such feedback is totally impossible, being forbidden by the "Weismann barrier", which supposedly prevents any communication of information from normal body cells back to the sex or "germ" cells of an organism – thereby making Lamarck's idea of the passing on of "acquired characteristics" from one generation to the next an absolute no-no. The influential Weismann apparently said just that: "It is impossible!" It sounds more convincing in German, I'm told.

Some scientists now describe the "Weismann barrier", which was simply a rule or convenient assumption anyway, as a "genetic chastity belt" around the sex cells, but one that is "selectively permeable", given the right circumstances. And so another scientific assumption bites the dust.

THE FINGERPRINT GENIUS

One of the opponents of Pangenesis was Darwin's clever cousin, Francis Galton, the inventor of finger printing.

As already noted, according to Pangenesis, the units of heredity that Darwin called pangenes were carried around the body in the blood, Seeking to disprove the theory, Galton took several rabbits of different colors and swapped their blood, and so presumably also their pangenes, by transfusions before then breeding them to find out what color their offspring would be as a result.

As Galton predicted, the transfusions had absolutely no effect – other than presenting Darwin with yet another headache.

The accepted theory of heredity in Darwin's day was that of "blending", and Galton's own particular version claimed that offspring received 25% genetic information from each parent and 12.5% from each grandparent. The consequent implication of blending was that interbreeding would soon dilute and destroy any new variation arising in an organism, like mixing colored paints together. This objection was a major problem for Darwin and was one more reason for his interest in Pangenesis. Another problem, according to Robin Hennig, was the fact that he was virtually innumerate and completely unable to understand Galton's mathematical theories of heredity anyway.

Little did Darwin know that even as he struggled with this problem, the monk Gregor Mendel had already proved that genetic traits are either inherited or not inherited, digital fashion, 0 or 1 as in computer code, and do not become blended and diluted. Recent research, however, has shown that in some organisms the traits do get blended – which is probably why Charles and his chums latched onto the idea in the first place.

2.5

THE ORIGIN OF VARIATION

As we saw at the outset, evolution requires a constant supply of variations for Natural Selection to work on – but where do variations come from? Darwin assumed that they just happened, and that was good enough – and also that those variations could go on accumulating, coordinating and extending ad infinitum, given a good slice of "deep time".

HUGO DE VRIES

In 1900 Hugo de Vries suggested a modification of Darwin's theory called "mutationism". Although other evolutionists, such as Haldane, rushed to discredit him, de Vries had concluded from his practical observations of nature that there are two distinct and very different kinds of variation in organisms:

The first kind were "Ordinary" variations, such as the tiny differences found in a litter of kittens or the offspring of any organism. According to de Vries, Natural Selection working on these "ordinary" variations could never, under any circumstances, even in millions of years, "lead to a transgression of species", as he put it.

The second kind were "Mutations" which were somehow caused, he suggested, by spontaneous and mysterious alterations in the genes, and which yielded significant modifications of the organism. Zillions of these, he speculated, might eventually accumulate to create new species. So Hugo was making the same assumption as Darwin and Lamarck, i.e. limit-*less* variation.

According to de Vries, mutations, which result in wholesale, coordinated modifications, rather than miniscule variations, never arise gradually, little by little, by the accumulation of small changes, but come about suddenly without any visible preparation or transition – a fact consistently confirmed in the fossil record, and still a source of dissension among evolutionists today as they ponder the problem of "punctuated equilibrium".

I believe it was de Vries who said, in his book "Species and Varieties: Their Origin by Mutation", that: "Natural selection may explain the *survival* of the fittest, but it cannot explain the *arrival* of the fittest".

Although Darwin was aware of "mutations" as exploited by plant breeders of the day, he had no credible explanation for them, and therefore preferred to focus on "ordinary" variations. Dr. Dawkins and his devotees, however, still expect us to believe that even these meaningful "mutations", and the genes involved originate from the fortuitous accumulation of random DNA copying errors.

POLYGENES

Even de Vries' "ordinary" variation in organisms such as puppies, for example, is not as simple as Darwin supposed, because it depends on two different factors. Part of the variation is simply due to variables such as the health of the mother, the nutritional intake of the puppies before and since birth, and even the position of a particular puppy in the womb. All of which, de Vries pointed out, can have no kind of evolutionary knock-on effect because the effect is not inherited by the next generation.

According to current theory, the remainder of this "ordinary" variation is due to the action of "polygenes". In contrast to traits such as eye color which may be under the control of a single "major" gene, quantitative variations, such as height or the size of a particular bone, are thought to be controlled by the cumulative action of several genes. If this were not the case, then, after allowing for environmental variation, all members of a population would be identical in every way. At least, that is the theory as of lunchtime today, but they might change their minds tomorrow.

Such is the complexity of the chromosome structure, which is still poorly understood, the several polygenes for a given trait may be located far apart, with "junk" genes interspersed between. Astonishingly, the polygene team players may even be located on different chromosomes, and may even help influence other traits as well.

Whilst some polygenes tend to maximise (+) a trait, others will tend to minimize it (-). With just a few polygenes at work (+ and -), a range of say a dozen discrete dimension values might be possible for a particular feature because of the possible combinations. However, when the environmental/nutritional factor is blended in, the illusion of a continuous height range is created.

Natural interbreeding will shuffle the distribution of the polygenes in a given population of organism, resulting in a typical average size with a range of sizes above and below. By selective breeding of taller members of a population, however, a tall breed could be created, which would have only the (+) polygenes in their sex cells for a particular trait, their "genotype". At that point, however, unless cross breeding or a mutation occurs, no further increase will be possible.

HAIRY STUFF!

The action of polygenes has been investigated using the Drosophila Melanogaster fruit fly, which is used in such studies because it breeds so rapidly – being able to produce a new generation every 12 days, or 30 times a year. One particular study focused on the number of bristles on the flies' bodies, which was found to vary in a certain population from 26 up to 55, with an average of 40. According to theory, those with more hairs had mostly (+) polygenes for hair count and those with fewest had mostly the (-) type. Incidentally, the impressive name Drosophila Melanogaster simply means "black bellied honey lover".

As expected, by carefully interbreeding those with average bristle counts, and selecting out those offspring with a higher count, scientists found that they could quickly create a population with the maximum possible number of 55, but no more – an interesting illustration of "micro-evolution", better described as simple variation. Without some kind of new mutation occurring, that was the limit of the variation for that particular trait.

QUESTION TIME

At this point, readers might like to test their understanding of polygenes by explaining the following historical fact: "Over a 75 year period, starting in 1800, selective breeding of sugar beet plants was able to increase the sugar content from 6% to 17% - but there the improvement stopped, and further selection did not increase the sugar content any further."

ALLELOMORPHS AND POLYMORPHISM

A major gene that controls a feature such as color will be located at a specific position on a chromosome called its "locus". In the snail Cepaea Nemoralis, for example, there are several genes for shell color extant in a typical snail population, including brown, pink and yellow. However, since the chromosomes are in pairs there will only be two "loci" available for color genes to occupy in a particular snail. As a result, no single snail can in theory carry the genetic information for all possible shell colors. Such a feature or locus is said to be "polymorphic", a term which simply means "many shapes or forms" – and the alternative genes for a given trait are called "alleles", or "allelomorphs".

Since in many organisms, such as insects and flowers, some 30 to 50% of the loci on the chromosomes may be polymorphic, the potential variety of combinations is vast – so that in a field of sunflowers, for example, which are visibly and evidently the same variety, no two individual plants might be identical in every detail – such as height, stem thickness, surface texture, petal width, shade of color, etc.,

As a result, a plant breeder let loose on our field of sunflowers could soon start "out-breeding" features he didn't want, and "inbreeding" to select those he did want – probably being rewarded along the way by a few interesting mutations generated by the creative action of the "Self-developing Genome" that has apparently been engineered into every organism.

By combining the action of allelomorphs and polygenes and a steady stream of mutations, a vast amount of variation is possible, again as demonstrated by dogs – but all of it within the basic design or "bauplan" of the "kind" of organism concerned, and none of it "evolution" in the deluded Darwinian sense. Which is why Professor Sheppard, in his book "Natural Selection and Heredity", frankly admits that: "No mutation converting one species into another has ever been observed". A revealing admission.

MUTATION OR MUTATION?
In 1927, de Vries' idea of variation by "mutation" as the mechanism of evolution was further developed by Russian entomologist Yuri Filipchenko, in a book entitled "Variability and Variation", where he introduced the terms "micro-evolution" and "macro-evolution", useful descriptors which we have already employed in our discussion.

The idea was that "micro-evolution" described the mutational variation within a species or "kind" of organism, such as those observed and exploited by plant and animal breeders – and that "macro-evolution" described the massive variation that evolutionists assume must have happened in order for fish, for example, to have developed legs and turned into land animals, etc.,

Although micro-evolution is a well established and useful fact of life designed to give mankind a creative handle on the earth's ecology, macro-evolution is a creation myth in the minds of evolutionists, a Darwinian delusion.

A ROYAL SOCIETY STATEMENT

Prompted by demands of creationists to have Intelligent Design (ID) taught in schools alongside evolution, the Royal Society in London issued a statement condemning ID. The extract that follows illustrates yet again the infantile Darwinian delusion of failing to distinguish between the reality of limit-*ed* micro-evolution and the mythical limit-*less* macro-evolution, as well as repeating Darwin's basic mathematical error of unwarranted extrapolation beyond the range of available data:

> "The process of evolution can be seen in action today, for example in the development of resistance to antibiotics in disease-causing bacteria, of resistance to pesticides by insect pests, and the rapid evolution of viruses that are responsible for influenza and AIDS. Darwin's theory of evolution helps us to understand these problems."

For "evolution" here, read "variation within their Genesis kind" or "micro-evolution".

INTELLIGENT DESIGN

Incidentally, ID, which is now seen as the major threat to the evolutionary establishment, is well described in the same Royal Society statement which continues: "Some proponents of an alternative explanation for the diversity of life on Earth now claim that their theories are based on scientific evidence. One such view is presented as the theory of *intelligent design.* This proposes that some species are *too complex* to have evolved through Natural Selection and that therefore life on Earth must be the product of a 'designer'."

Notice, in the phrase "evolved through Natural Selection", the misleading and actually un-Darwinian implication that Natural Selection somehow creates variation or mutation in organisms, rather than simply screening or acting on it when it occurs.

Sadly, perhaps as a consequence of the narrow specialization that necessarily denies virtually all scientists a comprehensive overview of the whole field, the spokesman for the august body then trots out the following favorite falsehood, claiming that ID supporters "make only selective reference to the *overwhelming scientific evidence that supports evolution*". The Discovery Institute (www.Discovery.org) has lists of hundreds of highly qualified and enlightened engineers, doctors, geologists, etc., who now refute the existence of that "overwhelming evidence".

A WISE MOVE
It is interesting that although creationists clearly see the errors of evolution, they in turn clearly see the key error of "creationism", namely the unscriptural claim that the earth is no more than six thousand years old, an easy target which they attack with enthusiasm.

The Intelligent Design movement has therefore been very wise in re-engineering the debate, so to speak, and removing barriers to the acceptance of their criticisms by confining their attention to the errors of evolution without making any counter claims regarding Genesis, the age of the earth, or even identifying God as the Intelligent Designer. Instead they focus on the infantile claims of Darwin and Dawkins, which are an affront to the common sense of any right-thinking person, namely that the mind-boggling complexity of life on earth somehow created itself accidentally by the endless accumulation of DNA copying errors.

SYNTHETIC EVOLUTION
The year Filipchenko published his book, a brilliant young member of his research team, Theodosius Dobzhansky migrated to the United States where he gained fame as the champion of the concept of "synthetic evolution" - which was a blend of Darwin's natural selection and Mendel's discoveries in genetics that had been developed a few years earlier by geneticists such as J.B.S. Haldane and R.A. Fisher, but published in such abstruse mathematical terms that most biologist simply could not understand what they were talking about.

What Dobzhansky did, in a book of his own entitled "Genetics and Origin of Species", was to explain the concepts much more simply, and attempt to apply them to practical problems of interest to evolutionists. As a result, by 1950 Darwin's theory of evolution by natural selection was universally believed by biologists, and the Synthetic theory version in particular had become widely accepted.

Note, however, that biologists at that time still had little notion of the massive complexity waiting to be revealed by the scanning electron microscope and the research of Watson and Crick – and even less understanding of how mutations could possibly arise. They simply let their imaginations take flight, assuming, like Darwin himself, that since "micro-evolution" was a fact of life, that any and all organisms therefore had the in built potential for the infinite variation required by "macro-evolution".

Modern evolutionists, such as Derek Hough, however, know better and openly admit that although they accept evolution as a "faith", they still have no clue, when confronted by the mind-boggling complexity of the cell, as to how it could possibly have originated.

IT AIN'T NECESSARILY SO!

Evolutionists of the 1960s, still pretty ignorant of the utter inner complexity of any and all living organisms, firmly believed and confidently taught an updated version of Darwinism. Namely, that evolution takes place by the steady accumulation, over vast eras of time, of small changes in the genes – claiming that the fossil record proved it.

So convincing was their specious reasoning, at least to young college students, that Stephen J. Gould, who later became an exalted grand master of the evolutionary cause, commented: "I well remember how the 'synthetic theory' beguiled me with its unifying power when I was a graduate student in the mid-1960s". Adding, however: "Since then I have been watching it *slowly unravel* as a universal description of evolution . . . I have been reluctant to admit it - since beguiling is often forever - that the theory, as a general proposition, is effectively *dead*, despite its persistence as textbook orthodoxy." Did somebody say "textbook"!

PUNCTUATED EQUILIBRIUM

In 1972, a more mature Stephen J. Gould, along with Niles Eldredge, published a paper challenging the synthetic model of evolution as a gradual process, proposing instead a "punctuated equilibrium" model, whereby, as apparently evidenced by the fossil record, major evolutionary changes took place step-wise in limited gene pools after radical climate changes – not at all in the gradual way Darwin envisioned or could possibly explain.

As often happens in science, Gould's term of punctuated equilibrium cleverly describes or labels a phenomenon without actually explaining it – namely the fact that the fossil record continues to show sets of distinct and fully formed organisms rather than the gradual gradation demanded by Darwin.

The paper, later described as a "time bomb", was apparently ignored by orthodoxy for some five years, until a second paper was published, the outcome of which was a special conference in Chicago where, according to a report in Science magazine: "Clashes of personality and academic sniping created palpable tension".

Much of the evidence for the new theory was provided by our old friends the trilobites – since in passing from one rock strata to the next, dramatically different fossil forms appeared. However, even today, trilobite buffs are still cracking open lumps of rock and shuffling fossil bits about hoping to discover evidence of some kind of gradual development of one trilobite variety into the next – which would of course simply illustrate micro-evolution.

Speaking of such extinct organisms, Gould said: "They appear in the fossil record looking much the same as when they disappear" – and even more specifically: "In any local area, a species *does not arise gradually* by the steady transformation of its ancestors; it appears all at once and *'fully formed'*". The late Dr. Gould seems to have been a bit of a heretic.

Incidentally, punctuated equilibrium seems to have been a simple reversion to the early days of evolution when two schools of thought emerged – the "continuous" school who thought like Darwin that evolution had occurred in tiny steps, and the "discontinuous" who saw change occurring in large steps, i.e. meaningful mutations.

CONVICTION
Despite his rejection of the synthetic theory however, Gould reaffirmed the "Faith", commenting that "Evolutionary theory is now enjoying this uncommon vigor. Yet amidst all this turmoil *no biologist has been led to doubt the fact that evolution occurred.* We are debating *how* it happened. We are all trying to explain the same thing: the tree of evolutionary descent linking all organisms by ties of genealogy. Creationists pervert and caricature this debate by conveniently neglecting the common *conviction* that underlies it, and by falsely suggesting that evolutionists now doubt the very phenomenon *we are struggling to understand.*" Keep struggling, chaps. Why don't I brew up another cup of conviction? Instant be OK. ?

THE "CREEPS" VERSUS THE "JERKS"
The embarrassing intellectual debacle of evolution to which Gould contributed was well reported in the prestigious British news magazine the Economist (December 2006 issue, article "Repeat after me") which described the two current and conflicting schools of thought. On the one side we have the "Creeps" who believe, like Darwin and Dawkins, that evolution must have

taken place gradually and over vast ages of time in order to lend the process any shred of credibility. On the other side we have the "Jerks", the "punctuated equilibrium" pundits who think that evolution must have taken place in jumps, in order to explain the absence of "intermediate" or "unfit" forms in the fossil record that Darwin required as the crucial proof of his theory.

FORGET THE FOSSIL RECORD!

Meanwhile, G-Theory suggests that the bulk of the fossil record, from the Trilobite to the age of the dinosaurs, from the Cambrian to the Upper Cretaceous, represents the flora and fauna of a previous, pre-Adamic world. If so, those exotic organisms did not evolve into present day plants and animals, because they were catastrophically destroyed and made extinct anyway. If that is so, then the findings of the fossil record would seem to be irrelevant to any discussion of the origins of present-day organisms. So that the plants and animals we know today are simply variants of the "kinds" whose creation is described in Genesis.

THE VIEW OF GREGOR MENDEL

Slipping back in time, Austrian monk, Gregor Mendel, "father of modern genetics", was busy carrying out his brilliant investigations into the genetic properties of garden peas at the very time Darwin was busy developing his theory of evolution. He published his findings in the transactions of the "Brunn Natural History Society" in 1866.

One year earlier, and evidently somewhat aware of the various evolutionary ideas that were brewing up, and the challenge being posed to the inspired Genesis account of creation, Mendel made the following comments in a lecture: "No one will seriously maintain that in the open country the development of plants is ruled by other laws than in the garden bed. Here, as there, changes of type must take place *if the conditions of life be altered*, and the species possesses the capacity of fitting itself to its new environment. [However,] *nothing justifies the assumption* that the tendency to form varieties increases so extraordinarily that the species speedily lose all stability, and their offspring diverge into an endless series of extremely variable forms."

Gregor seems to be suggesting that a change in environment can stimulate a creative response in a plant. Lamarck had a similar idea.

Notice that Mendel clearly perceived the Darwin delusion – understanding that although God had engineered into organisms the ability to adapt or "fit" themselves to altered "conditions of life" in "new environments", "*nothing justifies the assumption*" that "extraordinary" and "endless" variation can take place.

Mendel, incidentally, was only an amateur naturalist, which may help explain why he had long forsaken his research work to take on active and arduous duties in the Church and was in fact deceased before his outstanding discoveries were ever properly appreciated by the scientific community.

STABILITY AND CHANGE
Notice that Mendel was concerned with how organisms pass on their already existing features, such as tall and dwarfing growth habits – probably realizing that were it not for a steady flow of mutations, the variety of life would have stagnated long ago. Darwin, however, was more interested in change or "evolution", a term which first appeared in an anonymous article, possibly authored by his uncle.

Despite the occurrence of mutations, DNA is actually very stable and very resistant to change – with Professor Sheppard pointing out that there is a "complicated repair mechanism which *often* restores the molecule to its original form" if a mistake is made in the self-copying process. This, he says, is why mutations are very rare. He then tests our credulity by happily accepting that "new and striking varieties arise suddenly" - simply as a result of random individual DNA copying *error*s.

Amazing information on the processes by which each human cell identifies and corrects up to a millions lesions per day to the DNA molecules that encode its genome can be found on Wikipedia, article "DNA repair".

COMPOSER OR EDITOR?
According to G-Theory, all organisms contains versions of the "Self-developing Genome" postulated by Derek Hough which help fit them to purpose and enable them adapt to their environment, after the manner suspected by Lamarck.

Speculating on the origin of the variation required to feed natural selection, Darwin seems to have entertained a somewhat similar idea to Hough, as the following observation on breeding suggests, Quote: "Variability is not actually caused by man; he only unintentionally *exposes organic beings to new conditions of life*, and then nature acts on the organization and *causes it to vary.* But man can of course act on the variation given to him by nature . . . " Also: " . . . the organization seems to become plastic . . . it yields readily, when subjected to certain conditions . . . "

However, Hough would suggest that it is not "nature" that creates the variation but the organism itself responding to changed conditions. And the Darwin delusion, of course, was that such variation was limit-*less.*

In discussing the limitations of Natural Selection as an agent for change and adaptation compared to Hough's mechanism,   King and Jukes comment: "Natural Selection is the *editor*, rather than the *composer* of the genetic message.

MENDEL WOULD TURN IN HIS GRAVE
It used to be quite easy for evolutionists to hoodwink the scientifically uninitiated with their confident pronouncements as to the origins of man and the universe, but even the general public are now beginning to realize that scientists make an awful lot of mistakes and do an awful lot of changing their minds - notably in the area of nutrition and health, for example, where what was good to eat yesterday, such as full-fat butter or milk, is supposedly no longer good for us today, and what was once bad, such as coffee, may now help keep cancer at bay. According to the Da Vinci translation of the Bible discovered in my brother-in-law's garden shed last week, Moses actually led the people of Israel a the 'land of *low-fat* milk and honey'. What a visionary! I wonder how he knew all that stuff.

A significant recent overturning of a scientific absolute concerns Mendel's laws of inheritance, which figure prominently in "Neo-Darwinism".

Like people, cats and mice, for example, have "diploid" genes, which means that for each potential body characteristic, such as eye color, they have two genes, one from each parent. Which gene comes out on top in the ensuing sexual conflict, depends on which is "dominant" and which is "recessive". Incidentally, Mendel invented those terms.

Thus when two mice mate, the outcome for a particular trait will potentially depend on four genes, the two in each parent prior mating. In a pure breed, all four genes for eye color, for example, could be the same – so that only one color would be possible in the offspring. At least that is the theory, as currently taught in text books.

However, a recent article entitled "Mendel would turn in his grave", in the British New Scientist magazine says: "Another direct challenge has been posed to one of the cornerstones of biology, Mendel's laws of inheritance - which state that the characteristics of a particular offspring are dictated by DNA, by the combination of dominant and recessive genes in the two parents".

A SPOT OF BOTHER

Researchers at a university in Nice, France, have now discovered, in breeding experiments involving mice with brown tails and spotted tails, that even after several generations, and in direct violation of Mendel's laws, puppy mice may still be born with spotted tails when neither parent possesses the relevant genes. In the jargon, the spots had been "out bred".

The researchers suggest that in addition to DNA, the action of which is governed by Mendel's laws, molecules of RNA must also be transferred in the reproductive process and be instrumental in passing on genetic information no longer present in the genes, a kind of back-door delivery. How this happens is not yet understood, but the team leader stated that "such oddities are likely to be just the tip of the iceberg".

AN INSOLUBLE RIDDLE

Meanwhile, the lay observer could be forgiven for assuming from the confident and highly publicized assertions of evolutionists such as Richard Dawkins, who declares non-believers in the gospel of Darwin to be literally insane, that evolution already has all the answers - even attributing to DNA the creation of mind, personality, consciousness, emotion and instinct. When the simple fact is, as already noted, they do not even understand the function of the bulk of the DNA found in cells, casually dismissing it as so much genetic "junk".

Indeed, according to an article in the London Sunday Telegraph: "The most important scientific discovery of recent times is that the genes and their mechanism of inheritance are a *profound and seemingly insoluble riddle.*"

The author of the article points out in fact that: "the genes of man, mice and monkeys are virtually interchangeable, and not much different from a fly". Adding: "there is *nothing in the genes of a fly to explain why it should have six legs, a pair of wings and a brain the size of a full stop*", or for that matter why human beings should have two arms and two legs and "*a brain that is the most complex phenomenon in the universe*".

BAFFLED BOFFINS

According to the same source, boffins studying the human genome are "baffled" by the newly-revealed complexity of the cell, their findings "making uncomfortable reading for those who thought they understood the basics of biology" – as they realize that "junk" DNA is not junk at all, but is vital for staying alive. This, says the article, is yet another example of the "first law of biology", the simple fact that "life is always more complicated then you think". Such miraculous complexity not withstanding, the author's absolute faith in Evolution evidently remains unquestioned. A true believer indeed!

Perhaps the devout journalist could sympathize with a Dr. Rose recently quoted in the New Scientist as admitting: "*The tree of life is being politely buried* – we all know that. What's less accepted is our whole fundamental view of biology needs to change." Adding: "*Biology is vastly more complex than we thought* and facing up to this complexity will be as scary as the conceptual upheavals physicists had to take on board in the early 20th century." Cheer up chaps – it can only get worse!

2.6
A BRIEF HISTORY OF COMPLEXITY

Darwin knew nothing of chromosomes, genes and DNA, or even the genetic principles being investigated by the Gregor Mendel at the very same time he was writing his opus. As a result, the comparative ignorance of his evolutionary speculations put him on the level of a little child who squeezes a lump of modelling clay, pinches it a few times, then cries: "Look, mummy, I've made a doggy!"

The study of cells had begun with Robert Hooke (1635-1703) who used the newly available microscope to examine very thin slices of cork, and saw that they were composed of small segments that reminded him, for some reason, of the "cells" which monks occupied in monasteries. Hence the term we still use to today. His discoveries were published in 1665 in a book entitled "Micrographia".

Later, in 1805, the German naturalist Lorenz Oken stated what came to be known as the cell theory: "All life comes from cells and is made of cells", said to be the most important generalization in biology.

However, the importance of the cell as the basic unit of living organisms, let alone detail of its structure, was not firmly established until 1860 - one year after Darwin's book came out. Rudolph Virchow devised a Latin credo asserting that "All cells arise from cells". It was not until 1882, some 23 years after Origins, that German anatomist Walther Flemming was able to give a detailed description of the nine stages of change involved in cell division and reproduction, the process of mitosis that now figures in secondary school science texts.

CHROMOSOMES
The term "chromosome" was suggested by W. von Waldeyer in 1888 to describe the threadlike structures that became visible in dividing cells when dyed with "chromatin". By 1904, Theodor Boveri was able to count the numbers of chromosomes in the cell nuclei of several organisms, such as cats, wheat and tomatoes.

The removal of a chromosome, he found, caused offspring to be deformed in some way, leading him to conclude that Mendel's units of heredity, now called genes, must reside on the chromosomes in cells.

One year later, in 1905, ambitious Cambridge lecturer William Bateson proposed the term "genetics" to describe the rapidly expanding science of inheritance, basing it on the Greek word for "origins". Incidentally, Bateson was so excited about Darwin's theory that he once said in a letter to his sister "My brain boils with evolution!"

The term "gene" itself was not coined until 1909 when the wise Wilhelm Johannsen suggested it as a tool to facilitate fruitful discussion of the mysterious and as-yet-unidentified units of inheritance that had been investigated by Mendel and other workers.

CELL STRUCTURE

The detail observable through an ordinary microscope (its "resolution") is limited by the wavelength of visible light. This is because objects smaller than the wavelength of light will not disturb the waves passing over them enough to be detected - in just the way a pencil held in the path of a wave on the sea would also have minimal effect on its path or shape as it moved on to hit the shore. As a result, the maximum resolution of an ordinary optical microscope is about x3000, which although very useful, has severe limitations in investigating the structure of plant and animals cells which have a diameter of about a thousandth of a millimeter.

The scanning electron microscope however, developed in the 1940s, uses the extremely short waves associated with high-speed electrons as its "light", and has a resolution of the order of x1,000,000+. Suddenly a whole new cellular world of unsuspected complexity was made visible, and could even be viewed on the fluorescent screen of a TV monitor.

One of the complexities revealed is that every microscopic cell in our body contains several feet length of DNA -- so that one person's complete stock of DNA, stretched end to end, would reach to the moon and back several thousand times. Such are the miracles that Richard Dawkins happily attributes to the accidents of evolution.

But there is more -- because as millions of cells divide each second, we are actually generating thousands of miles of new DNA each minute!

MICRO-MANUFACTURING

It is well known that Darwin literally shuddered with fear when he contemplated the visible complexity of the human eye, knowing full well the futile inadequacy of his theory to account for its miraculous creation and design, as well as other wonders of nature he was well aware of. That probably explains why he suffered with severe psycho-somatic afflictions for many years. How astonishing it is, as he well knew, that the lens of the human eye is made thicker and thinner to focus on objects at different distances by a set of minute "ciliary" muscles that work without conscious effort.

That said, the detail revealed by the electron microscope would have surely given Darwin apoplexy – revealing structural detail of the cell such as the nucleus, chromosomes, genes, jumping genes, hox genes, DNA, RNA, chromatin, Golgi bodies, micro filaments, mitochondria, plastids, chromatin, micro-tubes, ribosomes, cytoplasm, enzymes, glycogen granules, selectively permeable membranes, lysosomes, micro-tubes, recticula, twisted strands, filaments, storage vesicles, secretory vesicles, etc.,   all vital parts of these incredible "micro manufacturing factories", and all of which then have their own internal molecular architecture. And all of which, Richard Dawkins still stoutly maintains, accidentally created themselves by the sifting action of Natural Selection on zillions of random DNA copying errors over gazillions of years! And he thinks creationists are the loony ones! I do wish he would shut up!

THE INTEGRITY OF THE CELL

In "The Chemistry of Life", Steven Rose attempts to explain for the layman some of what is presently known about the workings of a cell - the fact, for example, that the typical cell synthesizes several thousand new protein molecules per hour, using incredibly complex chemical reactions involving catalytic molecules called enzymes.

Incredibly, even after commenting that: "We have emphasized *the integrity* of the cell as a system, that *each part needs all the others in order to survive*", Rose remains a confirmed evolutionist, and happy to join in speculations as to how "life" accidentally arose out of mythical prehistoric pools of slime cocktail.

IS MAN A MONKEY?

Despite the genetic complexity already discovered, there is much left to learn. Rose points out, for example, that although human DNA is virtually identical to that of chimpanzees, about 97% , we not only look very different to chimps, but have vastly greater intellectual and creative capabilities. Clearly, there is something very different about the way those genes are "expressed". Why this should be, he happily admits: "We have no idea!"

The Bible gives a clue to help explain this mystery when it tells us there is a "spirit" in man, and almost certainly in animals – a spirit which imparts "understanding" (Job 32:8), and which evidently differentiates man from monkey, cat from dog, and so on. Clearly, there is more to man than mere atoms and molecules, and genes and chromosomes - as some evolutionists are actually beginning to suspect. Perhaps it is significant that Dr. Craig Venter of the human genome project   once commented: "In Vietnam, I saw people who gave up on life and died, and I saw other people who had no chance to live, yet did. The *human spirit* is a very powerful entity."

THE BIG QUESTION – GENE EXPRESSION AND REGULATION
A recent Yale University press release shares Rose's concern, saying: "The big question is why are humans so different (from apes)? What sort of changes in the environment or lifestyle could drive such a rapid shift in the *expression of genes* in humans and in no other primate?"

In classic Darwinian fashion, the Yale researchers seriously suggest that the differences between man and ape are explained in part by rapid alterations in diet, probably related to the acquisition of fire and the emerging preference for cooked food. "No other animal relies on cooked food," they say. "Perhaps something in the cooking process altered the biochemical requirements for maximal access to nutrients as well as the need to process the natural toxins found in plant and animal foods."

Although researchers do not understand these phenomena, they are still adamant that such mind-boggling and mysterious complexity simply created itself by the accidental accumulation of random DNA copying errors. Seemingly devoid of any sense of wonder, they happily make comments such as: "Each cell *expresses*, or turns on, only a fraction of its genes. The rest of the genes are repressed, or turned off. The process of turning genes on and off is known as *gene regulation.* "

They continue: "Gene regulation is an important part of normal development. Genes are *turned on and off in different patterns* during development to make a brain cell look and act different from a liver cell or a muscle cell, for example. Gene regulation also allows cells to react quickly to changes in their environments. Although we know that the regulation of genes is critical for life, this complex process is not yet fully understood."

THE EPI-GENOME

As noted, the fact that the human genome is said to be 97 per cent identical with that of a chimp suggests there is something very important here that we do not understand about the way those genes are *regulated* and *expressed*. Evolution's latest answer is to postulate the existence of even more miraculous complexity in the form of an "Epi-genome", a higher–level, or meta genome that tells the peasant genes, the workers, what to do and when to do it – especially at those critical moments when stem cells need to turn into specialist cells.

The protein materials produced by the worker genes, it seems, are like the paints on a palette, and the epi-genome is the artist who decides what to do with them - how and where to apply the colors and textures on the canvas of creation. Taken one step further, however, might the epi-genome in turn be no more than a paint brush in the hands of Sheldrake's morphic manager that we shall meet in a moment - the invisible, non-physical force this avowed evolutionist postulates as a necessary explanation of evolution's impossible antics?

EPIGENETICS

All this gene regulation is crucial because although every cell in the body contains the same set of genes, some have to do "liver" tasks, for example, whilst others elsewhere must do "skin" or "bone" or "brain" or "muscle" tasks, with some genes only functioning at certain stages in the development of a given tissue. Otherwise chaos would ensue.

An article in the authoritative New Scientist magazine comments: "Researchers are a *long way* from knowing exactly what mechanisms control all this". However, "they have made some headway". They are working on it!

The thrust of the article is the inadequacy of Darwinian evolution theory to explain the supposedly impossible influence of environment and parental experience on the genes in the germ cells, and the resurgence, as a result, of "the new Lamarckism". Remember the genetic chastity belt? Perhaps epigenetics explains why the Bible says that the sins of the parents can affect their children for three or four generations (Exodus 20:5).

An interesting and ancient illustration of epigenetics is the way bee larvae fed on royal jelly develop into queens rather than sterile workers, a process researchers have been able to replicate by feeding larvae a crucial chemical constituent of the jelly.

Recent post-mortem studies on the brains of schizophrenics now suggest that epigenetic mechanisms controlling some 40 genes are responsible for that tragic condition – leaving us to speculate as to what environmental factors might in turn trigger those mechanisms themselves. We can only wonder if the several thousand exotic man-made chemicals that are routinely added to the stuff that now passes for human food might possibly be the triggers. Such mechanisms, we are informed, are widespread, and may be at the root of a wide variety of problems, including tendencies to obesity and suicide.

ENTER DOCTOR SZYF

According to Professor Moshe Szyf of McGill University, *genes are not the whole story.* He says: *"The emerging field of epigenetics is revolutionizing the study of mental health - and challenging the belief that DNA is destiny.* So that nurture can trump nature, and good diet and exercise can *actually change our genes.* This is an entirely new way of looking at, diagnosing and treating human disease".

He continues: "Epigenetics will completely change the face of medicine." Which only goes to demonstrate that God's creation is mind-bogglingly more mysterious than Darwin et al ever imagined in their worst nightmares.

Dr. Szyf is a pioneer in the study of epigenetics, which is described as *the second genetic code.* While our genes act as a kind of blueprint for designing our body – for example, determining our hair color or height – the *epi-genome* provides the supervision by telling our genes what to do, where to do it and when to do it. Using a different metaphor, if DNA is the hardware of inheritance, the epigenetic operating system is the software - controlling the 25,000 genes in each of our cells.

While scientists are still deciphering the epi-genome, what is known is that numerous *chemicals* in our bodies *control which sets of genes are switched on* in any given cell. In effect, these chemicals give cells instructions on how they should function. The epi-genome regulates this entire chemical switching system.

When this switching system is working properly, the chemicals produced by the epi-genome activate the appropriate set of genes in different cells, critical for the normal functioning of the body. In *cancer* cells, this process is disrupted, leading to the inappropriate turning on of genes and the mass multiplication of unwanted cells.

Don't forget, folks, that according to Dawkins, all this complexity-within-complexity created itself by the fortuitous accumulation of accidental DNA copying errors. The comment of John McEnroe comes to mind: "You cannot be serious, man!"

MAKING THE IMPOSSIBLE POSSIBLE?

Marvelling at the structure of the cell, in both plants and animals, Rose is moved to comment: "Even the simplest of present day organisms are highly complex, highly improbable molecular structures, whose chance of assembly from their elements would involve *odds of such astronomical unlikelihood that we may regard it, for practical purposes, as impossible.*" Dr. Rose is clearly an impressive impossibility thinker. Darwin would be proud of him.

Not to be confused by the facts, however, Rose then asserts: "We must *assume* that these attributes evolved slowly over 4.5 billion years". It's a matter of "faith".

HOW DEY DO DAT?

Avowed evolutionist Rupert Sheldrake has the refreshing scientific honesty to ask difficult questions. He wonders with the childlike curiosity of genius how, for example, the molecules that come together to form a finger or an eye, a cell or a leaf or a root, "know" what shape and internal structure they are supposed to create, and how to coordinate their activities to achieve it.

Such situations seem to bear some similarity to phenomena such as the way shoals of fish, flocks of birds and armies of ants or hives of bees coordinate their activities. At an even more basic level, Sheldrake asks how a moving object, such as bullet speeding through the air, "knows" it has to obey the laws of mechanics. A short sequence of several such simple "yes, but why?" questions soon takes us to the frontiers of knowledge in any area and push any "expert" to the limits of his or her patience – and the realization that science really does not actually understand very much about the ultimate nature of time, matter, energy, electric charge, or space, let alone "life".

Sheldrake's solution to the mystery of morphology is to postulate the existence of an invisible "morphic field" which he compares to the one around a magnet that causes sprinkled iron filings to form interesting patterns. The suggestion that invisible "fields" shape the growth and development of plant and animal cells is in fact quite old, as he explains on his fascinating web site (www.sheldrake.org).

PANSPERMIA

Confronted by the impossibility of "life" having created itself on earth, the great astrophysicist Fred Hoyle effectively passed the problem over to the little green men from Mars by speculating in his theory of "Panspermia" (everywhere-life) that the earth was somehow "seeded" with pre-formed, ready-made, off-the-shelf, so-to-speak, nucleic acid units delivered from outer space on comets.

Supporters of Hoyle's theory now claim to have found organic-looking forms of microbial proportions on meteorites. If confirmed, this finding could be easily accommodated by G-Theory which would suggest that massive amounts of organic material could have been blasted into space by the incredible cataclysms that not only destroyed the pre-Adamic earth, but may also have devastated the moon and other parts of the solar system. Of course, we don't know what the other planets of the solar system were like before the catastrophic destructions that ended the world of the dinosaurs and wrecked the surface of the moon. Could they have had exotic flora and fauna? We do, of course, now know that there is water on the moon.

Panspermia speculates that living organisms exist throughout the universe. The more limited theory that life arrived on earth from somewhere else where it had accidentally evolved, possibly in one location, is called "Exogenesis".

THE VITALISTS

As microscope techniques improved, the question arose as to whether cells consisted merely of atoms and molecules, or whether there was a non-physical controlling mechanism at work, the principle of "vitalism". Interestingly, as the scientific merry-go-round continues, the vitalism concept that was very firmly kicked into touch a century ago is now making a come-back as evolutionists such as Rupert Sheldrake admit that nature is just too complex to be explained in simply mechanical terms – and that some kind of invisible, non-physical "morphic" (shaping) field must be at work controlling and directing the operation of the genes and chromosomes in cells as they work to create the internal and external architecture of organisms.

As the techniques of chemistry became more sophisticated, chemists were able to move on from discovering that water (H_2O), for example, is composed of simple molecules containing just three atoms, one of oxygen and two of hydrogen, and start to investigating the structure of molecules obtained from the organs of living things – whence the term "organic" chemistry. At first, they thought that the strange molecules obtained by distilling human urine, for example, or boiling masses of ants in water, were somehow magically different to those of non-organic compounds such as sodium chloride (common salt) or copper sulfate.

SIZE MATTERS

The key difference between organic and inorganic molecules, it was found, lay simply in their size and the predominance of carbon atoms in the latter. Whereas a water molecule contains just 3 atoms, organic macro-molecules, such as starches or fats, can contain thousands of atoms, all strung together along spines of carbon atoms.

A critical evolutionary event occurred in 1828 when chemist Friedrich Wohler, starting out with simple chemicals of non-organic origin, was able to synthesise molecules of urea, a compound which had previously only been derived from organic sources.

As a direct result, a major assumption was then made, a leap of erroneous understanding, reminiscent of that made by Darwin – namely that because an "organic" molecule could be synthesized from evidently non-living atoms of carbon, oxygen, nitrogen and hydrogen, all derived from non-organic sources, then "life" itself, as possessed by cats and dogs and on a lower level by apples and cabbages, must be no more than a bunch of atoms cleverly combined together. As a result, evolutionists also assumed the vitalists had been put to flight once and for all.

IS IT REALLY ONLY ATOMS?

So it was that when James Watson and Francis Crick finally worked out the chemical structure of DNA, they claimed to have discovered the "secret of life". It was Watson who later commented, in total ignorance of a spiritual dimension that: "In the last analysis, there are only atoms!" Why are these guys so dogmatic? Will they ever learn?

Coming from the same place as Watson, many molecular biologists now define life simply as "the capacity of accurate self-replication", as demonstrated by the mechanical self-replication of a DNA molecule . Despite his formidable knowledge of chemistry, and his stance as an evolutionist, Rose does actually admit that he cannot agree with that radical and simplistic claim – understanding intuitively, as a human being, that "there is more to life than replication".

AN ALMOST MIRACLE!

Sharing his colleague's belief that "life" somehow made itself from atoms and molecules, and also the hope that someday Darwin might be proved right, Francis Crick was moved to admit that: "An honest man armed with all the knowledge available to us now, could only state that in some sense, *the origin of life* appears at the moment to be *almost a miracle*, so many are the conditions which would have to have been satisfied to get it going".

SOME THINGS ARE ALIVE!

What, in fact, is the real difference between living and non-living things, Rose asks – and answers, saying: "Clearly some things – dogs, flowers, yeast cells – are alive. Others – such as molecules of salt, urea, or amino acids – are not". Good lad, he's making progress.

Despite the rapid progress of science, which is claimed to have reduced chemistry to a mere technology with nothing left to discover, evolution still cannot create "life", or any kind of organism - be it a fly or a worm, let alone a dog or a dinosaur, a man or a mouse, or even a blade of grass. There is clearly more to life and existence and mind and emotions than atoms and molecules. To misquote Shakespeare – "There are more things in heaven and earth than are dreamed of in your atheistic philosophy Dr. Dawkins."

2.7

COMPLEXITY WITHIN COMPLEXITY

As we have seen, Darwin's theory totally fails to satisfy the practical requirements of the scientific method on two counts out of two, using tests of his own devising. However, more and more biologists and mathematicians are beginning to fail it for a far more basic reason – the fact that evolution simply cannot provide a credible explanation for the recently uncovered intricacies of organisms that evolutionist Gordon Rattray Taylor described as "complexity within complexity". In particular, the mechanics of DNA and the logistics of the mind-boggling micro chemical factory we call a living cell.

JUMPING GENES
In "The Science of Life", Anthony Barnett, retired professor of zoology at the Australian National University and an evident evolutionist, comments that nothing can be "taken for granted" in biology, not even the so-called "fundamentals". He illustrates his point with the discovery by Nobel Prize winner Barbara McClintock that certain genes in maize chromosomes, now called "transposons", are able to detach themselves and actually move down the corridor, so to speak, to totally different locations, thereby generating mutations when the DNA is replicated later on.

These transposons are part of the so-called "junk DNA" for which scientists previously saw no possible use. Because McClintock's "wild suggestions" contradicted the fundamental principles of genetics as then understood, they were "brushed aside", says Barnett, by an incredulous scientific fraternity for some 40 years, in much the same way Lamarck's suggestions had been earlier.

It did not help McClintock's case, that she was once described as being "sharp tongued" and "indifferent to petty rules", as was Galileo - who sealed his own fate in his dealings with the Roman Catholic Church centuries earlier with his abrasive manner.

These so-called "jumping genes" have since been discovered in many kinds of organisms – such as bacteria, yeasts, insects and mammals. Notice that the mutations generated by the transposons are meaningful modifications, not the kind of accidental and usually damaging and disabling "DNA copying error" stuff beloved of Richard Dawkins et al. Incidentally, we are now told that jumping genes actually make up nearly half the human genome!

Astonishingly, it has been found that transposons can even move completely out of the sex cells of a fruit fly, for example, and be picked up by parasitic mites which may then transfer them to a different fruit fly. Was "nature" carrying out genetic engineering programs of its own long before scientists ever knew such a thing was possible?

Transposons illustrate just one aspect of the incredible complex mechanisms and sophisticated "intelligent design" systems originally engineered into organisms – enabling the Genesis kinds to spread, adapt as necessary and populate the ecological nooks and crannies of the world.

SOME GENES ARE MORE EQUAL THAN OTHERS
Another incredible feature of cells is the existence of "Master Control genes" whose function is to control other "slave" or junior genes. Since every cell in an organism contains the genetic code for the whole organism and the potential to multiply and form specialist cells for muscle, bone, eyes, heart, etc., it is very important that genes are strictly controlled and "told" when to operate and when not to.

Indeed, by interfering in these processes, at the level of a boy poking a stick in the wheel of a bicycle and watching his friend shoot over the handlebars, kindly men in white coats have induced fruit flies to grow extra eyes and legs on the wrong parts of their bodies.

Astonished by this information, I posed the following question to a geneticist over the internet:

Q: "How does a "master controller gene" which is apparently located at a fixed point on a chromosome switch other genes on and off when they are at different physical locations remote from it?"

I received the following answer:

A: "This is a great question. The way a master controller gene works is that the gene *codes* for a protein that can *turn on* other genes. The information from the gene DNA is *copied* into RNA. The RNA then *heads out* of the nucleus where it is *translated* into a protein. The protein then *goes back* into the nucleus and, because of the way it is built, it *looks the DNA over* for certain strings of bases. "

What I find as astonishing as the mechanics of the cell is the thinking of the geneticist in blithely believing that processes such those he describes so matter of factly could ever have been created by the fortuitous accumulation of zillions of accidental DNA copying errors.

Even a book on genetics already decades out of date provides the following amazing facts about mutational mechanisms:

1) a piece of a chromosome may be *deleted*;

2) a part may be *duplicated* at another location;

3) two sections may *change places* - "translocation";

4) a section may be *removed, turned end to end, then re-inserted* - "inversion";

5) a "*repair mechanism*" moves along and checks that the DNA has been correctly copied when a cell divides;

6) the mutations described here may later be *spontaneously reversed,* perhaps after several generations – which hardly seems like a random, accidental process.

DOES DNA TALK TO ITSELF?
In "Natural Creation or Natural Selection?", mystical scientific thinker John Davidson describes the research of a Fritz-Albert Popp who found that DNA molecules inside living materials are optically active, exchanging photons of energy internally and with other DNA molecules as well as neighboring cells. "What is going on?" asks Davidson. Could it be that the molecules are somehow "communicating" necessary information, after the manner of a computer, perhaps to help coordinate their actions in the formation of organs and limb shapes and structures?

DID THE JEWS INVENT DNA?

Ancient Hebrew text, we are told, was composed only of consonants, with suitable vowels being inserted where necessary by the reader in order to make sense. The amazing result, in some inspired sections of the Old Testament, such as the writings of Solomon, was that alternative and complementary messages could sometimes be generated by the insertion of different vowels into the same string of consonants. As a result, English translators of the Bible often have to decide which possibility to choose, and which to omit or perhaps offer as footnotes or "marginal" reading.

In similar fashion, we are told, the strings of A, C, T and G bases that make up DNA molecules can be "read" by the master controllers starting at different points in order to manufacture different forms of protein, a process known as "alternative splicing".

Describing such miracles as "wonderful tricks", brilliant Cambridge professor Denis Alexander has actually devoted seventeen years of his life to the study of just one such molecule, the CD45 gene, which can generate eight different proteins. And still he believes in evolution!

We are assured by Steven Rose that fascinating facts of the kind reported by Dr. Alexander, constitute just "an extremely superficial and brief look" at some of the discoveries of genetic research. And here are a few more…

CURIOUS MICROBES

A Google search for "curious microbes" digs up yet more recently discovered complexity that evolution cannot explain. For example:

Square Bacteria

"Why are they flat with square corners?" ask the experts. "We don't know, but at least now we are on our way to finding out". They may be small, but they have a big name: Haloquadratum walsbyi. To reproduce, they become rectangles, then split in two.

Giant Bacteria

One of the main characteristics of bacteria is that they are small, but Epulopiscium and Thiomargarita, found in fish guts, are big enough to be seen with the naked eye, approaching 1 millimeter in size.

Bacteria that give birth to live young

Bacteria normally divide by binary fission, by growing bigger then dividing in two, but there are exceptions. Some, such as Epulopiscium develop new cells inside, and then liberate these daughter cells as live young.

Bacteria that know where north is

Bacteria that travel north by following the earth's lines of magnetic force were discovered by Richard Blakemore in 1975. They contain tiny magnets made of iron oxide particles.

It is thought that the bacteria benefit from following the earth's magnetic lines of force because that leads them "down" into the mud on the sea bed, which seems good for their lifestyle. Astonishingly, those in the southern hemisphere swim south.

Microbes with too much DNA

Amoeba dubia, has 670 billion base pairs of DNA. That is about 200 times more than a human being. "Someday we may understand what it means" says an expert.

Microbes with too many genes

The human genome project revealed that humans have about 25,000 genes - not many more than the 20,000 of the worm Caenorhabditis elegans, or almost double the 14,000 of the fruit fly Drosophila melanogaster. However, Trichomonas vaginalis, a common sexually-transmitted protozoan, has about 60,000 genes. Clearly, genes are not the whole story – as science is starting to discover.

Bacteria that can count ?

Some bacteria can emit light - more or less as fireflies do - the phenomenon of bioluminescence. However, because the light from a single bacterium would be too dim to be of any use, isolated bacteria do not emit light. They only emit light when there are many of them together. But how do they know when to shine? Clearly, bacteria can count how many neighbors they have, a phenomenon called "quorum sensing". That is, the bacteria check to see if a quorum is present before emitting light, and do so by emitting special molecules. As a result of this communication they are able to act as a single organisms, somewhat like a shoal of fish or flock of birds.

According to Bonnie Bassier, an evolutionary biologist at the Howard Hughes Medical Institute: Quorum sensing involves the production, release, and subsequent detection of chemical signalling molecules called auto inducers, thus allowing bacteria to respond to changes in cell-population density. As a population of bacteria grows, the concentration of auto inducer increases.

When a threshold value is reached, the group responds.

A STITCH-UP

According to a New York Times report, some micro-organisms can live in such strong acid solutions that if you put your finger in, the skin would dissolve almost instantly.

Some organisms can even take three million rads of radiation and not be killed, a blast of radioactivity that is a good 1,500 times greater than is lethal to humans. "Its chromosome gets blown apart," Dr. Venter said, "but it stitches everything back together and just starts replicating again." Wow!

Dr. Ventnor is interested in the structures of these curious microbes because he is trying to "stitch" together off-the-shelf genetic modules to creates new and different microbes that do not exist in nature.

According to the same report, the biological engineering department at the Massachusetts Institute of Technology is putting together a registry of standardized biological parts, which they call BioBricks. These are components that can be pieced together by Dr. Venter and his crew to perform desired functions, rather in the way nuts, bolts, gears, pulleys, circuits and the like are assembled into the machines of our civilization.

Sadly, giving the glory for the creation of those complex BioBrick components to the impossibility of evolution rather than God, Dr. Venter comments: "Given the wealth of biological and metabolic *templates* that nature has *invented* over nearly four billion years of evolutionary tinkering, any sane program to synthesize new life forms must go hand in hand with a sustained sampling of the old."

By "evolutionary tinkering" Venter means the mythical accumulation of zillions of accidental random DNA copying errors. He does, however, have the humility to add: "My view is that we know less than 1 percent of what's out there in the biological universe." The explanation, for example, of why a lowly onion has more than five times as many nucleotides units as a human being!

As Cambridge professor Denis Alexander admits, the size of genomes "seem to bear no relationship to the complexity of the organism involved". Despite their ignorance of the creative genius of God, however, evolutionists have the incredible arrogance to inform us that such complexity actually created itself, error by error, and that the Genesis account of creation is a myth.

MEET SYNTHIA
According to recent reports, Venter has been able to combine DNA units to replicate the genome of the world's smallest bacteria, locate it in a cell that has had its DNA removed, and induce that cell to "work", to start multiplying. So, say hi to Synthia.

To use an incredibly generous metaphor, what Venter has accomplished by decades of effort is like a man shaping a flat piece of metal so that it can be inserted in the ignition of a Rolls Royce and start it up – then claiming to have "made a car", let alone its driver.

Impressive as Venter's feat is, it has absolutely nothing to do with Darwin or proving his mythical theory of evolution. It simply demonstrates the intelligent ability of one part of God's miraculous creation to actually investigate another.

PARANORMAL PIGEONS AND THE HOLY GRAIL
If evolution cannot cope with the physical complexity of even the "simplest" of organisms, how can it begin to explain the non-physical aspects of life, such as emotion, intellect, and instinct – something not even Darwin deigned to do?

A recent TV documentary described the intense competition between scientists in England, Germany and Spain to be the first to discover the "Holy Grail of Navigation" – i.e. finding the true explanation of how homing pigeons navigate, and find their way home from afar, as if drawn by invisible elastic bands.

The English group claims that the birds rely to a large extent on visual clues, so that in making their way home they tend to follow landmarks with which they are already familiar, such as roads and railway lines. This was demonstrated by tracking the birds using miniature satellite navigation systems – and using a computer to superimpose the flight paths taken over several trips to see how well they coincided.

However, when the birds' eyes were fitted with heavily frosted contact lenses, they could still find their way about locally, but with more difficulty and more indirectly.

In another experiment the birds were kept in closed cages where electric lights could be used to simulate and manipulate artificial sunrise and sunset times. Releasing the pigeons from a cage where they thought it was one time of day, out into sunlight that suggested that it was a very different time, also caused the pigeons some confusion and difficulty in sorting out the way home. This suggested their navigation system also relies in some way on the hourly position of sun.

MAGNETIC BEAKS

The German groups are convinced that the pigeons use mysterious magnetic organisms in their heads and beaks in order to navigate by means of the earth's magnetic lines of force, which run from south to north pole. In fact, they have just recently announced the discovery of a three-dimensional neural network located in the lining of the pigeon's upper beak which contains an array of microscopic magnetite particles which enable them to monitor and measure the strength and direction of the magnetic field as they fly. They now suspect that many other birds possess a similar mechanism.

For example, it is now thought that the humble Robin actually "sees" the magnetic field with its eyes, using an astonishing brain structure called "cluster N". Explain that as an accident of evolution, Dr. Dawkins!

OLFACTORY MAPS

The reality may well be that these astonishing creatures have been engineered with not one, but a variety of complementary fail-safe systems. For centuries many pigeon fanciers have claimed that the birds make their way home using their sense of smell, which is why some owners would accumulate massive heaps of droppings to assist the birds in that task. Astonishingly, the Italian group of scientists claim that this is indeed how the birds do navigate - not that they can smell their home from miles away, but that they are able to piece together an olfactory map of the locality in which they live, extending over many miles. The scientists demonstrated that if Novocaine is administered to paralyze the birds' sense of smell, they are unable to navigate properly.

Evolutionist Rupert Sheldrake, who is one of the English scientists investigating the phenomenon, is of the opinion that the invisible and intangible "morphic field", or the learning process he calls "morphic resonance" whereby the learnings of one generation are somehow inherited by the next, is at the bottom of the mystery. And how does Sheldrake think evolution created this morphic field, I wonder.

SEEING THE LIGHT

As noted earlier, in "The Making of the Fittest", Professor Sean B. Carroll promises to "vaporize" the views of creationists, but somewhat like a clumsy suicide bomber he actually succeeds in destroying the wrong target. By describing "seminal scientific discoveries" that afford the layman astonishing new insights into the complexity-within-complexity that God engineered into all living organisms at their creation.

One of those discoveries concerns "toolbox genes", and the fact that very similar or identical genes exist in a variety of organisms to perform similar tasks, such as the formation of compound eyes, or body segmentation, or fur or feather color. According to the Cladistic delusion, the existence of common toolbox genes supposedly proves common ancestry, rather than a common designer.

We know that Darwin himself trembled with fear when he contemplated the complexity of the human eye, understanding full well the sheer impossibility of it having been created by the accumulation of zillions of random variations like those found in a litter of puppies. Dr. Carroll, however, suffers no such qualms – clearly confident that since evolution is Truth, then the miraculous complexity he describes so well can easily be accounted for by vague verbs such as "evolved" or "invented" or "developed".

COLOR VISION

As already noted, Darwin understood and as is now taught in school science classes, the tiny ciliary muscles that surround the lens of the human eye automatically adjust its focal length in order to focus sharp images of objects located at various distances onto the retina. Amazing as that is, Carroll concentrates instead on the structure of that retina which contains three kinds of "cone" shaped photo receptors, sensitive to red, green or blue light, and a further kind of "rod" shaped receptor for seeing in dark conditions.

Each cone, he explains, contains a protein called an "opsin" plus a small molecule derived from vitamin A called a "chromophore" which "interacts" with it. The genes in the three kinds of cones are "tuned" to different colors of light – blue of wavelength 417 nanometers (nm), green of 530 nm, and red of 560 nm. The rods respond to 497 nm. In this way, humans can see a full range of colors in bright conditions, but lose color in dark conditions.

A similar arrangement is found in Old World apes and monkeys, showing that they also have full or "trichromatic" vision - but New World monkeys, rodents and other mammals only have dichromatic vision. As he explains, many birds possess opsins that are tuned to the ultraviolet region of the spectrum, outside the range visible to humans.

Carroll informs us that the electrical signals generated by these receptors "eventually reach and are integrated by visual areas in the cortex of the brain" and that the specific color perceived is "determined by the relative excitation of each kind of cone". He then proceeds to explain how the three opsins are controlled by genes that supposedly arose by "duplication" gazillions of years ago and then specialised for different regions of the spectrum.

Again, we are seriously asked to believe that all this incredible complexity originally arose by the accumulation of zillions of random DNA copying errors, as the ancestors reproduced, with Natural Selection preserving the useful ones and consigning the rest to evolutionary oblivion. Many people have nibbled the magic mushroom of Darwinism, but Carroll seems to have swallowed it whole – and is now suffering the inevitable evolutionary hallucinations.

As a result, he shares the Darwin delusion that because similar photo receptors are found in various animals, they must share a common evolutionary ancestor, rather than a common designer. No wonder we are told that "Of all the scientists in the world today, there is no one with whom Charles Darwin would rather spend an evening than Sean Carroll".

GENOMICS
Such is the sophistication of the new science of "genomics", the actual C, T, G and A base sequences in genes can now be identified and recorded as mumbo-jumbo "words" or sequences. As a result, the gene structures of various organisms can be directly compared and similar and even identical sequences identified. As we saw earlier, however, genes alone are not the whole story, which is why man has roughly the same number of genes as a mouse and only twice as many as a fruit fly.

Nevertheless, it is now possible to perform creative Cladistics exercises involving the use of "sophisticated mathematical and statistical formulas" to invent mythical evolutionary family trees on the basis of common gene sequences rather than visible traits – all based on the key evolutionary assumption of descent from a common ancestor. It used to be called "circular reasoning".

SOMETHING TO CHEW OVER
As result of his efforts, Carroll concludes to his "most profound surprise of all" that evolution has supposedly repeated itself - because identical "inventions" and common "problem solutions" are found in all sorts of different animals, supposedly widely separated in location and time. As we saw earlier, this phenomenon is called "convergence". Although convergence is obvious evidence of a common designer, Carroll prefers to believe that it demonstrates

how powerful evolution really is and how easily it achieves such creative miracles.

He informs us, for example, that unlike most primates, such as chimps and apes that feed on fruit and insects, Colobus monkeys have specialised as leaf eaters and are "ruminants" – having somehow "evolved" a large multi-chambered stomach like a cow! And in similar fashion to its farmyard friend, the Colobus has also "invented" a method of extracting nutrients from the leaves by the use of fermenting bacteria and a variety of enzymes in its fore gut. One of these enzymes, Dr. Carroll explains, is manufactured in the monkey's pancreas then conveniently transported and secreted into the small intestine. Simple!

As he then explains in a burst of vague verbosity, all it takes is a shift in lifestyle, a spot of gene duplication, some fine tuning, a spell of optimal activity, a few synonymous and non-synonymous mutations, the encoding of a few enzymes, a dose of Natural Selection and Bob's your uncle! Easy peasy!

Carroll et al are of course working with the sophisticated master/slave gene hierarchies of currently existing organisms, so that the detail being revealed is simply a revelation of the micro-evolutionary magic that God has engineered into the Genesis kinds – the ability to adapt to their environment, as with the icefish we met earlier, by means of constructive and coordinated mutations rather than random DNA copying errors. As Cambridge professor, Denis Alexander informed us earlier, however, they have no idea how those sophisticated structures originally arose from dead matter.

FOSSIL GENES
Genomics makes possible detailed investigations of the gene changes involved when organisms do adapt to new environments – such as creatures living underground or in caves. For example, in the owl monkey, said to be the only nocturnal species among the "higher primates", the short wave opsin genes in their eyes have been switched off by a "stop triplet" that has changed its TTG base sequence to TGA. Just tweaking a gene, old chap.

Dolphins, similarly, have little use for color vision. As a result, we are told, they have "tuned" their dim-light receptors some 10 to 20 nm closer to a blue end of the spectrum which fits them better to the filtered light conditions 100 metres or so under the sea.

Again, what Carroll is actually describing is Hough's super-sophisticated Self-developing genome at work, allowing Genesis kind organisms to monitor and actively respond to a changed environment, without generating oodles of rejects for the recycling bin as they do so.

When genes are switched off in such micro-evolutionary adaptations they are termed "pseudo genes" or "fossil genes", and remain in the organism's genome as "junk". Sharing the Darwin delusion that such limit-*ed* variation can become limit-*less* macro-evolution, and that all organisms share a common ancestor, Carroll claims that comparison of the "fossil genes" of various organisms demonstrates the path of evolution, just as the fossil record in sedimentary rocks is supposed to.

Other sources suggest that such inactive genes sometimes get switched on again, causing out bred traits to reappear generations later – so perhaps "fossilized" is not the best name for them.

IMMORTAL GENES
What Dr. Carroll finds "stunning" is that about 500 genes have been found to be common to all forms of life – archaea, bacteria, fungi, plants and animals. These "toolbox" genes perform common fundamental tasks in all living cells, such as decoding DNA and making proteins. Although these "immortal" genes clearly demonstrate a common designer, Carroll takes them as evidence of a common evolutionary origin. Unfortunately for evolutionists, only the former view is confirmed by the fossil record, as we saw earlier.

2.8

EVERY BODY NEEDS A BAUPLAN

After happily admitting that despite the title of the great book, Darwin never actually did explain how one species could possibly originate or change into another, or even offer a definition of the term, evolutionist Professor Anthony Barnett points out that science still cannot provide a watertight definition of what a "species" actually is. He then adds an interesting comment, saying: "However we define species, most organisms clearly fall into *kinds* sharply separated from similar types and do not breed with them". Notice the interesting recourse to the Biblical term "kinds".

Evolutionist Derek Hough comments: "the actual origin of a new species remains a *mystery to this day* . . . speciation forms the basis of a healthy debate in biological circles". Few true believers would openly admit that fact, I suspect.

DARWIN COMES A CROPPER
Even in a worshipful letter written to celebrate the 200th anniversary of Darwin's birth, professor Jerry Coyne is moved to comment: "On The Origin of Species was, admit it, a misnomer. You described correctly how a single species changes through time, but you came a cropper trying to explain how one species splits into two." Ah well, moving on from that difficulty!

In other words, Darwin correctly described "micro-evolution" within one species or a Genesis kind, but could not explain how one species could possibly change into another, the mythical process of "macro-evolution" or "speciation".

A SIGNIFICANT PROBLEM
That unsolved and insoluble problem is in fact the focus of Coyne's whole academic career, other than when he is lecturing a gullible public on the evils of creationism. He continues: 'Speciation is a significant problem, because it underpins the branching process that has yielded the tree of life – that extraordinary vision you bequeathed us of the natural world as one vast

genealogy." But Jerry, I thought your pals had chucked that grotty old tree in the recycling bin?

THE ENDURING MYSTERY
Coyne continues: "You once called speciation the 'mystery of mysteries', but it's a lot less mysterious these days. We recognize now that species are separated one from another by barriers to reproduction. That is, we recognize different species, like humans and chimpanzees, because they cannot successfully interbreed. " He concludes: "This is in fact the problem to which I've devoted my entire career". What a sad waste of a brilliant mind.

LUMPERS AND SPLITTERS
In "The Great Evolution Mystery", in a chapter entitled "The unsolved origin of species", the late Gordon Rattray Taylor says that when it comes to processing information, people are usually "lumpers" who want to simplify, combine and stress what things have in common, or "splitters" who delight in finding the most trifling of differences and exceptions.

Taxonomists, he says, fall into the second category – citing the example of Locard who classified the freshwater mussels of France into 251 species on the basis of shell shape and color. Today they are regarded as just one species. Similarly, the famous finches studied by Darwin in the Galapagos Islands have at different times been considered to constitute more than thirty species – although, in Genesis speak, they are clearly just one kind, or probably a subdivision of a kind.

Many biologists define species as a group of organisms that are able to mate with each other and produce offspring. Complications arise, however, when species A can mate with B, which in turn can mate with C – but A cannot mate with C.

THE BAUPLAN
As scientists discover more and more "complexity within complexity", says Taylor, the origin and nature of species still remains a mystery. One problem is that many organisms, a la Lamarck, even modify their appearance, their "phenotype", according to their surroundings, which makes it hard to classify them, although their genetic make-up, their "genotype", remains unchanged. Biologists have long recognized the informal concept of bauplan, a German word used by taxonomists meaning "body plan" or "blueprint", the acceptance, in so many words, of the common sense message of Genesis that God created

a core collection of "kinds" of plants and animals, each with its unique bauplan.

As a result, roses will remain roses and dogs will remain dogs, no matter how much variation occurs around that bauplan – just as when I change my clothes, cut and comb my untidy hair and trim my nails and don a hat and put on my reading glasses, it is still me inside it all. Biologists recognise that bauplans are remarkably stable and invariant.

THE MORPHIC FIELD
If evolutionist Rupert Sheldrake is correct, then the physical bauplan may simply be a reflection of an invisible spirit bauplan, the non-physical "morphic field" which he claims controls the shapes and forms of all organisms – as well as features such as mind, emotion and instinct. Perhaps that helps explain how the young of migratory birds are born knowing how to navigate by the stars.

If a cat could evolve into a canary, we might wonder at what stage it would start chirping instead of meowing, and develop a love for bird seed instead of mice. That would require evolution to move backwards to a common ancestor, then onwards and upwards again, I suppose, at least with regard to physical attributes.

SLIME MOULDS
As one of many amazing examples of inexplicable "complexity within complexity" that thinking individuals like Sheldrake seek to explain, we might briefly consider the "slime mould", an organism discovered by Kenneth Raper in 1935. Slime moulds possess both plant and animal properties and normally exist independently as amoeba which feed on bacteria, and divide up and multiply every few hours.

At certain times, however, apparently due to some kind of invisible signal from somewhere, some 40,000 or more amoeba will stream to a central point and assemble themselves into the form of a slug which then crawls about, and has been shown to respond, as if a single organism, to light and heat signals.

We are told that experimenters have investigated this mystery by dyeing the front end of such a "slug", then removing a thin slice and grafting it on the tail end of another "slug". To their amazement, the colored section migrated to the front end, as if, in Taylor's words: "they 'knew' it was their job to be front cells". Other, even more complex slime mould behaviors have also been observed.

The morphic fields of such creatures must be extremely sophisticated, if such exists, and Sheldrake's view of evolution requires the morphic field to do the evolving.

MECHANICAL MARVELS AND NEW INVENTIONS

Letting his evolutionary imagination take flight like a pterodactyl from a primordial swamp, Professor Sheppard easily accounts for what he rightly calls "the mechanical marvel of bird flight" as being simply "the culmination of a long series of changes – feathers replace scale, bones become lighter, the tail disappears, teeth are replaced by a beak", and much more! Jus' like that! Jus' like that - as Tommy Cooper used to say.

The "much more" the good professor dismisses so lightly would seem to include the ability to lay eggs as the outcome of sexual interaction between male and female birds, the development of claws, bird song, nest building, migration – and much much more. And all by the accumulation of accidental DNA copying errors?

Evolutionists become skilled as such soaring flights of fancy, as the professor again demonstrates in Natural Selection and Heredity, when he says, also referring to the fossil record, that the emergence of a new major group of organisms depends on a "new invention", which is why, for example, "the acquisition of lungs allowed the fishes to invade the land and evolve into amphibians".

For this amazing transformation to take place, numerous complicated and coordinated changes were also clearly required, as he does actually admit, saying: "Consequent upon this depended the evolution of an egg which could conserve water, and so did not have to develop in a pool" – a wondrous technological breakthrough which then made it possible for them to "live in more arid places and evolve into reptiles". Pause for applause, please! Ain't evolution wonderful!

Then, of course, came yet another "great invention", the wing, which - enabled reptiles to range further afield for food. Flight, he points out, was "a very effective way of avoiding earth-bound predators" - so useful that birds and bats and many insects all latched onto the same bright idea. Keep clapping folks!

Again, all this mind-boggling modification apparently originated from the miraculous accumulation of zillions of accidental but   fortuitously complementary DNA copying errors. Put politely, Sheppard is talking infantile nonsense.

Hoping that such superficial reasoning will convince the reader, Sheppard concludes that: "not only has Natural Selection occurred, it is *competent to account for the facts of adaptation and evolution as we know them*". If anybody finds that convincing, I can introduce them to a friend of mine who has a London landmark for sale, very cheap – with excellent potential for a lucrative toll bridge operation over the River Thames.

STANLEY THE KNIFE FISH
With regard to inventions, I wonder what Sheppard would make of the Amazonian knife fish, in particular a specimen that engineers at Bristol University have named "Stanley", evidently because it has a ribbon or knife-shaped ventral fin running the length of his body. By means of some marvellous muscular mechanism, Stanley is able to make the ribbon fin undulate in such a way that a wiggly wave motion runs along its body – thus pushing him smoothly through the water.

Engineers were amazed to observe that Stanley can also run the fin in reverse and move backwards, even through dense weeds that would soon enmesh a motorboat's propeller and render it useless. They are now busily trying to copy the mechanism for use on submarines, using a "fin" composed of metal plates oscillated by a rotating cam shaft running the length of the boat.

The project leader said that there were many technical fluid flow problems to be solved before they could come anywhere near approaching the efficiency of Stanley's motor – which is, incidentally, over 90%, better than any propeller.

Little Stan truly is amazing, but what about the Star Nosed Mole, a land-based mammal which is able to hunt under water by blowing out bubbles from its nostrils then immediately sucking them back in to see if they have picked up any scent of worms for dinner? Darwinize that, Dr. Dawkins!

ORCHID YOU NOT!
As scientists struggle to understand how evolution could have created identical and even seemingly surplus genes in many different plants, workers at Kew Gardens have discovered that one petal of the orchid is controlled by a different gene to the others, giving it the ability to morph into the shape of

a female bee, thereby attracting males to pollinate it. How tragic that this discovery is somehow seen as a tribute to the madness of Charles Darwin.

ODONTOMACHUS BAURI

Bauri is not another Russian geneticist, but a lowly ant from South America. Its claim to fame being the fact that it clamps its deadly mandibles around its termite victims with a force equal to 300 times its own body weight and in record time of 0.13 of a millisecond – which scientists have calculated to be a speed of 145 mph.

According to a newspaper report, little Bauri is "operating in the outer known limits of biology". Apparently scientists have had the little chap under close observation since the 1800s, and have finally agreed that as well as using his mighty jaws to chomp his victims he also uses them to leap about, ejector seat fashion, to escape predators, able to bounce a distance of one foot with a trajectory reaching as high as 3 inches in one go.

To catch his prey, the jaws are slowly ratcheted back and cocked and ready for instant action by means of massive muscles which are located inside his oversized head. Such is their power that Bauri is equipped with a self-protection mechanism just in case he misses his victim and the jaws power into each other. Oh, the wonders of Evolution! It must be time to practise our "Darwin woz right!" mantra again!

DARWIN DEFEATED!

About a century prior to the publication of Origins, Italian professor Luigi Galvani observed that the leg muscles of a partially dissected frog would twitch if in contact with surgical instruments made of different metals. As a result he theorized that the frog was acting as a source of "animal electricity". Another Italian, the physicist Alessandro Volta doubted the truth of that theory and set about investigating the matter more thoroughly, finally proving that any two different metal plates held in a conducting liquid, such as a dilute acid or salty water, will generate a steady flow of electric current. Hence the word "volt" for electrical potential difference.

By stacking up pairs of metal plates, such as copper and zinc, separated by bits of cloth moistened with salt water or a dilute acid, Volta was able to build a "voltaic pile" of much greater power, in other words, a battery – like a common 9 volt battery, which, when broken open, is seen to contain six cells, each of 1.5 volts.

In theory, by making a pile containing hundred of plates, a battery capable of giving a nasty shock could be constructed – which is precisely the principle found in electric eels, except that in their case the voltage is generated by hundreds of pads of muscle running along the creature's body that discharge electricity when flexed.

Commenting on this incredible phenomenon, in a chapter entitled "Difficulties of Natural Selection", Darwin himself says: "*It is impossible to conceive by what steps these wondrous organs have been produced*". Truth at last!

Darwin's favorite strategy, of course, when confronted by the complexity of nature, such as the human eye, was to dream up a vast number of tiny steps in order to demonstrate, for example, how a single light-sensitive cell could gradually "evolve" into a human eye. Of course, the biochemistry of even a single light-sensitive cell is horrendously complicated – but Darwin didn't know that.

In this case, however, even Darwin had to admit defeat, totally unable to concoct any kind of credible tale – so notice that phrase again: "It is IMPOSSIBLE TO CONCEIVE" – a rare admission for Darwin's fertile imagination.

Darwin's puzzlement was greatly increased by the fact that several kinds of totally unrelated fish also possess such electric organs - and often located in different parts of their bodies, and sometimes with no apparent function. Ah well, moving on from that difficulty!

2.9

NEO-DARWINISM

Neo-Darwinism is simply another name for "Synthetic Evolution", the modernized and made-over theory we briefly discussed earlier which attempts to blend Darwin's original theory with Gregor Mendel's genetic discoveries and make is seem more modern and "scientific".

PHENOTYPE AND GENOTYPE

In modern parlance, what Mendel discovered was that the physical appearance of organisms, their "phenotype", is controlled by the genes they inherit from their parents, their "genotype". Although organisms such as dogs and cats carry two genes for each characteristic in their genotype, one from each parent, only the dominant genes manifests themselves in their outward appearance, the phenotype.

Incidentally, the terms phenotype and genotype were invented by Wilhelm Johannsen, the man who also invented the term "gene".

If genes were totally invariant, and no mutations were to occur, no variation would be possible in populations even over many generations, other than that created by shuffling and dealing out new combinations of the existing genes.

Mendel's peas, for example, carried two genes for height, and two genes only, thereby causing their offspring to be either tall (T) or dwarf (t) – with tall being the dominant factor.

What Mendel's inspired work demonstrated was not a magical mechanism to fuel evolution, but an inherent stability, whereby the genes acquired by offspring are simply a random mix of genes acquired from ancestors. As we now know, of course, and as Lamarck evidently suspected, a mutational mechanism has been engineered into all organisms which allows them to respond and adapt to the needs of new environments – sometimes manifesting traits not logically present in the parental genes.

These constructive and complex mutations, which have been the stuff of plant and animal breeding throughout the centuries, should not be confused with the tiny puppy-litter type variations that Darwin hoped could be accumulated ad infinitum.

All Neo-Darwinism does is assume that Mendel's hereditary units, now called genes, are prone to DNA copying errors each time they replicate themselves in the process of cell division. Consequently the incredible complexity and variety of life on earth is attributed to the accumulation of zillions of random copying errors. Even dyed-in-the-wool evolutionists are beginning to find such infantile nonsense very hard to swallow as they daily discover more and more of the mind-boggling complexity for their juvenile theory to explain.

BINOMIAL NOTATION
Mendel realized that each pea plant he crossed contained two "units" of heredity for each trait, which we shall now call genes for convenience. Thus, using the "binomial" notation system he invented, the genotype of pure breed tall plants could be written TT and that of a pure dwarf as tt.

By "crossing" we mean that he took male pollen from a flower on a pure tall pea plant and daubed it on the female stigma of a dwarf plant, or vice versa. He then covered the plants up to keep the bees out in case they messed it all up with pollen from elsewhere.

Mendel realized that only one of the two genes in each parent can be passed on in sexual reproduction, so that crossing a pure tall pea plant (TT) with a pure dwarf (tt) would produce "daughters" with seeds having the following identical genotypes hidden away inside them: Tt, Tt, Tt, Tt. In other words, all the seeds of this "first filial generation", known as F1 hybrids had the same genetic make up (Tt), at least with regard to height.

DOMINANT AND RECESSIVE GENES
Mendel found, however, that although each of the four F1 hybrids contained a (t) gene, they all produced peas that grew to be tall (T) plants. The reason he realized was that the tall gene was "dominant", as he described it, and the dwarf gene (t) was "recessive".

In this way, Mendel was able to explain why a trait, such as dwarfing, could by chance result from the crossing of tall plants. Things became very interesting when two of these F1 hybrid plants were crossed – i.e. Tt with Tt – because this time the possible genotypes combinations of the daughters became: TT, Tt, tT, tt. By this time, the brilliant monk also realized that he was dealing with matters of chance, and that in order to obtain the reliable statistics required to test his hypothesis he had to grow hundreds of plants, not just a dozen or so – in which case he could predict that 25% of the daughters' genotypes would be pure tall (TT), 50% would be mixed (Tt and tT), and 25% would be pure dwarf (tt). This he did repeatedly over a number of years growing thousands of plants in order to confirm his findings.

Notice that because of the dominance factor, three seeds out of four of these hybrids (those with TT, Tt and tT genes) would still produce tall plants, and one in four (having only tt genes) would produce a dwarf plant.

MENDEL'S LAWS
Determined genius that he was, Mendel then proceeded to consider how combinations of traits, such as height with color, would be inherited. Although the mathematics became more complicated and the logistics very demanding, Mendel saw that the principles was the same, and was able to deduce two important facts, or "laws", as follows:

The first, the law of "Segregation", simply states that the two parental genes for any trait have equal chance of being passed on in reproduction, so that a Tt hybrid had an equal chance in the fertilization process of passing on the T gene or the t gene – just like tossing a coin to get a head or a tail. We are told that Mendel was the first person to apply statistical methods like this in science, basing his measurements and conclusions on large samples of plants, rather than just a handful which would have given unreliable results.

The second, the law of "Independent Assortment", simply says that the genes for various traits all operate independently – so that pea plants could be tall and purple or tall and green, or dwarf and purple or dwarf and green. The genes did not interfere with each other.

THE EVOLUTIONARY RAINBOW
Thus Mendel had disproved the ancient "blending theory" of inheritance that had bothered Darwin. Traits were either passed on or not passed on – a kind of digital system, like the 0 and 1 binary system used in computer code. They did not get mixed up and diluted, like mixing colored paints. No wonder evolutionists were excited when three of them independently re-discovered Mendel's writings some years after his death – hoping that Mendel's insights would lead them closer to the end of the evolutionary rainbow.

Although he himself remained in scientific obscurity, Mendel was well aware of Darwin's ideas. As the comment quoted earlier and repeated here suggests, his understanding of genetics coupled with his knowledge of Genesis told him that Darwin's evolutionary theory was complete nonsense: "No one will seriously maintain that in the open country the development of plants is ruled by other laws than in the garden bed. Here, as there, changes of type must take place *if the conditions of life be altered*, and the species possesses the capacity of fitting itself to its new environment. [However,] *nothing justifies the assumption* that the tendency to form varieties increases so extraordinarily that the species speedily lose all stability, and their offspring diverge into an endless series of extremely variable forms."

HUMAN NATURE AT WORK

Mendel's personal trials and tribulations and the astonishing diligence and determination of this lone genius over a period of some eight or nine years are beautifully described by Robin Henig in her book "A Monk and Two Peas". Apparently, Mendel lived in a monastery where the cooking was outstanding - and smoked 20 cigars a day to try to lose weight.

As Henig explains, real progress in understanding genetics by the scientific community at large began to take place around 1900 when, as just noted, three leading biologists re-discovered Mendel's writings independently, and set out to repeat and improve on his work.

Henig's extensive research leads her to suspect that all three men actually made their own "discoveries" only after reading Mendel's papers – rather than before, despite their having claimed to simply having had their own brilliant findings confirmed by reading Mendel later on. It is interesting that a copy of Mendel's historic paper was found amongst Charles Darwin's personal effects, but the fact that the page edges of the primitive publication had never been cut showed that he had never got around to reading it. Might have changed history if he had – if his maths could have stood it, that is.

In fact, in describing the undignified scramble of biologists to attain fame and possible fortune by being the first to nail the genetic problems that had puzzled Darwin, Henig feels called on to employ words such as arrogance, frenzy, anger, fury, sarcasm, rage, accusations and even murderous.

CO-DOMINANCE

As often happens in scientific matters, however, the situation with regard to heredity was not as simple as it first appeared. Although Mendel had made some amazing basic discoveries of how both plants and animals inherit and pass on traits, it was found when others tried to repeat his experiments using different plants, that there were many exceptions to the basis rules.

Some cattle, for example, have "co-dominant" genes, so that if a "red" shorthorn bull, for example, is crossed with a "white" cow, the calves will not be red or white, but "roan", a mixed color due to their possessing a mixture of both red and white hairs. Mendel's basic statistics still apply however, Co-dominance is apparently caused by additional genes that interact, in this case, with the action of the red and white hair color genes.

SEX LINKAGE
In some organisms, such as the fruit fly, the inheritance of certain traits has been found to be linked to sex, causing the male and females to differ in various ways. As we saw earlier, French scientists have discovered other situations where Mendel's laws appear to be violated in a mysterious fashion, such as offspring acquiring traits for which neither parent has the relevant genes - an apparent impossibility.

As already stated, Mendel's discoveries simply demonstrate that organisms are inherently stable and invariant, subject only to the sudden appearance of the mysterious complex and meaningful variations known as mutations – variation within the Genesis kind.

FORTUNE FAVOURS THE BRAVE
It is now known that genes operate independently if they are located on different chromosomes – and the amazing fact is that the seven visible traits that Mendel investigated in peas are in fact separately located on the seven different chromosomes that the pea plant possesses. He was, therefore, astonishingly fortunate in both his choice of plant and also the traits he chose to study. Is it possible that Mendel did try some other traits but found the results too complicated to understand.

Incidentally, Mendel's laws were later confirmed to work in animals by Thomas Hunt Morgan, working with red and white-eyed fruit flies. Because the flies reproduced so quickly, Morgan could carry test in a matter of months that would have taken Mendel decades to perform.

2.10

CUVIER THE CATASTROPHIST

Evolutionists are stumbling around in a daze, like children lost in a very complicated maze, desperately looking for a way out - turning this way then that, searching for any kind of theory that could begin to explain the complexity of even the supposedly most simple of organisms. As they do so, new theories are scrapped while old ones are brought back out and refreshed.

As we have already seen, even Lamarck's old ideas are making a comeback. Researchers now confirm that organisms can creatively respond to the needs of a new environment, rather than helplessly "waiting" for the fortuitous accumulation of accidental DNA copying errors to come to their rescue, before Natural Selection gives them the thumbs down of death. The principle is demonstrated by the way microbes become immune to drugs.

In similar fashion, the old catastrophe and mass-extinction theories of French naturalist Georges Cuvier (1769-1832) are also being called back into service.

The brilliant Cuvier, famed in his youth for his prodigious memory, was a student and later professor of comparative anatomy. He developed techniques to flesh out the original form of a fossilized organism by studying the curves and contours of their bones, looking for clues to the shapes and sizes of the muscles and sinews that had once been attached to them.

KANGAROO MAN?
Imagine for a moment that all life on earth had been destroyed and a little green anthropologist from Mars arrives and digs up a complete human skeleton, twisted and distorted in the ground. He might at first understandably assume that a human being was a four legged animal, and that since the back legs were so large, that it might have resembled the kangaroos he had found earlier in Australia – having a squatting posture and moving about by leaps and bounds. He might also assume, because of the British climate, that it once had a furry coat to keep it warm.

Thanks to the pioneering work of men like Cuvier, such initial impressions would soon be corrected – although, as happens with man's alleged ape-like ancestors, the fur coat might still be retained as an interesting adornment, despite the fact that there was no actual evidence for its existence.

Cuvier's interest in the study of fossils and their origins, led him to publish several books, two of the most important being: "Research into the Fossilized Bones of Quadrupeds" and "Discourse on the Upheavals of the Earth's Surface". It was Cuvier, incidentally, who named the famous "pterodactyl" (flying reptile), or "pterosaur (winged lizard).

Cuvier, a Christian and never an evolutionist, saw organisms as integrated wholes, holistically engineered by the hand of God, with each part's form and function integral to the entire body – and no part able to be modified without a knock-on effect on the others.

Darwin's own comments in his later book "The Descent of Man", suggest that he was also aware of this unfathomable complexity, causing him to say: "In man, as in the lower animals, many structures are *so intimately related*, that when one part varies so does another, without our being able, in most cases, to assign any reason. We cannot say whether the one part governs the other, or whether both are governed by some earlier developed part."

Convinced that plants and animals had been created for their particular roles in the earth's ecology, Cuvier saw no developmental scale of perfection or complexity in the fossil record of the kind imagined by evolutionists of the time in their "great chain of being" charts. Instead, he insisted that any similarities between organisms were due to common functions, not to common ancestry - since function determines form, form does not determine function. Darwin, of course, believed just the opposite – claiming similarity in structure as irrefutable proof of descent from a common ancestor, rather than a common designer.

It is instructive to contrast Cuvier's wise insights into the complexities of organisms, such as the giraffe, with the naive speculations of Lamarck: "The component parts of each must be so arranged as to render possible the whole living being, not only with regard to itself, but to its surrounding relations, and the analysis of these conditions frequently leads to general laws, as demonstrable as those which are derived from calculation or experiment."

ANATOMICAL RECONSTRUCTION

It was because Cuvier regarded organisms as delicately balanced functional wholes that he refused to believe in evolution. Each part of an organism, he maintained, no matter how small, bore signs of the whole – as we now know it does even internally in its cells, each of which supposedly contains the genetic blueprint of the whole body.

Able to identify fossil animals from their teeth and pelvic bones, Cuvier said: "If an animal's teeth are such as they must be in order for it to nourish itself with flesh, we can be sure without further examination that the whole system of its digestive organs is appropriate for that kind of food." It was guiding principles like these that made his anatomical re-construction techniques so successful.

EXTINCTION

Based on extensive research on fossils from the Paris Basin and other parts of the world, and his expert knowledge of comparative anatomy, Cuvier came to the conclusion that most fossils were from organisms that no longer existed and which had *no connection to present-day organisms.* "No connection". Hence no evolution.

The ancient organisms, he maintained, had been destroyed by repeated catastrophes, and made extinct. They *had not evolved* into other forms in the manner Darwin later believed. Another clue to the existence of Buckland's prehistoric world.

Although a life-long Protestant Christian, Cuvier believed that the Earth was immensely old, and that periodic "revolutions", or catastrophes, had rendered numbers of species extinct.

Although Cuvier's theory of "revolutions" was later rejected by Lyell and Darwin in favour of infinitely slow change, it has been resurrected in recent years, as we shall see in part three, to help explain the several mass extinctions of species evidenced by the fossil record, such as the major K-T (Cretaceous-Tertiary) event that wiped the dinosaurs from the earth.

The following extracts from Cuvier's "Discourse on the Upheavals of the Earth's Surface" (Paris, 1825), are well worth reading, and show his awareness of the wild evolutionary ideas that were already extant - in particular those of his contemporary, Lamarck, no doubt.

"Someone will say to me, Why would the present species not be modifications of these ancient ones which we find among the fossils, produced by local circumstances and climatic changes, carried to this extreme difference by the long succession of years. This objection must appear especially strong to those who believe in the *indefinite possibility of changes* in the structure of forms in organic bodies and who think that through habit over centuries all species could change themselves from one species into another or result from a single one of their species."

Note Cuvier's awareness of the delusion later embraced by Darwin, that given enough time, and a mechanism for "indefinite" modifications, modern species might have descended from those found in the fossil record.

(2) "However, we can reply to them following their own logic that if the species have changed by degrees, we ought to have found traces of these gradual modifications, that we ought to have discovered certain *intermediate* structures between the palaeotherium and today's species, and that up to the present time this *has not happened* at all."

Here we find Cuvier fingering the fatal flaw in evolutionary theory that Darwin himself was forced to admit half a century later – namely the fact that the fossil record simply does not show the gradual changes, or "degrees", the "intermediate forms" that evolution demands. Darwin must have read these very same comments during his researches. Nevertheless, he pushed madly on, driven by his desperate agenda, as we shall see later.

(3) "The varieties keep within certain limits fixed by nature. In order to respond to them, we must examine just how far these limits extend, a curious study, extremely interesting in itself in all its ramifications, a subject which, however, people have concerned themselves with *very little* up to now."

Once again, Cuvier queries the early evolutionist assumptions of the day that organisms can be infinitely varied, and raises the interesting and neglected question that modern biologists would do well to investigate—namely, what are the limits God has imposed on micro-evolution within a Genesis "kind"?

(4) "The most marked effects of the influence of man are revealed in the animal of which he has made the most complete conquest, the dog."

"Subjected to all causes capable of influencing their development, matched in their unions at the will of their masters, dogs vary by color; by the abundance of their hair, which they even lose entirely sometimes; in their nature; in their height, which can differ by a factor of five in linear dimensions (equivalent to more than a factor of one hundred in weight); in the shape of the ears, nose, and tail; in height relative to the legs; in the progressive development of the skull in domestic varieties, from which the very form of their head develops, sometimes skinny with a tapering muzzle and a flat forehead, sometimes a short muzzle and a bulging forehead; to the point where these apparent differences between a mastiff and a water spaniel or a greyhound and a pug are stronger than those of any wild species of a similar natural genus. "

"Finally, and this is the *greatest amount of variation known up to this point in the animal kingdom*, there are types of dogs who have one digit more on the rear foot along with the corresponding tarsal bones, as there are in the human species some families with six digits."

"But in all these variations, the relationships of the bones remain the same, and the structure of the teeth never changes to an appreciable degree."

Darwin made a big thing of natural selection mimicking the work of plant and animal breeders. How interesting that here once again, as if prescient or inspired by God, Cuvier points out that despite the incredible variety that exists among dogs, they all remain dogs, with the same basic bauplan or body structure – precisely in line with G-Theory.

(5) "Thus, in the known facts, there *is nothing which can in the least support* the public opinion that the new genera which I have discovered or established among the fossils, any more than those which other naturalists have established, the palaeotheriums, anoplotheriums, megalonyx, mastodons, pterodactyls, ichtyosaurus, and so on, could have been the ancestors of some animals today."

Even today, evolutionists still look wistfully to extinct organisms in the fossil record, vainly imagining that their disappearance somehow proves that they must have evolved on into something else more "modern", when they were not the "ancestors" of anything, but actually belonged to a pre-Adamic age, a different world.

2.11

THE SELF-DEVELOPING GENOME

We have already referred to evolutionist Derek Hough, whose excellent book "Evolution – a case of stating the obvious" provides interesting insider insights into the current terminal state of evolutionary thinking. Hough's main concern is the inability of Darwin's theory to explain the origins of utter complexity of any and all organisms and the need, therefore, to find a new mechanism. That quest appears to have taken him back to the ideas of Larmarck that we looked at earlier.

THE HUMAN EYE AND THE HAND OF GOD
Oddly, although Darwin himself admitted that the idea of even the human eye being created by the action of Natural Selection was "absurd in the highest degree", he still felt driven to embrace such insanity – admitting on one occasion that his mind was "haunted" evolution!

Derek Hough's rejection of Darwinism, after having been a "true believer" of missionary zeal for many years, has nothing to do with the Bible or geology or rock strata or fossils or extinct life forms or the age of the earth.

It is just that with the discovery of the micro-structure of the cell and its constituent parts, as made visible by the electron microscope, biologists now realize that even "simple" organisms have an inner complexity far more massive than anything Darwin ever dreamed of in his worst nightmares.

A PILE OF SCRAP METAL
According to Hough, the chance of even a plant or animal cell having been developed by the fortuitous combination of zillions of DNA copying "errors" is just not credible, especially to mathematicians, who, he says, regard the acceptance of such impossibility thinking by biologists as ignorance and "sheer arrogance".

The mere possibility, he asserts, is as likely as "throwing ten tons of scrap metal into the air and having it come down as an aero-engine". Clearly mindful of the desperate and highly publicized claims of his more illustrious fellow believer, who apparently belongs to a more fundamentalist sect, he adds: "No, Mr. Dawkins, you would not get an aero-engine in a thousand years, not in a million years, not in the total age of the universe". Actually, I think Derek is actually misquoting the great Fred Hoyle, a confirmed atheist, who actually said that the chance that "a tornado sweeping through a junk yard might assemble a Boeing 747 from the materials therein" was more likely than the simplest living cell assembling itself.

THE MISSING MECHANISM

Nevertheless, Hough affirms his faith that "Evolution" must somehow have occurred, because the only alternatives are magic and divine creation, and he is not prepared to accept either of those. And so his search for a credible creative mechanism continues – and it seems unfortunate that some Christians, blinded by science, so kindly let evolutionists off the hook of their own error and provide the missing miracles by suggesting that perhaps "God made it happen that way", when the Bible plainly that he did not.

A CREATIVE GENOME

The intellectually honest Hough therefore postulates the existence of a "Self Developing Genome" - a complex master controlling mechanism in cells that somehow orchestrates and regulates the DNA copying process in order to prevent "errors" and the creation of "unfit" forms that would then have to be weeded out by a process of Natural Selection. That genome, Hough predicts, is "likely to consist of a complex multi-hierarchal process which will astound us with its ingenuity". N.B. *It will "astound us" by its "ingenuity"*.

Again, Hough is simply trying to explain why the fossil record does not demonstrate the existence of zillions of "unfit" organisms, the discovery of which Darwin said would be absolutely essential to the truth of his theory, and that he predicted would very soon be found. Time to face the facts, Derek - evolution ain't never happened, not nowhere, not nohow.

MEANINGFUL MUTATIONS

If Hough is correct, then it becomes clear that "mutations", the sudden unexpected changes in organisms, which resulted in Mendel's tall and dwarf peas, for example, were not due to accidental "DNA copying errors" as cells divide and multiply, as evolutionists have hoped, but are purposefully generated by an astonishing meta mechanism – the "Self Developing Genome"

- which can actually sense and respond to the needs and pressures of the organism's environment.

But where does Hough think the first magical Self-developing Genome came from? Since it must be far too complex to have possibly evolved on earth, he seriously suggests that it may have *arrived on a comet* from a distant galaxy, or one of the infinite number of parallel universes cosmologist talk about.

Notice that Hough envisions the self-developing genome as a totally creative mechanism, always coming up with something new and different – but might it not be possible that the mysterious mass of "junk DNA" in every organism could also hold in store a range of useful mutations already pre-engineered into it, and tucked away in the closet, ready to appear or re-appear when the time is right? That is clearly the inference of the Genesis statement that would have organisms reproducing "after their kind".

GENE SWITCHING
Astonishingly, an article in the "Economist" reports that a "gene switching" mechanism, has now been discovered in dogs – a mechanism which can explain how one ancient pair of dogs could have made possible all the breeds we now have, all of which are still "dogs". I wonder if Noah called them Rover and Lassie?

DARWIN'S INVISIBLE INK
Troubled by the occasional and sudden emergence in organisms of significantly different mutational forms, called "sports", and in an attempt to speed up the work of Natural Selection, Darwin came up with the Pangenesis theory we examined earlier. In a mystic moment, he suggested that the "germ" or sex cells, were "crowded with invisible characters . . . separated by hundreds or even thousands of generations from the present time. These characters like those written on paper with invisible ink, lie ready to be evolved *whenever the organization is disturbed by certain known or unknown conditions*". Did he but know it, Darwin was talking G-Theory there.

A FORENSIC RECORD OF EVOLUTION?
Recent discoveries in genetics, as revealed to the layman for the first time by Dr. Sean Carroll in his book "The Making of the Fittest" begin to afford insights into the utter complexity of Hough's Self-developing genome, and the mysteries of gene mutation in response to a changing environment as postulated by Lamarck prior to Darwin.
Carroll's hero, however, is Darwin, not Lamarck. And for him the amazing

complexity and wondrous harmony revealed by genomic techniques are simply visible evidence of macro-evolution at work. Enthusing that we live in the golden age of evolution, miracles of genetic manipulation are seen as mere "tweaking of genes". A pathetic over-simplification on the level of explaining that a computer "works" by "pressing buttons". First catch your computer!

As noted earlier, for example, body structures seem to be controlled or influenced by master and slave genes that are arranged in multiple tiers – and similar "toolbox genes" are found performing similar specific tasks in a wide variety of organisms, such as body segmentation, color vision, and fur and feather color. Add to that "immortal genes" that perform more common tasks in virtually all organisms.

No wonder his publishers inform us that of all the scientists in the world, there is no one with whom Charles Darwin would rather spend an evening. The reason being that Dr. Carroll evidently shares his hero's gargantuan capacity to believe the impossible. I wonder if there is a gene for that?

The fact that organisms that have changed habitat (from light to dark conditions for example), are found to have "fossil genes" for vision that are no longer active is taken as "forensic evidence of evolution". With his over-confident understanding of these matters, Carroll assumes that those genes have perished and can never be brought back into use because bits and pieces appear to be missing. Don't bet your pension on it Sean!

THE TECHNICAL ACCURACY OF GENESIS
If God did indeed engineer such mechanisms into each "kind" of organism, as he clearly did, then evolutionists now have even more massive complexity of which to explain the origins.

Meanwhile the new discovery serves to confirm the scientific accuracy of the Genesis account - namely that all the organisms we now know are simply breeding variations of the set of original "kinds" of organisms God created - which is why dogs will continue to be dogs, and roses continue to be roses, no matter how exotic they become, and why endless breeding of fruit flies over zillions of generations has produced only more fruit flies.

Incidentally, another reason fruit flies were favoured for genetic research was Edouard Babiani's discovery in 1881 that the chromosomes in their salivary glands are some 100x the size of normal chromosomes, making them much easier to study. Of course, they also had other advantages including a gestation period of just a few days, low cost, small size and the fact they can survive on a simple diet such as ripe bananas. Some early cash-strapped researchers, we are told, found that the flies could be bred very well in milk bottles stolen from doorsteps on the way to work!

Evolutionist Gordon Rattray Taylor comments: "In all the thousands of fly breeding experiments carried out all over the world for more than fifty years, *a distinct new species has never been seen to emerge.* Only in bacteria, where drug resistance emerges rather readily, too readily, and where the ability to subsist without some normal dietary component can emerge, do we see anything approaching evolution in the act. In short, *the case for Darwin's theory has never been conclusive.*" N.B. "Never been conclusive". And never will be conclusive.

Taylor adds an even more telling comment on the failure of Darwinism when he says: "A still more extraordinary example of failure to evolve is found in the bacteria. Since they reproduce themselves, in favorable conditions, every twenty minutes, they might be expected to evolve faster than any other organism - but fossil bacteria going back three and a half billion years, to the threshold of life itself, have been recovered and are virtually identical with modern forms." N.B. No evolution over millions of years!

THE NATURE OF LIFE
Perhaps we should stress once again that all of this discussion of the physical structure of organisms ignores the fact that there is more to man and animals, than mere atoms and molecules - and that there is more to intelligent life and consciousness than repetitive, self-sustaining chemical processes and organic electronic circuitry. As already noted, according to the Bible, there is a non-physical element, in man at least, a human "spirit" that imparts intellect and which departs at death and returns to God who gave it. The inspired genius Solomon suggests that the situation may be just the same with animals.

2.12

ANOTHER LOOK AT NATURAL SELECTION

THE UNIFYING FORCE

Long before "Origins" was published, radical evolutionary ideas were already the subject of intense discussion, especially amongst atheistic intellectuals. In fact,   some ten years earlier, a crude but comprehensive theory of cosmic and biological evolution entitled "Vestiges of the Natural History of Creation" had been published by Scottish journalist Robert Chambers. Anticipating the considerable political controversy that its radical and unorthodox views would stir up, Chambers chose to publish the book anonymously.

We are told that Darwin took a lesson from the ensuing furore and deliberately toned down his own work, eliminating any claims to explain the origin of life or the universe. Interestingly, one of Darwin's criticisms of Chamber's theory was that it favoured Lamarck's ideas and preached an early version of "punctuated equilibrium", whereby new species arose spontaneously, not gradually.

The creative key to Darwin's dominance was the addition of an extra unifying ingredient, a notional driving force. That organizing principle, namely the "seductive idea" of Natural Selection, was neatly described by him as "relentlessly sifting and sorting all organisms on earth" and in order to ensure the "survival" only of "the fittest".

Even that contribution, however, was not strictly original, because Darwin's thinking was evidently influenced by a Dr. Wells who suggested, in a presentation to the Royal Society, that just as plant breeders improve crops by exploiting variations and selecting out those best suited to their purpose, so nature slowly shapes organisms to the habitats and climates they occupy. According to the record books, it was in the year 1813 that Wells actually came up with the crucial phrase: "a theory of natural selection by the survival of the fittest". The good doctor was of course simply describing the limit-*ed* variation within Genesis kinds that we now know as "micro-evolution".

As we have also seen, however, Wells and Darwin seemed to have had things back to front, in that it was the proactive organisms that originated the required changes in their physiology in a constructive, coordinated fashion in response to, or stimulated by, the needs of the habitats in which they chose to live – rather than the environment sifting and selecting their ancestors over millions of years on the basis of tiny random DNA copying error variations that somehow got accumulated until they were finally "fit" to occupy a particular ecological niche.

PREGNANT SUGGESTIONS
Some eighteen years later, in 1831, the very year that Darwin set off on his tropical jaunt to the Galapagos Islands as an amateur naturalist aboard HMS Beagle, botanist Patrick Mathew discussed the same theory of natural selection in a book on forestry. Although Darwin was undoubtedly aware of these ideas, historians tell us that the "pregnant suggestions" of Wells and Mathew were, for some strange reason, practically ignored for more than another twenty years, until Alfred Russel Wallace came up with same ideas in 1858.

Incidentally, the Beagle's professional naturalist got the sack en route and had to make his own way back from South America. Better than cutting his own throat I suppose, which is what the previous captain of the Beagle did – as a result of depression brought on by the long sea journey. That is why Darwin was taken on to give the new captain a bit of stimulating company.

DARWIN AND WALLACE
It was only after returning from South America, still puzzling over the amazing diversity of living things he had observed there, that Darwin's cogitations were crystallized as a result of reading the works of Thomas Malthus. They concerned the coming threat to mankind of supposedly unavoidable competition between members of rapidly expanding populations (geometrical progression) for less rapidly expanding food supplies (arithmetical progression). This combined with a clever adaptation of Adam Smith's idea in "The Wealth of Nations" that capitalism was guided by "an invisible hand" directing affairs, led to Darwin's meta-principle of Natural Selection.

As a result he formally proposed the principle of Natural Selection as the engine of evolution, a mechanism for weeding out the less fit organisms in a population from the more fit, which would then be left free to breed and increase in numbers. Hence the notion of the "survival of the fittest" supposedly leading to the creation and accumulation of an endless chain of small but beneficial modifications which could ultimately transform a frog, for example, into an elephant, or even vice versa – given enough time.

Thus it was not until 1859, after working quietly on his theory for some twenty years, that Darwin was shocked into going public with his ideas by the news that Wallace had written a paper, also inspired by Malthus, outlining an identical theory of evolution. One year prior to the publication of Origins, Wallace sent Darwin a copy of that paper requesting his comments. It was entitled "On The Tendency of Varieties to Depart Indefinitely from the Original Type". Notice how the title reveals that Wallace also shared Darwin's delusion of limit-less variation, the myth of macro-evolution.

Although the two evolutionists then became friends, and made a joint presentation of their ideas to the Linnaean Society that same year, Wallace, who was from humbler circumstances and who also dabbled in spiritualism, soon took second place in the public eye - and the more respectable Darwin came to be the generally acknowledged as the creator of the theory. His landmark book, "The Origin of Species", was published the following year, and sold out in record time, all 1,250 copies in just two days. Apparently a library group purchased some 500 copies for distribution to its members, a move that greatly helped in the promotion of the book.

So, what Darwin had done was to unify several ideas, whose time had apparently come, into one simple, and seemingly logical theory. He suggested that all organisms are "plastic" and can, "given enough time", be infinitely varied by the power of the master controller. So a fish, for example, could indeed, as the ancient Greeks had imagined, be changed step by tiny step into a man, or a cat, or a cow. As we have seen, that idea is simply not supported by the facts of the fossil record, and should be absurd to any right-thinking person.

A FALSE TERM

When "Origins" was published there was some confusion, as there is today, over the alternative terms Darwin employed for the same process. It helps to understand that: Natural Selection = Survival of the Fittest = Preservation of favorable individual differences. It also helps to understand, as Darwin stressed, that Natural Selection does not and cannot *create* differences or variations between organisms – but can only *sift* and choose between those already existing in populations and offered up to it, so to speak.

As Darwin also pointed out, Natural Selection is actually a "false term", being simply a metaphor used to summarize in a clever phrase the unfathomable interplay of forces at work in the earth's incredibly complex ecosystems. An interplay described by him as a battle for survival as organisms struggle to cope with changing factors such as climate, micro-climate, food supply, synergistic relationships and predators that can kill and control populations.

After discussing Darwin's and Wallace's speculations in this area, Professor P.M. Shepherd, in his book "Natural Selection and Heredity", comments: "It is a sobering thought that after 100 years later in *not a single instance* are all the controlling factors for a wild population known, and, in fact, *hardly one such factor is fully understood*".

Such is the amazing complexity of creation. Yet evolutionists claim it all happened robotically and mindlessly by the fortuitous accumulation of zillions of DNA copying errors.

THE FATAL FLAW
As we have seen, despite its popular acceptance, evolution continues to fail as a scientific theory because the predictions it generates are simply wrong for the following reasons:

A) because the fossil record does not demonstrate or consist of the overwhelming mass of failed, unfit transitional organisms it requires;

B) because the fossils in the very lower and supposedly most ancient strata, such as those that make up the famous "Cambrian explosion", are not those of "primitive" organisms, but incredibly complex creatures, such as the Trilobites.

Such a massive failure suggests that the theory itself is fundamentally flawed, and since in most such situations the problems lie in the unquestioned assumptions on which the theory is based, perhaps we should identify and examine a few of Darwin's dodgy assumptions.

DODGY ASSUMPTION NUMBER 1 – INFINITE VARIATION
In his brilliant book, "The Origin of Species", Darwin devotes page upon page to specific and detailed examples of variation in nature, comparing variation in the wilds to that exploited for thousands of years by plant and animal breeders. One specific example, of course, concerned the famous finches of the Galapagos Island, one of which was a rare example of a tool-user, able to use a twig to prise grubs out of their hiding places.

Everything Darwin said was factually correct, except for the fatally flawed deduction on which he then based his whole theory. Namely, the assumption that since all organisms are found to be "plastic", they must be infinitely plastic, so that, given enough time, they can be transformed or "evolved" in totally new and different organisms. In which case man, for example, may well have evolved from some primitive organism in a pool of prehistoric slime.

All Darwin ever observed, however, was **limit-***ed* variation within the Genesis kinds, what is now termed "micro-evolution" – as well demonstrated by his personal experiments in pigeon breeding, which produced only more pigeons. This truth was more recently confirmed by the many years' breeding of rapidly reproducing organisms such as fruit flies which continue to produce nothing but yet more fruit flies.

Thus the totally unfounded assumption that organisms are infinitely plastic, the myth of **limit-***less* "macro-evolution", is the fatal flaw of evolution – the Darwin delusion - which explains why Darwin's personal predictions regarding the fossil record have proved totally wrong.

DODGY ASSUMPTION NUMBER 2 – EXTINCT ORGANISMS AS THE ANCESTORS OF MODERN FORMS
Realizing that his imagined accumulation of enough tiny random but beneficial variations to transform any kind of organism into something new and different would clearly required zillions of millions of years, Darwin was delighted when the infant science of geology made those massive slices of "deep time" available to him.

Ignoring the evident complexity of the extinct organisms whose fossils were found in even the most ancient of geology's rock strata, such as the Trilobites - which are, of course, far and away more complex than Darwin ever dreamed of now that we know about cell structure and DNA - Darwin next assumed that our present flora and fauna must have evolved from those pre-historic forms, as if they were somehow primitive and less complex.

This delusion was then compounded by imagining that "life" had begun in the sea and therefore marine organisms must somehow have evolved legs and later wings in order colonize the land and then the air. This was pure speculation, not supported by the fossil record which simply shows fully formed organisms, without the required zillions of intermediate forms. The theory of "punctuated equilibrium" was devised to try to explain that glaring fault. There's that "trade secret" of paleontology again.

The G-Theory truth is that there was a pre-Adamic age, or possibly ages, which were destroyed and their flora and fauna rendered extinct. As a result the earth's present flora and fauna, whose creation is described in Genesis, have an ancestry of just a few thousand years, although the earth itself may be millions of years old.

DODGY ASSUMPTION NUMBER 3 – THE STRUGGLE FOR LIFE
Darwin assumed that all living things are engaged in a desperate and relentless "struggle for life" or "struggle for existence", as he called it. That continuous struggle in which only those currently the "fittest" survive is the key driving force of the mythical process of macro-evolution.

NATURE, RED IN TOOTH AND CLAW
In his book "Parasite Rex – the bizarre world of nature's most dangerous creatures", evolutionist Carl Zimmer quotes some comments from Charles Darwin about the upsetting evils found in "nature", for example: "We behold the face of nature bright with gladness . . . we do not see, or we forget, that the birds we see idly singing around us mostly live on insects and seeds – and are thus constantly destroying life . . . or we forget how largely these songsters, or their eggs, or their nestling, are destroyed by birds and beasts of prey". Incidentally, in his latest book, Zimmer describes the way E-coli microbes move about using reversible propellers, making them his personal favorites.

Such violence in nature, which was famously described by one author as being "red in tooth and claw", greatly disturbed Darwin, evidently a gentle person who had in his youth trained for the Christian ministry. How could a loving God, he reasoned, allow or, worse still, have created such wickedness? It seems clear that, unlike the atheistic Greek evolutionists, Darwin's private agenda was not necessarily to eliminate God from the picture, but to let him off the hook, so to speak, suggesting that He had originally created only a handful or benign organisms that had, purely by the accidental attention of Natural Selection, become violent and evil. Darwin's personal agenda and the problem of evil will be looked at in more detail later.

One of the most disturbing things Darwin observed in nature was the action of vile predators, which are in fact the focus of Zimmer's scary book - in particular the action of a wasp that parasitizes fruit flies by laying eggs inside them. In due time, the eggs hatch out into larvae which gobble away the insides of their hosts for food, leaving them dying empty shells.

IS THE EARTH FLAT?
Thanks to the media's relentless propaganda, the Darwinian view of nature as a deadly struggle for survival, which by his own admission was based on a very imperfect understanding of its unfathomable complexity, now seems obviously correct to most people. As obviously correct as man's belief seemed in the Middle Ages that the earth was flat with the sun rotating around it as it rose and set each day. In both cases the truth was just the opposite.

A DISSENTING VOICE
As already noted, confident that the battle against Genesis has been won, many evolutionists have now been emboldened to admit their secret doubts, and disclose the problems and internal squabbles of the evolution movement.

One such dissenter is committed evolutionists Jonathan Balcombe, who, in his book "Pleasurable Kingdom", takes issue with the view that nature is "red in tooth and claw", and the popular notion that animal lives are a desperate struggle for the survival of the fittest.

REINFORCING THE MYTH
Decrying the way Darwin's cliché that animal life is harsh and joyless is repeatedly promoted in the media, Balcombe compares it to the distortion created by newspapers, whose gloom and doom reporting of bad news leaves many readers with the impression that it is not safe to leave their homes, that they will probably be mugged in the street, that the empty house will almost certainly be raided by burglars, and that their children will all be abducted on the way to school.

"Nature is not nearly so grim as she is made out to be" he concludes, adding: "Reinforcing the myth, we perpetuate a one-dimensional perception of the animal kingdom. Cougars are seen only to snarl, snakes to hiss", a myth that is subtly reinforced by appropriate music and sound effects.

Stressing that animal life is not the relentless battle for survival that Darwin claimed, Balcombe says that once an animal "gets past the precarious infancy", about which we shall have more to say in a moment, "he or she has good prospects of a long and mostly peaceful life". However, he says, such is the power of the Darwinian myth that, until very recently, suggestions that animals might even experience pleasure in their lives were dismissed as "anthropomorphism", i.e. comparing them to man – so that birds kissing is labelled "beak rubbing" and open-mouthed kissing as "false feeding".

INTELLIGENCE AND AWARENESS

Perhaps coming around to the realization that there may be more to animals than what can be explained in terms of mere atoms and molecules, Balcombe says: "Natural history writing is strewn with incidents in which writers are moved to awe by the intelligence, sensitivity and awareness of animals they have lived with".

Balcombe's claim that animals experience pleasure is confirmed by ancient scriptures such as Psalm 104:26 – and, in sharp contrast to the callous idiocy of Descartes that we shall discuss in a moment, the wise Solomon observed some three thousand years ago that: "A righteous man cares for the needs of his animal, but the kindest acts of the wicked are cruel" (Proverbs 12:10).

Birds, it has been realized, do sing for pleasure – and a study of the taste buds of cows has suggested that they pass their days in ecstasy. Darwin's and Dawkins' crude view of creation is evidently seriously inadequate and distorted.

SEXUAL PLEASURE

As Balcombe also points out, the fact that the female sexual organ of pleasure, the clitoris, occurs in all mammals strongly suggests that animals do not indulge in sex simply for the purpose of procreation.

The existence of this unnecessary organ is a major problem for even the most fertile evolutionary imagination – to the extent that Elizabeth Lloyd, in "The Case of the Female Orgasm", dismissed some 20 explanations for its origin, concluding that its existence is no more than a happy accident, a vestigial organ. The erect clitoris of the elephant is over a foot long – hardly vestigial!

Incidentally, it should not surprise us that sexual perversion is common in the animal world, as is violence and killing, conditions that will be corrected in the world to come, when, as the Hebrew prophets foretell, the original benign ecology of Genesis will be restored. More about that later.

DODGY ASSUMPTION NUMBER 4 – THE SURVIVAL OF THE FITTEST

Evolution is supposedly driven by the principle of the "survival of the fittest", otherwise known as Natural Selection. Darwin eloquently described this as "daily and hourly scrutinizing, throughout the whole world, the slightest variations; rejecting those that are bad, preserving and adding up all that are good; silently and insensibly working, whenever and wherever, opportunity offers, at the improvement of each organic being."

In another place he claims that: "Individuals having any advantage, however *slight*, over others, would have the best *chance* of surviving and procreating their kind" - and that: "On the other hand we may feel *sure* that any variation in the least degree injurious would be rigidly destroyed". However, can we be sure of that?

Notice the claim that the "chance" of surviving rather than dying early in that battle depends on even the "slightest" advantage or disadvantage - which might be due, for example, to an organism being a tiny bit bigger or smaller, faster or slower, stronger or weaker, etc. However, might not the differences he speaks of be so slight as to actually be irrelevant?

TIME AND CHANCE
Like Darwin, King Solomon of ancient Israel, the wisest man and probably the greatest genius who ever lived, was also an avid observer of nature, even lecturing and writing books on the subject. However, whereas Darwin speaks of the certainty of the survival of the fittest members of a population and the surety of the death of the less fit, Solomon points out that life is not that logical – so that even in human affairs, where people can consciously attempt to control events, seeming absolute certainty can commonly be defeated by the operation of time and chance - so that: "the race is not (always) to the swift, or the battle to the strong . . . or wealth to the brilliant – time and chance happen to them all . . . so that men are trapped by evil times that fall unexpectedly upon them".

DUCKING AND DIVING
Each year in the village where I live, it is a delightful sight to see a mother duck and five or six babies swimming in a local stream, disappearing from view now and then as they dive under the water in search of a tasty morsel. Sadly, a few days later there may be only two or three babies left trailing behind their mother. In the lush surroundings, it seems unlikely that the lost ducklings perished for lack of food – but it does seem highly likely that they were taken by predators, such as pike, birds of prey and vermin.

Would Darwin seriously suggest that the ducklings which survived did so because they were a bit bigger or stronger, or had feathers of a slightly different shade of color – or that the eggs of those stolen from the nest were somehow less fit to survive and hatch out, or were in some way more attractive to vermin?

Or might he concede that time and chance can play a far more important part in survival than slight variations in physical and even mental attributes. How fast can duck eggs run when they see a predator anyway?

In the same way, as already suggested, Lamarck's reasoning regarding the giraffe's neck seemed to be an over-simplification, because the giraffe not only needs food to survive, but also the fleetness of foot to escape its predators. Common sense would suggest that the longer the giraffe's neck, other things being equal, the heavier, more ungainly, slower-moving and more unfit to survive it will become. However, the unfathomable complexity of our planet's ecology renders all such seemingly logical reasoning suspiciously simplistic.

THE GOOD DIE YOUNG?
Darwin himself points out the interesting fact that the key to maintaining a "shoot" with a good stock of partridge and grouse is to keep strict control of the vermin that destroy the eggs and devour the young. Once again, small individual differences amongst the eggs and the young chicks are clearly insignificant as the voracious predators move in for the kill.

Although Darwin desperately wanted slight individual differences to matter and be the stuff of evolution, many of his comments seem to suggest that the crucial mechanism preventing vast overpopulation of both plants and animals is actually the operation of time and chance – particularly with regard to the destruction of eggs and the very vulnerable young. He states, for example, that "Eggs or very young animals seem generally to suffer most". Time and chance are blind to the very slight differences that occur at that stage.

Many plants likewise perish very early on in their existence, as the industrious Darwin investigated by observing the growth of common weeds in a 3 foot by 5 foot plot of ground that he had carefully cleared and dug over. He noted that of 357 weeds that came up, some 295 were destroyed at the seedling stage by slugs and insects. Again the same question needs to be asked: Were the 295 seedling that were destroyed, picked at random by the greedy, marauding slugs or carefully selected on the basis of slight individual differences?

RUN RABBIT, RUN!
As a final example of time and chance in operation - if, when walking my Jack Russell terrier, Ollie, I come upon some rabbits lazily nibbling choice bits and

pieces of vegetation in a field, will it necessarily be the weakest or slowest running rabbit that becomes dead meat for my dog? Or might it not be the one which, purely by chance, is the farthest from the safety of its burrow?

Even in human affairs, in business and show business in particular, it is well acknowledged that "luck" plays an important part. It's not always the most talented, clever and diligent who get the big breaks and achieve fame and fortune.

Even on the most fundamental level of physics, that of the quantum theory, time and chance are dominant players. The probability of any event occurring is a matter of percentages as the wave forms associated with supposedly solid particles are partially reflected and partially transmitted at potential barriers.

Bear in mind, however, that no matter how ruthlessly Natural Selection happens to operate, it can only process already-existing variation. i.e. variations about the basic bauplan of the Genesis kinds.

FORTUITOUS DESTRUCTION
Darwin does recognize the existence of time and chance in a paragraph devoted to "fortuitous destruction". Although he states that a "vast number of eggs or seeds" are destroyed annually by "accidental causes", as well as a "vast number of mature animals and plants", he claims that this can have no effect on the course of Natural Selection.

Sounding a touch desperate to dismiss this chance factor, he adds: "But let the destruction of adults be ever so heavy . . . or again the destruction of eggs or seeds be so great that only a hundredth or a thousandth part are developed . . . those that do survive will tend to propagate their kind in greater numbers than the less well adapted".

THE MOTH MYTH
The inherent adaptive power engineered into organisms that enables them to vary and adapt or "fit" to new conditions is well demonstrated in school biology books where the story of the peppered moth is held up as a model example of Natural Selection and evolution in action.

According to the story, the pale or white Peppered moths, so named because of the spotted pattern on their wings, thrived many years ago in England - in the days when the climate was free of industrial pollutants - by resting on the trunks of trees that were adorned with pale patches of lichen growths that served as camouflage against predatory birds. However, with the coming of pollution, the lichens died out, leaving bare and dark trunks on which the white moths then became conspicuous. As a result, their numbers were decimated by the birds – the white moth having proved "unfit" to survive in the new darker environment.

The outcome was that a black variety of peppered moth, which had previously been in a tiny minority in the population, then thrived and its numbers greatly increased. Ergo – behold natural selection working the magic mechanism of evolution.

However, was this really an illustration of Natural Selection on its way to creating a new and different kind of organism – or simply an increase in numbers of an already existing variant of moth?

Notice also that the advantage which rendered the black moths "fitter" to survive, was not "slight" in the way Darwin claimed, but highly significant – a meaningful mutational difference, not some imagined accidental DNA copying error of the kind imagined by Dr. Dawkins.

DODGY ASSUMPTION NUMBER 5 – EVOLUTION IS TRUTH
As we have already seen, even today the checks and balances of the earth's ecology, the stomping ground of Natural Selection, are still poorly understood. So it is little wonder that Darwin had to admit that: "The causes which check the natural tendency of each species to increase are most obscure . . . We know not exactly what the checks are *even in a single instance*". N.B. Even in a *single* instance? You cannot be serious Chas!

Darwin illustrates this unfathomable complexity of nature when he informs us that although a condor lays only a couple of eggs each year compared to the score produced by an ostrich, the condor is usually far more numerous – adding that the Fulmar petrel lays only one egg, yet is said to be the most numerous bird in the whole world!

Even more than a century after Darwin, such matters are still poorly understood – so that despite the confident pronouncements of evolutionists regarding fossils, extinct organisms, and even the origins of life on earth, they do not even understand the incredible complexity of organisms that exist now and are readily available for study. Even the humble squirrel, for example, as evidenced by the following information:

THAT'S NUTS!

One authoritative web site gives the weight range of grey squirrels as 400-600 grams, but another as 350-800 grams One site says that reds live about 7 years and another that they only live 3 years. One says that reds eat acorns and another that only greys eat acorns because reds cannot digest them. What are we to believe? But there is more!

Although red and grey squirrels are clearly "cousins" and belong to the same Genesis kind, they seem unable to live with each other for some mysterious reason. Despite the best efforts of ecologists, nobody understands why the British red squirrel has virtually died out in the hundred years since the American grey was introduced to the country. The popular notion that the greys are violent towards the reds and drive them away is now said to be a fallacy.

However, some people claim that disease may be the key factor – citing the Parapox virus, for example. It is supposedly fatal to red squirrels but does not affect the greys, which are even thought to be carriers. Some other ecologists dispute this difference in immunity.

I KNOW NOTINK MR. FAWLTY!

In the final paragraph of his chapter on the "Struggle for Existence", Darwin says that it is interesting to try to imagine what changes a biologist might make, if he had the power to do so, to give one species a competitive edge over another. He answers that "Probably *in no single instance should we know what to do*" – adding the astonishing comment: "This ought to convince us of *our ignorance* on the mutual relations of all organic beings". I for one am totally convinced of your ignorance, Chas!

Despite such open admissions of ignorance in the face of the unfathomable complexity of the natural world, where shoals of fish in the ocean will migrate hundreds of miles due to a degree or two change in water temperature, Darwin confidently pronounced his infantile theory of evolution as the new Truth anyway. And the world applauded, understandably so impressed by his brilliance as a naturalist that they simply assumed he must know what he was talking about.

INFINITE COMPLEXITY

From what we have seen so far, it would be a bold biologist who would claim to understand the vagaries of nature, and the checks and balances of complex food webs - where certain butterflies, for example, feed only on certain flowers, which may or may not survive the agricultural activities of man, and where, as a recent study showed, slugs and snails in the garden use each other's mucus trails to save energy and hence reduce their food requirements.

Almost daily, reports appear in the press describing the discovery of yet more incredible complexity in nature. For example, bees can apparently assess how much honey they have stored up and so decide whether or not they need to venture out of the hive. And a dog can read the expression on his master's face.

Consider also the fact that baby birds learn to sing by replaying songs in their heads while they sleep. Recordings taken from electrodes implanted in dozing birds' brains showed they flickered with bursts of activity that corresponded to songs they had heard their parents sing the day before. Incredible!

Appreciating such matters more than he cared to admit, perhaps, Darwin himself said: "Let it be borne in mind how *infinitely complex and close fitting are the mutual relations of all organic beings to each other* and to their physical conditions of life". Ironically, it is this utter complexity combined with the ignorance of most other people of it that enabled Darwin, and still enables Dr. Dawkins, to bamboozle most of the world with evolutionary bunk.

The key phrase in Darwin's comment here is "infinitely complex", for the more science investigates the handiwork of God, the more the unsuspected sophistication they discover – a complexity that is very unwelcome to evolution's True Believers and mechanical reductionists.

Little wonder, therefore, that scant attention is paid to the work of Scottish ecologist V.C. Wynne-Edwards, published in 1962, which suggested that Scotland's native red grouse do not breed willy-nilly like mindless machines and so create starvation conditions for themselves, but rather somehow sense the amount of food available on the moors and adjust their breeding behavior accordingly. This led Wynne-Edwards to conclude that the interests of the group override those of the individual. It is claimed that similar "sacrificial behavior" has been observed in ants and bees – conduct quite opposite to that envisioned in Darwin's selfish and desperate struggle-for-survival model.

MUS DOMESTICUS
The unfathomably complex in-built ability of organisms to adapt or fit themselves, a la Lamarck, to the needs and pressures of a new environment

is well illustrated by Mus Domesticus - the common mouse, which manages to find habitations in almost all parts of the world, from the tropical to the sub-Antarctic.

Confirmed evolutionist Anthony Barnett describes how kindly biologists have investigated mouse adaptability by breeding them in a variety of simulated environments - such as in a refrigerator at near zero Celsius. The few survivors of the trauma and the widespread sterility it induces were actually able to produce offspring. After ten generations, as a result of the females secreting a very concentrated milk, their young then grew to an average body weight of 40 g, compared to the 16 g typical of some tropical cousins.

Falling into the same trap as Darwin himself, Barnett then lets his vivid imagination extrapolate this amazing adaptability in a totally unjustified and unscientific manner, saying: "If such diverse populations were isolated for a long time, they would perhaps evolve into separate species". Notice particularly, the word "perhaps", because such "macro-evolution" has never actually been observed, and never will be.

Such reasoning is about as infantile as predicting that because an athlete running at 5 mph, can speed up to 10 mph and then 15 mph, he will soon be running at 100 mph. There are barriers and limitations in nature about which Darwin seemingly knew nothing – or declined to dwell on if he did.

OUR AUDIO-VISUAL ENVIRONMENT
Despite his theological training, Darwin apparently failed to perceive the fact that the whole world is metaphorical – in particular that the gruesome evils of nature he found so upsetting were merely demonstrations to mankind of the end results of the self-sufficient and Godless way of life opted for by Adam and Eve in Eden - and followed by most people ever since, as typified most immediately by the thorns and thistles that began to spring up on the earth, and the hard labour and striving typified by the sweat of Adam's brow. In other words, nature began to illustrate the hell-on-earth that mankind has been busy creating ever since – with its lust, pride, greed, deception, exploitation, violence, cruelty and oppression.

It is no accident, therefore, that people have been able to draw endless informal parallels between human society and the natural world – the loan shark, the dirty pig, the sloth, the cunning fox, the stupid donkey, the snake in the grass, the slimy low-life under the stone – and also the protective mother hen with her chicks, the majestic eagle, the wise old owl, and the industrious ant.

A widely recognized metaphor from nature is that there is food for the body and food for the mind – and just as there are poisonous plants and snakes, so there are toxic ideas and poisonous people, which is why Jesus compared the Pharisees to vipers. Perhaps the theory of evolution should be compared to a "magic mushroom", an hallucinogenic plant that distorts reality for those who nibble or swallow it.

AND IT WAS VERY GOOD
Darwin also seemingly overlooked the fact the original ecology created for man as described in Genesis was benign and "very good". There was no violence or death in Eden – and Adam and Eve did not eat animals, nor did animals attack or eat one another. In fact, one newspaper report a few year back reported the discovery of a crocodile whose teeth showed it to be a herbivore.

All that changed, however, when our ancestors decided that they could work out how to live and operate this planet without God poking his nose into their affairs, and that the devil's advice seemed more appealing anyway – including the insanity, despite a stern warning, of experimenting with the forbidden fruit for themselves, confident that because it looked good and was found to taste good, then it must be good. But it killed them.

At that point, an ecological transformation took place, and good turned to evil, and Pandora's mythical box was opened. As the Old Testament prophets predict, and Christian Churches should be proclaiming, that benign original ecology will one day be restored – when the viper will become a child's plaything, and the lion will eat straw with the ox, and violence and warfare will come to an end once and for all and for ever. *(Isaiah 11:6-9 & Micah 4:1-7)*.

OF OLD MAIDS AND MICE
As already noted, I strongly suspect that the success of "Origins" was not due to the actual theory itself, but Darwin's evident and impressive genius as a practical botanist. This is nicely illustrated by the following summary of the findings of an investigation he carried out into an ecosystem in a field near his home:

1) the red clover out in the fields is pollinated only by bumble bees, because ordinary bees cannot reach the nectar and so do not visit the plants;

2) the bumble bees live in small colonies in nests at ground level which often get attacked and destroyed by field mice;

3) the mice are hunted by cats, especially near villages;

4) old maids tend to keep a lot of cats, so that;

5) the number of red clover plants in the fields around a village depends on the number of old maids!

2.13

THE MISSING LINK

Although the term is commonly misapplied, as it has in this very book, the description "Missing Link" strictly applies to the imagined evolutionary ancestor of modern man that was invented by German zoologist Ernst Haeckel – rather than to the zillions of "intermediate forms" postulated by Darwin as an essential part of the evolution of any and all organisms.

COME IN NUMBER 21 – YOUR TIME IS UP!

After reading Darwin's seductive theory in translation, Haeckel became the leader of the evolutionary crusade in Germany, emulating the efforts in England of Thomas Henry Huxley, "Darwin's bulldog". By the time he published his "History of Creation", in 1868, Haeckel had dreamed up a twenty-two link chain of evolutionary development leading from the denizens of the mythical primordial slime pool to Homo sapiens - i.e. large-brained, upright-walking, talking, clothes-wearing, tool-making and wielding, TV-watching, car-driving and creative modern man.

All this evolutionary nonsense, which was foisted on a gullible and scientifically ignorant public, was just pure wishful thinking coupled with a vivid creative imagination. Coming into the charts at link number 20 was the existing Ape, a creature bearing some resemblance to Man, but unable to speak, and clearly many orders of magnitude different in mental prowess to Man, i.e Homo sapiens, who then topped the inverted chart as the final link, number 22.

Perhaps you are ahead of me again – in realizing that the problem Haeckel had to solve was to identify mystery entry number 21, the speech-less ape-cum-man to whom he assigned the title of "Missing Link".

On reflection, Haeckel's bid for fame seems to have been based on a misunderstanding of Darwin's theory, which would require not just a couple of dramatic jumps from Ape to Man, but zillions of gradual changes, with Natural Selection ruthlessly assessing each one for fitness to purpose. In other words, from a Darwinian point of view, all talk of one unique Missing Link was nonsense anyway.

Nevertheless, ever since that time anthropologists have been hot on the trail of this mythical being – despite the fact that even Alfred Russel Wallace, cofounder of the theory of evolution by Natural Selection, apparently drew the line at Haeckel's proposal, pointing out that man was too perfect a creature to have been formed accidentally and without "spiritual" intervention.

SAFETY IN NUMBERS

Haeckel found himself in safe company, however, a few years later when Darwin took the same line in his book "The Descent of Man" in 1871 – devising an evolutionary history of mankind, led only by his fertile imagination, and a good dose of wishful thinking. It was in fact Ernst who claimed that "ontology recapitulates phylogeny" – i.e. that the stages of development of an egg into an adult in the womb demonstrate the imaginary evolutionary history of the organism. The claim was, of course, utter nonsense.

Darwin himself was evidently greatly encouraged by Haeckel's book, which is why, in "The Descent of Man", he comments: "If this work had not appeared before my essay had been written, I should probably never have completed it. Almost all the conclusions at which I have arrived I find confirmed by this naturalist, whose knowledge on many points is much fuller than mine."

Fully aware in his heart of his error, and desperate for the support of others in his foolishness, Darwin also commented: "The conclusion that man is the co-descendant with other species of some ancient, lower, and extinct form, is not in any degree new. Lamarck long ago came to this conclusion, which has lately been maintained by several eminent naturalists and philosophers; for instance, by Wallace, Huxley, Lyell, Vogt, Lubbock, Buchner, Rolle, etc." There's safety in numbers, I suppose.

NEANDERTHAL MAN

An earlier discovery that must have colored Haeckel's thinking was that of Neanderthal man, an early contender for the title of Missing Link, whose remains, were discovered in a cave in the Neander Valley in Germany in 1856 – the bits and pieces consisting of the top of the skull plus some leg and arm bones.

The enormous eyebrow bulges, "super ciliary ridges", on the skull and the great thickness and bowed shape of the leg bones apparently suggested a "brutish", "uncouth" appearance and a stocky, powerful build – features that soon made Neanderthal a kind of Fred Flintstone star, the archetypical cave man with walk-on parts in endless evolution textbooks and comics ever since.

Incidentally, measurements on a number of Neanderthal skulls have now shown his average brain size to have been about 1600-1700 ml., somewhat greater than that of "modern man", suggesting great intelligence. Studies of other remains found since also indicate the possession of vocal cavities and connecting points for the musculature required for speech.

On the basis of extensive studies of those further discoveries, now numbering some 500, it has been decided that although Neanderthal was human, he was not a direct ancestor of modern man - but rather an earlier sideshoot running parallel that mysteriously and suddenly petered out.

In 1908, a near-complete Neanderthal skeleton was discovered in a cave in France. On the basis of very meticulous studies at the "Museum of Natural History" in Paris, Marcellin Boule then classified Neanderthal as a separate species, Homo Neanderthalenis, rather than as a subspecies of Homo Sapiens, modern man – again, a separate branch from a common ancestor.

DNA TESTING & THE EVE HYPOTHESIS
Boule's opinion has recently been confirmed by studies of mitochondrial DNA, which suggests that all peoples now on earth descended from one original female - the "Eve Hypothesis". However, the same studies suggest that the once-rampant and violent Neanderthal hordes did not carry this Eve's mitochondrial DNA and so could not be ancestors of modern man, but, again, were, perhaps, merely a defunct offshoot of the family, an anthropological cul-de-sac, so to speak From the Genesis viewpoint, of course, the only "Eves" to survive the Flood and be ancestral to modern man would be the wives of Noah and his sons.

THE NEANDERTHAL ENIGMA
The sudden disappearance of Neanderthal man is one of the great mysteries of anthropology. In "The Neanderthal Enigma", James Shreeve explains that Neanderthals were typically thick-boned, barrel-chested and with enormous physical strength - in addition to possessing greater brain capacity than modern man. In a struggle for survival with modern man's forebears, such as Cro-Magnon man, Neanderthal was all set to take over the world. "They could not lose!" says Shreeve, yet they did lose. In geological terms, they "suddenly vanished from the earth". The latest theory is that they simply intermarried and

got mixed in.

The obvious solution to this inexplicable mystery, if the Bible account is to be trusted, must be that the Neanderthals perished in the Flood of Noah, which destroyed everyone on earth other than Noah and his wife, and their three sons and their wives.

EXPERT OPINION

The sheer speculative nature of the evolutionary quest in which anthropologists are involved is illustrated by earlier expert opinion regarding the origins of Neanderthal. One scholar, for example, suggested that the legs were bowed by rickets caused by a vitamin D deficiency – and that the pain of this illness had caused the man to furrow his brow, thereby creating the prominent ridges!

Yet another expert suggested that the bones were actually quite recent and had belonged to a ferocious Russian Cossack cavalry man – his legs having become bowed from sitting astride his horse for long periods.

The pronounced eyebrow ridges on the skull were also thought to be the result of a disease. A theory proved wrong when other specimens were discovered in other locations with the same features.

THE QUEST

Although a number of apparently-human fossils finds had been made by pure accident over the preceding decades, it was not until 1887 that the young Belgian doctor, Eugene Dubois, born the year before "Origins" was published, set out with his wife Anna on a deliberate quest for the "Missing Link" on the islands of Indonesia. Hoping to make a new find of his own that would "open the book of human prehistory", Dubois may well have been drawn to Indonesia rather than Africa by tales of the cave-dweller culture that apparently persisted there.

Dubois' zeal was well rewarded with his discovery of "Java Man", said to be the "most famous, most discussed, and most maligned fossil" of all, more correctly named Homo erectus because his upright walking posture. Homo erectus is supposed to have lived some 2 million years ago, whereas Homo sapiens, modern man, supposedly came on the scene a mere 200,000 years ago, as already noted.The suspicious and subjective nature of the whole evolutionary enterprise, especially with regard to the origins of humanity, was illustrated by the comments of British anthropologist Sir Arthur Keith, who said of the revered Dubois: "His mind tended to bend the facts, rather than alter his ideas to fit them".

By the 1950s the competition for glory was so fierce that fossil men were being discovered on a regular basis, each one being given a unique species name. Such was the profusion and confusion that the "lumpers", led by Harvard biologist Ernst Mayr had to intervene and sort out the "splitters" who kept on inventing new species, by getting everybody to agree to classifying all the supposed intermediates between Homo erectus and Homo sapiens as Archaic Sapiens.

Wether or not those hominid skulls were human is a matter of contention. And it may be significant that, according to Professor Peter Andrews of University College, London, no decorated artifact or other artwork of any kind has ever been discovered with remains thought to be older than 40,000 years, with even that date being questionably old.

A BRAWL IN A BAR
Inspired by a newspaper cartoon drawing of that time, creationists are fond of depicting Neanderthal Man, the eponymous cave man, in a suit and tie, suggesting that he would not be out of place on the modern day streets of New York or perhaps in a bar anywhere in the world – with one anthropologist joking that he sees Neanderthal in his bathroom mirror each morning.

Incidentally, the evolutionist authors of "Java Man" admit that the heated debate among "supposedly objective scholars" over human origins has been "more like a bar brawl than objective scientific discourse". How, they lament, can the same evidence, scrutinized by different experts equipped with the same sophisticated technology, lead to completely opposite conclusions? How indeed? Ah well, moving on from that difficulty!

In discussing the actions of some of their own scientific contemporaries, the same authors feel called on to employ phrases such as "looking for public aggrandizement", "hungry for acclaim", "high decibel personal verbal assaults", and "the tossing around of books". All this in the ivoried temples of the evolutionary establishment.

LUMPS AND BUMPS
The detailed conclusions regularly drawn from fossil fragments are often quite astonishing, bearing in mind that, as the authors of "Java Man" put it, paleontologists often cheerfully distinguish one species from another on the basis of *a few lumps and bumps* on fragments of petrified bone. Of course, the definition of a species as organisms that can breed to produce viable

offspring is of absolutely no use when dealing with fossils.

The uncertainty of the conclusions drawn in such work is illustrated by the comment of biologist Alan Walker who points out that if the dozens of species of monkeys living in the trees of Kenya were killed and all the flesh and other soft tissue removed from the bones, it would probably be concluded that they were all one species.

PALEO-ANTHROPOLOGY'S GREATEST CHALLENGE

According to James Schreeve, even now science still does not know just how or when the all-important but imagined transition from ape to man was made. This problem, he informs us, is "the biggest remaining challenge to paleo-anthropology".

THE APE THAT STOOD UP

However, such is their absolute faith in evolution, anthropologists are convinced that someday, somewhere they will find the remains of the elusive ape that did cunningly transformed himself into modern man.

According to one group, the transformation was effectively instantaneous – rapidly endowing our star performer with three key distinguishing characteristics:

A) bipedal gait — the ability to walk upright habitually and with a free striding gait;

B) the ability to make and use tools and weapons;

C) high intelligence, and a large brain capacity.

Another group maintains that the magical transformation took place very gradually, a la Darwin. As the authors of "Java Man" put it: "the resourceful ape transformed adversity and potential disaster into evolutionary opportunity". In so doing, it apparently "followed an evolutionary path down which no other ape had ever ventured". One of the smart moves it apparently made on the way was to decrease the inconvenient size of its very long canine teeth, simply by not using them so much. Easy when you know how! Given enough time, of course.

UPWARDLY MOBILE APES

According to one expert, after our ape had come down from living in trees it (he?) acquired bipedal gait because it helped him see further across the savannah and spot potential enemies. According to another expert, however, the male apes sometimes stood up straight to warn off rivals, and it just became a habit. Yet another claims that it happened because of a change in diet that required them to reach for things to eat.

More recently, however, it has been suggested that standing erect reduced the area of body surface exposed to the burning sun, thereby making it less tiring to forage for food at midday. Naturally, the loss of body hair also helped ape man keep his cool. However, Darwin's pet theory was that standing upright freed the ape's front legs to become hands, so he could carry things and make things, like tools and weapons.

Notice yet again that although a faith in evolutionist demands that these imagined changes took place, they have no credible mechanism and no idea *how* they could took place, since, as they admit, the anatomical differences between humans and "our closest relatives" are, in the words of one, "quite substantial" and "profound". Not to be confused by the facts, however, Curtis, Swisher and Lewin sum up the magical leap of imagination in one phrase: "Bipedalism was an ape's way of living where an ape could not live". So there you have it. Those go-getter apes simply got what they wanted, probably Dawkins' selfish genes at work! You can, if you think you can

UNSCIENTIFIC "EXPLANATIONS"
Darwin's "explanation" that the ape acquired an upright posture, or the slightly knock-kneed leg joints that enable humans to walk more efficiently. *because* that freed its "hands" to make and use weapons is a model for all evolutionary "explanations" that are in reality no explanation at all. All Darwin does is to describe the change he would like to have happened to support his theory, and then the advantage such a change would have imparted for Natural Selection to work on - if it really had taken place in the first place. No cause-and-effect connection.

Like a magician using misdirection to draw attention to his right hand while his left hand is surreptitiously extracting an item from under his coat, Darwin and Dawkins focus attention on the advantage the magical change would impart to an organism, all the time ignoring the mechanism, the problem of the zillions of accidental but fortuitous DNA copying errors required to make the desired change take place to begin with. In effect saying: a) It would be nice if evolution had done this, and b) since I have total faith in evolution, c) that proves that evolution did do it. As Hough discloses, evolution is a theory without a credible mechanism -- a car with no engine.

AN AMATEUR OPINION

According to the "Institute of Human Origins" at Arizona State University, human fossil remains cannot be dated directly, but only by inference from the age of the strata in which they are found. Sometimes, as with the famous Lucy skeleton, remains found buried in volcanic ash are dated using the Argon-40/Argon-39 technique which is claimed to be infallible – in her case yielding an age of some 3 million years. Incidentally, that particular skeleton got the name Lucy because when the anthropologists were celebrating the find that evening, somebody played some Beatles songs.

If we entertain the possibility that the age assigned to the Neanderthals by the same dating method might be in error, perhaps for technical reasons and assumptions not yet appreciated by science, an interesting parallel emerges between those mysterious Neanderthal people and the descendants of Cain, the disgraced son of Adam and Eve as described in Genesis.

According to the well-known account, which has inspired a number of novels and Hollywood films, Cain, the first son of Adam and Eve, killed his younger brother Abel in a violent fit of jealousy. When later asked by God where his brother was, he replied in the famous phrase, after the manner of an insolent teenager: "Am I my brother's keeper?" - a phrase that inspired the cartoon in Darwin's time showing a puzzled monkey in a cage in the zoo asking: "Am I my brother's keeper - or am I my keeper's brother?"

As a punishment from God, Cain, who had become a farmer, was put under a curse and told that he would be driven out to become a restless wanderer in the earth, and that wherever he went the ground he cultivated would be poorly productive.

The implication seems to be that Cain and his descendants would live a kind of subsistence nomadic existence on the margins of civilization – perhaps becoming cave dwellers and reduced by their isolation to a crude stone-age culture. Incidentally, when anthropologists hold up primitive artefacts as evidence of the evolution of human society, they seem to forget the simple fact that a primitive and debased culture may well be the result of degeneracy and retrogression from an earlier more civilized level. Thus the cultural isolation of Cain's descendants from the mainstream, may well have reduced them to the level of Neanderthal man, despite their evident intelligence and creativity also described in the Genesis account.

THE MARK OF CAIN

The Genesis account tells us that God put a "mark on Cain" so that nobody who came in contact with him would kill him. The nature of that famous "mark" has been a subject of speculation for centuries. Some scholars have suggested that it was horn growing out of his forehead, others that he had a Hebrew letter stamped there, and even that the mark consisted of having a dog always trailing along behind him.

If the parallel between Neanderthals and the descendants of Cain suggested above is correct, the simple truth of the matter may well be that the "mark" was in fact the massive double-arched eyebrow ridge possessed by Neanderthal Man, the same mark having been passed on from Cain to his children – a mark that, according to many artistic renderings, gave him an appearance matching his temperament – one of brutishness and violence, a physiognomy that has made Neanderthal skulls immediately recognizable wherever they have been unearthed around the world.

In true Darwinian manner, and attributing all change, no matter how complex or inexplicable, to the magic of Natural Selection, the evolutionist authors of "In Search of Neanderthal Man" make the following fascinating and perhaps significant comment regarding the Neanderthal's massive double-arched eyebrow ridge: "Perhaps it provided a *signal*, even a threat, to others". Astonishing!

Notice yet again, in their evolutionary "explanation", the magical misdirection to imagined effect and away from non-existent cause – suggesting that Neanderthal magically evolved a brutish countenance because it would be an advantage in protecting him from enemies. With evolution, all things are possible, if only you can believe!

THE DESCENT OF MAN

In "The Descent of Man", published in 1871, a dozen years after "Origins", Darwin becomes ever bolder in his assertion that man has descended, together with all other creatures, from just one primitive ancestral organism, portraying this belief as almost a visionary insight.

So fully convinced was he by then, it seems, that the need for corroboration by the fossil record was no longer necessary.

The only evidence Darwin needed to satisfy himself was:
A) his burning belief in the absolute truth of evolution;

B) the acclaim of an equally deluded intelligentsia;

C) the observed physical similarities between man and ape and other creatures – stressing the accepted fact, for example, that: "Man is constructed on the same general type or model as other mammals. All the bones in his skeleton can be compared with corresponding bones in a monkey, bat, or seal. So it is with his muscles, nerves, blood-vessels and internal viscera."

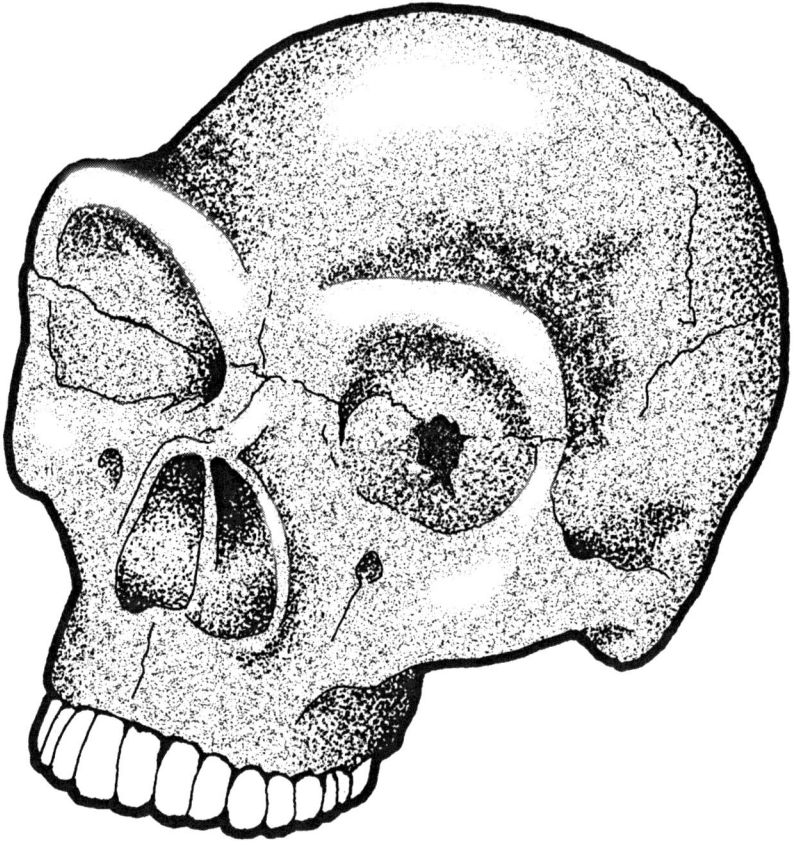

Neanderthal man

The Neanderthals may have been descendants of Adam's violent son Cain. After killing his brother Abel , Cain was condemned to be a nomad and mysteriously "marked" by God so that he would not be hunted down and killed. The fierce appearance imparted by the Neanderthals' pronounced eyebrow ridges may well have been that warning mark. Having existed on the fringes of society, Cain's descendants would have perished in the Flood of Noah.

Seeing commonality of design elements as irrefutable proof of descent from a common ancestor, Darwin asserts: "The grounds upon which this conclusion rests *will never be shaken*, for the close similarity between man and the lower animals in *embryonic development*, as well as in innumerable points of structure and constitution are *facts which cannot be disputed*". Darwin here appears to be appealing to Haeckel's claim that ontology recapitulates phylogeny in the womb.

Although these similarities of design are clear fact, they do not warrant Darwin's triumphant claim that consequently: "The *great principle* of evolution stands up clear and firm, when these groups of facts are considered in connection with others." Adding that: "It is *incredible* that all these facts should speak falsely". It seems significant, that by this point, Darwin's belief in the theory of evolution had become more important than fact and reality or physical evidence. It had become TRUTH!

Clearly on a roll and getting carried away, Darwin continues: "The close resemblance of the embryo of man to that, for instance, of a dog . . . the construction of his skull, limbs and whole frame on the same plan with that of other mammals . . . *all point in the plainest manner* to the conclusion that man is the co-descendant with other mammals of a common progenitor."

The whole theme of "Descent" is in fact the need to believe in the implications of evolution, a faith that makes all things possible. I suspect that by this time, Darwin knew his theory would never be proved by the fossil record, and so he embraced it as a Faith, just as well-informed evolutionists like Hough are forced to do today.

Had he been on the other side of the argument, Darwin would, no doubt, have pointed out that similarities between organisms, plus the unfathomable complexity of the component parts involved, simply demonstrate that all such organisms had been designed and created to exist and function in the same earthly environment – all generally requiring food for nutrition and energy, oxygen for respiration, some kind of digestive system, circulatory system, plus a means of locomotion, and of course a brain and nervous system to operate the muscles and sense the environment – all demonstrating intelligent design, the infinite creative genius of God in every detail of their anatomy.

THE BRAIN AND THE MIND
Darwin continues: "The brain, the most important of all the organs, follows the same law . . . every chief fissure and fold in the brain of man has its analogy in

that of the orang". However, he adds: "At no period of development do their brains perfectly agree; nor could perfect agreement be expected, for otherwise their mental powers would have been the same."

Here Darwin makes the usual erroneous evolutionary assumption that "brain" and "mind" are synonymous, so that the massive gulf between man and ape has to be explained by quite small physical differences in physiology. As we have seen, however, because the study of DNA has shown that the physical difference between man and ape is apparently even far less than Darwin suspected at the cellular level,   the massive gulf between the two beings becomes even more difficult to explain in terms of mere atoms and molecules, as evolutionists such as Derek Hough and Rupert Sheldrake willingly admit. Evolution, of course, is a matter of atoms and molecules, and only atoms and molecules.

EJECTING OBJECTIONS - AS SIMPLE AS ABC
In disposing of the petty annoyance of the lack of fossil evidence to support his assertion that man descended from apes, Darwin resorts again to the illogical syllogism, of the form:

A) Although there is no evidence to prove that evolution made this thing happen;
B) I have complete Faith that evolution could have made it happen;
C) Therefore, evolution did make it happen!

A GRAVE OBJECTION
Which is why when he admits that: "The great break in the organic chain between man and his nearest allies, which cannot be bridged over by any extinct or living species, has often been advanced as *a grave objection* to the belief that man is descended from some lower form". That said, he still reassures the Faithful, adding: "But this objection will not appear of much weight to those who, from general reasons, *believe in the general principle of evolution.*" So there you have it – objection ejected, as easy as ABC. All your need is Faith.

THE POWER OF POSITIVE THINKING
Admitting to yet more problems, Darwin continues: "The high standard of our *intellectual powers* and *moral disposition* is the *greatest difficulty* which presents itself" – adding: "There can be no doubt that the difference between the mind of the lowest man and that of the highest animal is *immense*". And your point is, Chas?

Still niggled by the lack of evidence to support his infantile assertions, Darwin then trots out the illogical syllogism once again, saying: "Every one *who admits the principle of evolution, must see* that the mental powers of the higher animals, which are the same in kind with those of man, though so different in degree, are *capable of advancement.* Thus the interval between the mental powers of one of the higher apes and of a fish, or between those of an ant and scale-insect, is immense; yet their development does not offer *any special difficulty.*" So even "special difficulties" disappear like magic for those who can "admit" that evolution is true!

Pausing   to ponder the immensity of this gulf, Darwin says: "An anthropomorphous ape, if he could take a dispassionate view of his own case, would admit that though he could form an artful plan to plunder a garden - though he could use stones for fighting or for breaking open nuts, yet that the thought of fashioning a stone into a tool was quite beyond his scope."

He continues: "Still less, as he would admit, could he follow out a train of metaphysical reasoning, or solve a mathematical problem, or reflect on God, or admire a grand natural scene". I guess they really need to go to school.

WHAT IS MAN?
However, mental and emotional similarities or commonalities between creatures do not prove common descent any more than physical parallels do. What is interesting, is that just as science is increasingly discovering organisms to be unfathomably complex in their physical structure, so they are discovering that animals in general, even "stupid sheep", are far and away more sophisticated than they or Darwin ever suspected in their mental powers, emotional make-up and instinctive behavior – as stressed by evolutionist Jonathan Balcombe in "Pleasurable Kingdom".

Recent research has shown, for example, that the Great Apes can recognize themselves in a mirror - and will reach up and remove a strip of paper that a researcher has stuck on their head. Elephants and dolphins have also passed that same self-recognition test.

Chimps and some birds, we are told, can make and use a variety of crude tools, sometimes fashioning probes from leaves in order to extract grubs and insects from crevices. And primates, for example, are able to learn by imitation – and many creatures can learn to respond to dozens of word commands.

As already noted, however, the Bible does not say that man alone is a sentient being and that all other creatures are mere robotic assemblages of atoms and molecules. As recent research clearly indicates that there is a non-physical component in both man and animals - a "spirit" that imparts intellect, as the Bible suggests.

Again, if we accept the Bible accounts, man and a variety of angelic beings also have much in common, and on a very high plane, whilst still remaining different kinds of being – with man at the moment being "a little lower than the angels" with regard to his mortal, fleshly physiology (Hebrews 1:1-14 & 2:5-8).

ENTRAPMENT BY GOD?

As we have seen, in the dozen years that elapsed between the publication of "Origins" and the "Descent of Man", Darwin seemingly became seduced by the ancient atheistic idea that similarity between creatures absolutely proves evolution from a common ancestor, a point he hammers at continually, concluding: "Consequently *we ought frankly to admit* their community of descent." Sorry, Chas, but I don't ought to admit it at all.

Apparently irritated by the opposite and quite logical view that commonality of design simply demonstrates a common designer, i.e. God, Darwin complains: "To take any other view is to admit that our own structure, and that of all the animals around us, is *a mere snare laid to entrap our judgment*".

In other words, Darwin seems to blaming God for his belief in evolution, implying that by employing common design elements in various creatures, God actually tricked him into thinking they all descended from a common ancestor.

Straying even further into the jungle of emotive opinion, Darwin declares: "It is only our *natural prejudice, and that arrogance* which made our forefathers declare that they were descended from demi-gods, which leads us to demur to this conclusion". So If we disagree with Darwin we are arrogant – and according to Dawkins we are also ignorant, stupid or totally insane!

Then, in a prophecy that has sadly proved all too true, he predicts: "But the time will before long come, when it will be thought wonderful that naturalists, who were well acquainted with the comparative structure and development of man, and other mammals, should have believed that each was the work of a separate act of creation". By "wonderful" he apparently means "incredible" or "unbelievable", I suppose.

In summary, it should be clear by now that cladistic-based attempts to create an evolutionary ancestry for man are nothing more than wild speculation and wishful thinking based on the unproven assumption that evolution must be true.

In summary, G-Theory would suggest that any hominid remains dated in excess of six thousand years cannot be of human origin. In this regard, the limitations of C-14 dating are well established and other methods, as discussed later, are under intense suspicion.

Nevertheless, as we have seen, the notion that man descended with apes from a common ancestor is nothing more than unfounded evolutionary myth and wishful thinking, all based on a false metaphor and the assumption that evolution is Truth.

2.14

FAITH, CONFESSION AND DOGMA

Evolution is a theory in crisis. In fact, the authors of "Lamarck's Signature" compare the entrenched and desperate position of Darwin's fundamentalist followers, such as Richard Dawkins, to that of the Roman Catholic bishops in Galileo's time who even refused to look through the telescope and see with their own eyes that the planet Jupiter did in fact have phases, like those of the moon, which were only explicable by the fact that it too, like the earth, moved around the sun.

However, encouraged by the shameful connivance of the mass media, including the BBC, and the scientific ignorance and the intellectual capitulation of too many religious leaders, the process of peddling evolutionary myth in every biology text, ancient history book and encyclopaedia continues. Consequently, as already noted, many evolutionists have understandably but mistakenly assumed that the battle against the Bible and divine creation has finally been won. In fact one webmaster I spoke to, has stopped updating his anti-creationist web site for that very reason. Big mistake!

EMBARRASSING ADMISSIONS

As a result, some members of the brotherhood have been emboldened to make astonishing admissions in print – in particular, as we have seen, that Darwinism is simplistic nonsense, and that a magical new mechanism is urgently required in order to restore its credibility.

In his entertaining book already mentioned, "Evolution – a case of stating the obvious", Derek Hough, for example, describes how, after being a true believer for many years, and spreading the Darwin doctrine at every opportunity, it being "the most intellectually seductive idea in scientific thought", he suddenly had "a gut feeling" on the way to work one morning, on the London underground ride from Piccadilly Circus to Charing Cross, telling him that the theory was actually totally incapable of explaining the recently discovered complexities of the cell. That's only a two-minute ride. Must have seen the light at the end of the tunnel!

FAITH

However, Hough avows, he still accepts the reality of evolution with a capital "E" as a matter of *faith* - so despite this sudden enlightenment, he remains a confirmed believer that the process of macro-evolution did somehow take place – all it needs is a viable mechanism to explain how.

The present situation amongst evolutionists is very much like a man sitting in his favorite armchair, surrounded by travel brochures, planning the details of holiday of a lifetime - a week in a five star hotel in Paris, a penthouse in Cannes for a few weeks, a cruise around the Med, a flight to the Bahamas for Christmas, then on to Austria for the skiing, etc. He has it all logically organized in every detail. The only problem is, he is over 100 years old, out of work and bankrupt, and has no money, so it never will happen – just as macro-evolution never did happen!

CONFESSION

Although Hough openly admits that his book "*takes for granted that evolution has occurred*", and that: "*it is assumed to have occurred*", he does admit in the very first chapter that: "*There is in fact no definite proof*" – the reason being that: "it is difficult to conduct experiments over millions of years". As a result, he stresses, we have to: "*convince ourselves* that the theory is adequate to explain all the complexities of life". Perhaps a spot of self-hypnosis would help!

The problem is, as he then explains in detail later, that the theory is not adequate to explain that complexity at all. N.B. "takes for granted", "assumed", "no proof".

Astonishingly, Hough states that the main evidence of evolution is the fact that "organisms of all types appear to be well adapted to their environments" – an observation that would surely serve equally well as major evidence of intelligent or divine design.

Adding to the confusion in evolutionary circles is the fact that, as a result of the incredible complexity of living things, and the expansion of biochemistry and geology, more and more scientists work in isolated, specialist disciplines – with the consequence that virtually none has a complete overview of the whole field, each worker relying on the assumed expertise of others, each trusting that the others know what they are talking about. One such top scientist I know, deflects difficult questions with the comment: "I only work on single cells!

DOGMA
It is strange how circumstances can radically change, so that what was once the "under dogma" can sometimes become the "top dogma". It seems significant, for example, that words such as "faith" and "dogma" even appear in scientific literature, as an increasing number of believers start to question the growing power of evolutionary orthodoxy, comparing it, as we have just seen, to that exercised by the Roman Catholic Church in earlier centuries - even pointing out that those who do foolishly dare to publish heretical views critical of Darwinism put their academic careers at risk, and may find it difficult to obtain research grants.

VE HAVE VAYS OF MAKING YOU LISTEN!
The pressure put on young people to compromise their beliefs is illustrated by the Church of England web site, where they have an official postumous apology to Darwin for ever having doubted his wonderful theory. What a monumental and tragic betrayal of rank and file believers! One of the misguided authors of the site reveals that he asked a Kansas university biology professor "how he coped with teaching Darwin's theories to students whose churches insisted that evolution was heresy and whose schools taught creationism."

"No problem," replied the professor, "the kids know that *if they want a good job* they need a degree, and if they want a degree *they have to work with evolution theory*. Creationism is for church, as far as they're concerned. Here, they're Darwinists."

"Perhaps he was over-cynical", says the author, "but he was also pointing to young lives which could not be lived with integrity – the very opposite of how Christians are called to live." And your point is, Reverend?

Little wonder then that the Discovery Institute (www.discovery.org) actually has lists of scientists who have been sacked for speaking out against the doctrines of the great Lord Darwin. See also www.DissentfromDarwin.org In fact, such is the sinister stranglehold of evolution on western academia that it was reported on the BBC news that the education director of the British Royal Society was forced to resign by enraged evolutionists simply for suggesting that science teachers should take time to discuss objections to evolution raised by pupils who have been brought up to believe in the Bible account of creation.

Academic freedom at its very best!

ANCIENT GREEK THINKERS

Earlier "orthodox" authorities, the same ones that dealt with Galileo and his alleged unscriptural astronomical theories in the Middle Ages, also did a good job of holding back the development of the infant science of geology at that time.

The study of fossils apparently began with Greek thinkers such as Eratosthenes, and also Strabo, who puzzled over the vast quantities of fossil sea shells found inland in Egypt. However, for a long time, perhaps because most fossils are no more than stone patterns and nobody had any idea how they could have been formed, there was some doubt as to whether they had any real link to once-living organisms at all. Incidentally, Eratosthenes was the clever chap who used measurement of an obelisk shadow length at one place in Egypt , when the sun shone vertically down a well some distance away, to calculate the radius of the round earth to be about 4,000 miles and hence the circumference to be 24,000 miles. I wonder why Columbus and his mates never knew that?

In subsequent centuries, as the power of the religious authorities in Europe grew, the orthodox teaching about Genesis was the same as that of today's "Young Earth" creationists – and any suggestion that thick fossils beds and even sedimentary rock strata thousands of feet deep might have resulted from anything other than Noah's Flood, "the Deluge", attracted unwanted attention and the risk of being severely proceeded against as a heretic. It could, of course, be a mite painful when those kindly religious gents got their hands on you, in order to purify your thinking! As a result, those who did teach the orthodox explanation, the "diluvalists", held sway until the late 1700s.

Orthodoxy has therefore been turned on its head – so that geological ideas that were once heresy are now mainstream belief, and Biblical belief has become sidelined.

AN ANCIENT IDEA

Evolution was, of course, a very ancient idea, and in the first few pages of "The Origin of Species", Darwin explains how he found his famous principle of Natural Selection foreshadowed in the writings of the Greek philosopher Aristotle -- who claimed that no matter how well-designed or adapted to purpose things in nature appeared to be (such as our chisel-shaped front teeth for cutting and the flat-topped molars for chewing and grinding) all had come about by accident - by "spontaneity", with the result that things not well fitted to purpose would in time naturally perish, having proved "unfit" for purpose.

GETTING RID OF GOD

Aristotle, one of a band of Greek philosophers whose aim was the deliberate elimination the idea of divine interference in man's affairs, even devised a "ladder of nature", similar to the "tree of life" or "descent" charts found in modern biology textbooks, in which he attempted to demonstrate that so-called "higher" and "more complex" organisms had evolved from supposedly "simpler" or more "primitive" ones.

Notice that the use of adjectives such as "higher" and "more complex" assumes that evolution is a fact, a demonstrated reality, a foregone conclusion, when honest evolutionists will readily admit that is no real proof of the theory at all. It is a faith.

WAS MAN ONCE A FISH?

Equally "modern" in his thinking was Aristotle's fellow philosopher Anaximander who is on record as saying that: "Living creatures arose from the moist element (water) as it was evaporated by the sun" and that, in the beginning, man "was like another animal, namely the fish". However, Darwin's secret agenda, as we shall see, was somewhat less radical than that of these atheistic philosophers.

ARE ANIMALS MERE MACHINES?

The French philosopher and mathematician Renee Descartes (1596-1650), like the Greeks much earlier, also taught that all organisms, no matter how complex, had arisen from inert matter, claiming that animals are no more than mechanical devices, or, in more modern parlance, mere chemical combinations of atoms and molecules.

Like Aristotle before him, Descartes was also seduced by the simplistic notion that similarities in the structures of organisms demonstrated and "proved" development from a common ancestor, an approach that became more systematized after Karl Linnaeus (1707-78) developed the taxonomy system, still used today, for classifying all known organisms according to similarities of structure – extending the then existing system by adding the categories of class, order, genus and species.

SCIENTIFIC BARBARITY

In his superb book "Pleasurable Kingdom", evolutionist Jonathan Balcombe discusses the apparently surprising realization by scientists that many animals may actually have emotions and intelligence, and be able to experience pain, pleasure, love and relationships.

Obvious as this revelation has been to pet owners over the millennia, the thinking of scientists has until very recently been dominated by the crude ideas of our friend Descartes, whose mechanistic theories led to the development of the "stifling behaviorist psychology dogma that rejected the idea of animals as conscious feeling beings", regarding them instead as mere machines, robotic mechanisms totally under the influence of environmental factors, and slaves of stimulus-response behavior. There's that word "dogma" again.

Balcome even describes medical experiments, conducted with Decartes' blessing, in which dogs were actually nailed to wooden boards by their paws then slowly flayed alive to remove layers of skins and flesh in order to allow kindly scientists to observe the working of their exposed blood circulation systems. It seems ironic that to one of the influences that put an end to these diabolical "scientific" practices was Darwin's theory that animals shared a common evolutionary ancestry with man, and were therefore due some measure of respect.

A GAPING VOID
The sheer arrogance of evolutionists' confident claim to understand the origin of living things despite their abysmal ignorance of the complexity of nature is revealed by Balcombe's admission that: "Our past failure to even acknowledge, never mind investigate, animal feelings represents a gaping void that wants filling".

THE REDUCTIONISTS
Most dog, cat and horse owners, I suspect, would strongly disagree with atheistic "reductionists" such as Descartes, and their modern counterparts -- men such as Watson and Crick, who claimed they had discovered the "secret of life" when they worked out the chemical structure of DNA.

It was Crick who claimed in an article in Icarus Magazine in 1973 that because life on earth is too complex to have made itself, space aliens must have sent some "spores" here by rocket? An idea as screwy as a chromosome.

As noted, pet owners know better, intuitively understanding that there is more to the objects of their affections than mere atoms and molecules – as did Solomon, the wisest man who ever lived, who taught that, like man, some animals at least have a non-physical element, a "spirit". If Solomon was correct, then even if by some miracle of transplant surgery a rabbit could be turned into a dog, it would still instinctively want to dig burrows to live in, and eat lots of lettuce.

RUPERT SHELDRAKE'S MORPHIC FIELD

Recognizing the total inability of evolution to explain the complexity of living things, let alone mysteries such as bird migration and animal instinct, thoughtful evolutionist Rupert Sheldrake now suggests that all organisms possess an invisible "morphic (shaping) field", which somehow directs their growth and development into adulthood in the same way the invisible field around a magnet guides sprinkled iron filings into the well-known patterns most of us played with in school science lessons. Ever the evolutionist, however, Sheldrake now maintains that it is the morphic field that evolves, not the DNA. What the "field" actually is, or how it could possibly exist and evolve, he has, of course, no idea.

As Sheldrake points out, despite all we claim to know about DNA (which is actually just the tip of an iceberg of unknowing), we still do not understand how the cells of a developing embryo "know" how to coordinate their activities in order to form and shape a nose or an arm or a liver, for example. They therefore need the help of the morphic field which acts as an invisible mould.

A CRUMBLING THEORY

Avowed evolutionist Gordon Rattray Taylor admitted some years ago that Darwinism was "crumbling under attack" – and that not just from creationists, but from high powered university mathematicians who saw that the chance of scores of accidental miniscule mutations fortuitously combining in even one aspect of one organism's physiology was insanely unlikely. Scientists are just human beings, inside those white lab coats, and Taylor speaks of meetings between evolutionists and mathematicians where tempers often "ran high" – the meetings having been called to discuss problems with Darwin's theory that biologists themselves had become aware of decades earlier, but had quietly ignored.

Derek Hough also admits that the idea of innumerable random copying errors in the DNA of a "primitive" organism ever leading to something much more complex is simply "inconceivable on the grounds of improbability". Hough also assumes, of course, that all organisms are nothing more than a clever combinations of atoms and molecules.

Using similar language to Taylor, Professor Frazzetta of the University of Illinois is reported as saying: "With each passing year, the once rather simplistic views on evolution continue to crumble". Crumble, crumble, crumble! I prefer apple crumble, personally.

A TRUE BELIEVER
Amazingly, despite the openly admitted inability of the random processes of evolution to cope with the complexities of any and all living things, Taylor, still a true believer, asserted: "The fact that an evolutionary process has taken place is *not in doubt*", adding "It is only the *mechanism* which brought it about which is being questioned. No problem!

Like Hough, who is still desperately searching for that elusive mechanism, Taylor was also unwilling to accept the obvious "mystical" alternatives i.e. God, or magic, or little green men from Mars – and therefore hoped for some kind of "third way" to emerge, but in his book he never found it. G-Theory is that third way.

HAVE I WON A PRIZE THEN?
Reading what we have seen about the derisive state of evolution, it is a marvel that any thinking person can continue to give it serious consideration – but many still do. The situation seems reminiscent of a lady who phoned in to a radio programme I was listening to, where she was asked to identify a mystery voice. After she had failed abysmally, the DJ said, with silences interspersed, words to the effect of: "Sorry Mrs. Bloggs, that's wrong", but got no response. Then, after a long pause, he continued: "It's not correct …You failed to name the person … You didn't get it right … The names you gave were wrong … Time is up … We have to move to the next contestant…" to which the woman finally replied: "You mean I didn't win the prize then?"

So let's be very clear before we proceed any further: Evolution is bunk. It's wrong. It is incorrect. Darwin and Dawkins have been rumbled. The theory is infantile and stupid. It has hit the buffers. It's kaput. It cannot cope with the complexity of any single organism on the face of the earth. It is nonsense. It does not explain the origins of life, mind, emotion or instinct. The game is up. It don't work. It ain't never happened and never will. If evolution was a parrot, then to quote Monty Python, "Look, matey, I know a dead parrot when I see one, and I'm looking at one right now!"

SWEPT UNDER THE CARPET!
On the very last page of Taylor's treatise, just before the massive technical

bibliography, a number of other interesting and telling comments appear. For example: "Most of the unexplained phenomena of macro-evolution were first minimized, then *swept under the carpet*" – "Many facts remain *inexplicable*" – "The attempt to present Darwinism as an established dogma, immune from criticism, is *disintegrating*" – "Evolution has been *blinkered* by a too narrowly materialist and reductionist approach". And perhaps most telling of all, confirmation of the fact that scientists who wish to criticise the faith have been "in fear of having their *careers damaged* by the awful charge of unorthodoxy".

EATING HATS
Such is the internal dissent among the faithful, according to evolutionists Steele, Lindley and Blanden, in "Lamarck's Signature", that the current high priest of Darwinian orthodoxy, Richard Dawkins has now offered to eat his hat if what he terms "the Larmarckian scare" proves to be correct.

Incidentally, Steele et al candidly admit that error sometimes becomes scientific orthodoxy, so that, at times, large numbers of scientists become "held in thrall by erroneous concepts". Eeeh bah gum, there's trouble at mill.

THE PRIESTHOOD
Perhaps we should end this chapter with a comment from free-thinker Rupert Sheldrake: "Science is the last unreformed institution in the modern world today. It's *like the church before the Reformation.* All decisions are made by a small powerful group of people. They're authoritarian, entrenched, well-funded *and see themselves as a priesthood.*" Amen, brother.

2.15

DARWIN'S PERSONAL AGENDA

Many Christian people, I understand, avoid reading sections of the Old Testament of the Bible because they may appear, on the surface, to present God out of character, as some kind of angry monster. As a result, they are happy to accept the theories of erudite scholars who claim that the Old Testament is nothing more than a collection of myth and metaphor, mixed with the superstitions and exaggerations of ancient and ignorant peasant peoples.

Darwin likewise, who had earlier studied for the Christian ministry, found the fact that Genesis attributes to God the creation of all living things, including, therefore, the vicious wild animals, poisonous snakes and all manner of pests and parasites, an unbearable thought.

It was to solve this problem that Darwin suggested that God had originally "breathed life into a *few* forms or into one", with the word "few" apparently meaning just a handful of benign prototypes which then seemingly became subverted by the action of natural selection. That motivation drove him to forsake whatever faith he had, much to the distress of his believing wife, who must have thought her dear husband was doomed and lost forever.

More specifically, Darwin seems to have been the victim of warped evangelical Christian teaching, in particular the claim that any person not coming to repentance in this present life is "lost", and doomed to burn in torment in hell fire for ever, supposedly at the hand of the God of love. That would, of course, include his atheistic relatives. What misery those scripturally ignorant hell-fire preachers have caused – and what widespread deception they helped provoke by driving the desperate Charles Darwin to devise the theory of evolution in his attempt to escape the clutches of their false god.

THE BABY AND THE BATH WATER

As mentioned elsewhere, the Bible is brought into disrepute when Church leaders defend "orthodox beliefs" that are simply not scriptural – such as the claim that because the linking together of ages, dates and figures gleaned from the Old Testament suggest that man was created 6,000 years ago, then "the Bible says" that the physical earth is also six thousand years old, when a simple common-sense reading of Genesis chapter one quickly negates such a claim, as we shall see.

It seems significant, therefore, that just one year after "Origins" was published, a group of Church of England clergymen were emboldened to publish "Essays and Reviews", a book promoting scholastic criticism of the whole Bible, not just Genesis, claiming that much of the Old Testament was riddled with contradictions, myth and allegory, and should not be taken literally.

We are told that their book ran to thirteen editions and caused much greater furore amongst Christians then than the current debates about women vicars and bishops and gay clergy do today. Sadly, the ideas those men promoted are now the standard fare for candidates training for the ministry of the Anglican Church - the proverbial baby of Truth having been thrown out with the dirty bath water of "orthodox" error.

I was not surprised, therefore, at a recent Darwin event, to hear a professor of divinity from Oxford University, comment that of course "the Bible is just a book", much to the pleasure I imagine of the atheists and humanists in the audience.

EXTREME VIEWS
In Darwin's day, even naturalists such as the great Carl Linnaeus held the extreme and unscriptural view that all organisms then extant, including all known breeds and varieties, had existed that way since creation. It was Darwin's attempt to go to the opposite extreme that actually created the error of evolution – when the Truth of the matter, as is often the case, lay in the middle.

The simple fact, according to Genesis, is that God created a limited number of "kinds" of plants and animals, from which those we know today must have descended - a number which must have been sufficiently limited for some of each kind of land creature to have been carried by Noah's ark.

Once this simple fact is understood, the problems melt away, and we realize that "micro-evolution" is simply the expression of the potential for variety and adaptation to purpose and environment that God engineered into organisms at creation - but that "macro-evolution" is a myth.

A FEW ORIGINAL FORMS
Towards the end of "Origins", Darwin says that he saw "no good reason why the views given in this volume should shock the religious feelings of anyone" – pointing out that a famous author and divine, had written to him saying that he had "gradually learnt to see that it is just as noble a conception of the Deity to believe that He created a *few original forms* capable of self-development" than the myriad forms that were extant at the time. That "divine", apparently, was Charles Kingsley, famous author of "The Water Babies".

Although the wise and diplomatic Kingsley was probably comfortable equating Darwin's "few" to the "kinds" of Genesis, we can only wonder what he thought when Darwin then moved the goal posts, saying that "analogy" would lead him "one step further"—to the belief that all organisms had descended from just *one* original form.

THE HIGH PRIESTS OF EVOLUTION
In the "Dark Ages", when religious authorities ruled supreme, a corrupt priest could preach from the pulpit that the Bible said such and such a thing, and the ignorant and illiterate peasants would be unable to challenge his pronouncements, or even check them – not having access to a Bible, and being illiterate anyway in most cases. Of course, the priest might simply be passing on false teachings that he himself had unthinkingly accepted from his superiors without himself ever checking them properly against the scriptures.

Today many of those supposed Biblical teachings would be based on the warped ideas of learned "scholars" who make a living and seek reputation by dissecting and criticizing scripture, claiming most of it to be myth and mistake.

In a very similar manner, because of the complexities of biology and the scientific illiteracy of even highly educated individuals in non-scientific fields, the high priests of evolution, such as Professor Richard Dawkins and Dr. Steve Jones, are likewise able to confidently pronounce and have widely published unproven and erroneous evolutionary assertions.

But it is not just the public at large that has been duped. Many college students in the life sciences, like their peers in theology, have uncritically swallowed the evolutionary teachings regurgitated to them by their professors and their textbooks. Of course, they had to learn the "right" answers to pass their exams, like those kids in Kansas.

2.16

THE BIRTH OF GEOLOGY

The emergence of structured evolutionary ideas coincided with the birth of the new and complex science of geology. This led in particular to intensive scrutiny of the orthodox religious teaching that the earth was only six thousand years old, and that all or most of the earth's rock strata and their fossil content had been formed by the great Flood of Noah described in Genesis. At the time, however, fossils were poorly understood patterned lumps of stone, and even the suggestion that they had any connection with once-living organisms was severely frowned on.

THE ITALIAN JOB

One man who dared to dissent, however, was the Italian Nicolas Steno (1631-1687), an expert anatomist who became interested in geological matters - risking the wrath of the establishment by claiming that some fossils found in the his country's northern hills had once been shark's teeth, actual parts of living creatures.

Steno realized that many rock strata were formed by sediments deposited by turbulent water – currents moving first this way than that, transporting and depositing particles of various weights and sizes depending on their densities and the speed at which the water moved. He also suggested that the tilted, arched and even vertical strata he examined had originally been deposited horizontally over extended areas - and had been disturbed by massive earth movements, including volcanic activity, on land and under the seas, the heat of which also served to bake and harden sediments, sometimes forming "metamorphic" rock, such as marble which started out as limestone.

All this activity, Steno realized, clearly required far more time than the few months allowed for in the Genesis account of Noah's Flood – a fact that he saw as an insuperable barrier to the popular acceptance of his theories.

As a result of his contributions, however, Steno is regarded by many as the father of modern geology, a title conferred by others on the great James Hutton.

SOME INTERESTING CLUES IN GENESIS

As we shall see in more detail later, some interesting clues in the Genesis account of Noah's flood suggest that its effects were not as cataclysmic as modern young-earth creationists claim. Firstly, for example, as the flood waters subsided, Noah sent out a dove that brought back a freshly plucked olive leaf - which suggests that the trees were still standing, and that the flood's impact on the earth's topography was minimal. At least, in the mountainous area where the ark came to rest. What mountain building or other terrestrial landscaping took place elsewhere, we cannot tell, except that on the basis of their fossil content, some or all of the Cenozoic strata appear to have been formed by the Flood.

Secondly, when building the ark, Noah sealed the seams inside and out with pitch, an extract of fossilized plant matter – suggesting the fossilization of organisms in an earlier, pre-Adamic age, as the precise wording of Genesis chapter one clearly allows.

Incidentally, the fact that Noah took specimens of all kinds of land creatures onto the ark to ensure their survival would seem to suggest that none were made extinct by the flood – another hint, perhaps, that bizarre extinct organisms and their rock strata belonged to a previous, pre-Adamic world.

JAMES HUTTON

Scottish geologist James Hutton (1726-97), who was born about a century after Steno, reached similar conclusions concerning the origins of the earth's rock formations. As a Christian person he strongly believe that the earth was a kind of machine created and provisioned by God for human habitation – but that the present land and geological strata were not the primordial ones, having been "formed by the operation of secondary causes". In other words, the useful soil that he had learned to cultivate in this fourteen years as a farmer, the gravel beds, the clay and chalk, the limestone, the coal and oil and rich metal ore deposits so useful to man had all been created by God from the original pristine igneous rock material by slow processes of erosion and sedimentation – all in preparation for human habitation of the globe, and possibly over vast periods of time.

The fact that Hutton suggested that "a preceding world" had been destroyed by such processes, suggests that he too had rejected the orthodox young-earth teaching of the religious establishment.

Envisioning the endless operation over millions of years of what he called "the great geological cycle", Hutton stated that earth offers "no vestige of a beginning - no prospect of an end", hence the concept of "uniformitarianism", the idea that the geological forces that created our world were the same as those now at work - a deliberate attempt, perhaps to counter the claim that all had been produced by Noah's world-wide flood. Uniformitarianism does not, however, exclude the possibility of catastrophes – such as earthquake, flood or volcanic eruption.

One wonders also if Hutton's thinking here was influenced by the Bible, for example by the metaphors in Psalm 102 and other places that compare the heavens and the earth to garments gradually wearing out and needing to be changed.

One wonders also if other scriptures inspired Hutton's model of the earth as a kind of machine made for the service of man – for example, Moses' brief description of the geological treasures locked up in the land of Canaan, Quote: "God is bringing you to a good land, a land of brooks of water, of fountains and springs, flowing forth in the valleys and hills . . . you will lack nothing, land whose stones are iron, and out of whose hills you can dig copper".

Those mineral deposits must have existed long before Noah's flood, as evidenced by the fact that one of Adam's immediate descendants, Tubal-Cain made implements of bronze and iron – and that one of the rivers flowing out of Eden traversed a land where gold and precious stones were to be found. Incidentally, this same section, written after the Flood of Noah, suggests that the original geography, including the river courses, had remained unchanged by the Deluge.

THE NEW ATHENS
It is said that the Edinburgh of Hutton's day was called the "New Athens" and was probably the most intellectually stimulating city in the world - a society inhabited by the likes of the poet Robert Burns, the chemist Joseph Black, the engineer James Watt and the economist Adam Smith. In this environment Hutton found people who welcomed new ideas. However, despite his intellect, his own writing was characterized, we are told, by "a degree of obscurity astonishing to all who knew him".

Hutton was, incidentally, the first person to explain how rain forms from the condensation of water vapor when warm air masses saturated with moisture are cooled by collision with cold air masses from more northern latitudes. He also speculated as to the nature of "reality", in language reminiscent of articles in modern scientific journals, suggesting, for example, that what we perceive is not physically real, but merely a construct of the mind.

However, in matters geological, his thinking was based on many years of practical hands-on observation of rock formations in various parts of the world. Like Steno, Hutton found it impossible to accept that Noah's flood had not only created all the rock strata, but in some locations had also turned them vertical, eroded the ends level, and then deposited more layers on top in giant T-formations – as demonstrated at Siccar Point, in Scotland, a formation once described as "the daddy of all British unconformities".

THE SURVIVAL OF THE FITTEST
According to a document not discovered until 1947, Darwin's crucial concept of the "survival of the fittest" in the struggles of life had been suggested a hundred years earlier by none other than James Hutton - who speculated that organisms best suited to their surroundings were the ones "*most certain of surviving*". However, credit for coining the famous phrase itself, which did not actually appear in "The Origin of Species" until the fifth edition, is usually given to the philosopher Herbert Spencer.

LYELL'S GEOLOGICAL YO-YO
Sir Charles Lyell, born a couple of months before James Hutton died, carried the new science of geology forward with immense energy, and popularized Hutton's teachings in his classic book "The Principles of Geology – an Attempt to explain the former Changes of the Earth's Surface by Reference to Causes now in Operation".

Much to Darwin's delight, Lyell thus rejected rapid-acting mechanisms such as massive floods and cataclysms as geological agents, teaching instead the uniformitarian principle that strata were deposited extremely slowly over millions of years – a process evidently made possible by continents repeatedly rising and falling at convenient intervals to enable gradual ingressions and regressions of the sea.

According to Lyell, the hundreds of coal beds that exist in some parts of the earth were also produced by this giant geological yo-yo acting over zillions of millions of years, despite the fact that multiple beds of coal are sometimes found to be pierced by a single fossilized tree trunk - a "polystrate" fossil.

Creationists, who imagine that most sedimentary strata resulted from Noah's flood, suggest that the most of these multiple beds were all formed at the same time by great masses of vegetation being transported and deposited in haphazard fashion by powerful currents of water.

On a trip to the United States, we are told, Lyell applied uniformitarian principles in estimating the annual rate of regression of Niagara Falls due to the friction of the moving water – and likewise the rate of accumulation of silt particles at the mouth of the Mississippi River.

THE GEOLOGICAL COLUMN
One of his major contributions was to help organize the systematic naming and dating of rock strata on the basis of the fossils they contained - leading, thanks to the coordinated efforts of a number of workers, to the drawing up of the notional "Geological Column", the whole of earth history consisting of the Pre-Cambrian age, followed by three major *Eras* – the *Paleozoic (ancient life)*, the *Mesozoic (middle life)*, and the *Cenozoic (recent life)* each broken down into *Periods,* and then, in some cases, *Epochs.* As we shall see, the bizarre and unfamiliar fossil content of the *Paleozoic* and *Mesozoic* eras suggest they belong to a separate, pre-Adamic age.

Lyell was personally responsible for naming three Epochs of the *Cenozoic* Tertiary Period - the "Eocene" (Dawn or recent), the "Miocene" (More recent), and the "Pliocene" (Most recent).

Lyell also refined the technique of using "index fossils", whereby strata, independent of whether they consist of sandstone or chalk, for example, are dated by their fossil content. Simple as that may sound, very similar fossils may appear mixed with other forms in several strata, and Lyell devised a complicated dating method which involved comparing the relative percentages of the several fossils in each in order to assign the appropriate label.

DEEP TIME
The concept of "deep time" afforded by Lyell's yo-yo was to prove crucial to Darwin because it conjured up the vast ages required for the relentless operation of "Natural Selection" to supposedly sift and accumulate tiny and very occasional random variations in organisms – a process eloquently described by him as: "daily and hourly *scrutinizing,* throughout the world, *the slightest variations*; rejecting those that are bad, preserving and *adding up all that are*

good; silently and insensibly working, whenever and wherever opportunity offers, at the improvement of each organic being . . ."

There was a temporary scare for Darwinism in the 1890s when the great physicist, and thermodynamic expert Lord Kelvin estimated the age of the earth to be relatively young, a mere 30 million years, far too young for geologists' liking, by calculating how long a sphere of molten magma of the same size would take to cool to its present temperature.

FAULTY SCIENTIFIC ASSUMPTIONS

So confident was Kelvin that his figures were correct and that geologists were wrong, he said: "A great reform in geological speculation now seems necessary . . . a great mistake has been made". As it happened, however, it was Kelvin who had made the "great mistake", with the result that what seemed like absolute certainty turned out to be wrong because of a faulty assumption.

Kelvin had obtained such a young age for the earth because he was not aware that much of the heat being lost from its surface was being compensated for by nuclear energy still being released in its interior – without which the earth would now be far cooler and hence appear to be much older.

A few years later, just after the turn of the century, the phenomenon of radioactivity was discovered, enabling Kelvin's younger contemporary, Ernest Rutherford, to use measurements on the decay of uranium into lead, and the subsequent release of helium, to date the age of the earth as some 500 million years. When it was later pointed out that much of the helium created and trapped in rocks must have diffused out and so escaped Rutherford's detection, the age figure was again revised radically upwards – and evolutionists could smile again. Current estimates are in excess of four billion years.

However, according to G-Theory the actual or imagined age of the earth has no relevance to the origin of the plants and animals with which we are familiar.

PRE-CAMBRIAN ROCK

In keeping with the expectations of the G-Theory of creation and James Hutton's suggestions, geologists tell us that the bulk of world's valuable minerals – gold, silver, nickel, copper, iron and chromium – are found in the most ancient of all rock strata, the Pre-Cambrian.

ERAS
As already noted, geological time since the Pre-Cambrian is divided into three "eras" – the *Paleozoic* (i.e. ancient life, supposedly a time before land creatures had evolved), the *Mesozoic* (i.e. middle life, the Age of the dinosaurs, previously named the Secondary era), and the *Cenozoic* (i.e. recent or familiar life, previously the Tertiary era).

MESOZOIC ROCKS
Geologist also tell us that 50% of the world's oil reserves, fossilized remains of sea creatures, were formed in ancient Mesozoic times, in the pre-Adamic age postulated by G-Theory, when the Earth's climate was much warmer with temperate conditions at the poles, and with lush tropical forest conditions extending to latitude 45, north and south. Europe's massive North Sea oil and gas deposits, however, are said to be of Paleozoic origin, having later diffused and been trapped in porous Permian sandstone formations. Clearly, these are very complex situations with great scope for misunderstanding and error.

A DRAMATIC TRANSITION
The final period of the Mesozoic era, the Cretaceous, has been described as the *"transition between the very different earlier Earth and the Cenozoic, a world relatively similar to that of the present day"*. This evidence of a dramatic transition from an alien prehistoric world to our present age is one of the key discoveries of geology – the implication of which is that the array of bizarre and grotesque creatures evidenced by Paleozoic and Mesozoic fossils were not the ancestors of the earth's present flora and fauna, and were, in any case, all fully-formed complex organisms in their own right, not the unfit, failed primitive transitional forms Darwin's theory required.

THE MOST PUZZLING EVENT
As already noted, George Gaylord Simpson, said to be the most influential paleontologist of the twentieth century, once commented that: "The *most puzzling event in the history of life on the earth is the change from the Mesozoic Age of Reptiles, to the . . . Age of Mammals*. It is as if the curtain were rung down suddenly on a stage where all the leading roles were taken by reptiles, especially dinosaurs, in great numbers and bewildering variety, and rose again immediately to reveal the same setting but an *entirely new cast*, a cast in which the dinosaurs do not appear at all, other reptiles are supernumeraries and the leading parts are all played by mammals of sorts barely hinted at in the previous acts" (*Life Before Man*, 1972). G-Theory solves that puzzle.

CENOZOIC ROCKS

It was during the Cenozoic, also called the Cainozoic, era that placental mammals came on the scene, leading the "Encyclopaedia Britannica" to comment: "the Cenozoic *placental mammals were poised to take over* the terrestrial environment, as soon as the dinosaurs vanished". Some kind of dramatic terrestrial transition clearly took place.

Early in the Cenozoic era, for example, in the Eocene period, mammals, such as horses, sheep, pigs, dogs, cats, giraffe and deer make their first appearance in the fossil record. Some of those were the first ruminants, creatures such as cows that chew the cud, one of the guidelines in the Law of Moses for the identification of "clean" animals – i.e. those fit for human consumption, in contrast to "unclean" creatures such as slugs and snakes and even pigs.

Some of these creatures grew to very large proportions, for example, the mammoth, its cousin the mastodon, the sabre-toothed tiger, and the famous Irish Elk, which was seven feet tall at the shoulder, with an antler span of 12 feet. Although these creatures are now extinct, they were clearly mutant varieties of kinds now existing. Their disappearance from the scene is another mystery, and one suggestion is that they were hunted out of existence by early man – rather than perishing due to severe constipation, one of the theories seriously proposed to explain the demise of the dinosaurs, a suggestion probably resulting from a consideration of the practicality of vast amounts of food and faecal matter needing to be transported long distances through very large bodies!

According to G-Theory, the latter part of the Cenozoic era would seem to equate, basically, to the age between Adam and Noah – the pre-Flood world whose creation is described in the Genesis account of Creation Week, the world that was destroyed in the Deluge. Although scientists divide the era up into seven epochs and attempt to trace some kind of evolutionary trail through them, their findings are confused and the subject of much disagreement.

It was during the Cenozoic, also, that the world assumed its modern continental configuration, the one shown on any school atlas.

THE DELUGE

Young-earth creationists are thought to bring the Bible into scientific disrepute by rejecting these findings of geology and insisting not only that the earth is only six thousand years old, but that much or most sedimentary rock strata and their fossil content were created by the waters of the great and apparently world-wide flood of Noah.

At the time of Adam, according to scripture, God had no intention of bringing a future Flood on mankind, as the Genesis account makes clear when it says: "The Lord saw that the wickedness of man was great in the earth, and that every imagination of the thoughts of his heart was only evil continually. And *the Lord was sorry* that he had made man on the earth, and it grieved him to his heart".

If the flood was not originally intended when man was created, then the earth on which Adam and Eve walked must have been already equipped, like Hutton's "machine", with all the coal seams and other natural resources needed by man to live a good and constructive life.

Is it possible, therefore, that much or most of the earth's massive rock strata and their fossils were formed in a previous age, in a mysterious and violent pre-Adamic world that perished prior to the so-called seven days of creation? That was in fact the belief of some early Christian geologists.

If a pre-Adamic world did indeed exist and was totally destroyed, G-Theory suggests that all or most of its fossil record has no connection, evolutionary, with the flora and fauna of this present world.

THREE TYPES OF ROCK
Early geologists identified the three kinds of rock. The first, *Igneous* rock, like granite, is formed by the cooling and solidification of molten material either inside the earth or in lava flows from volcanoes. Igneous strata contain crystals of various sizes and show signs of having been molten. They do not contain fossils.

The second, *Sedimentary* rock, such as sandstone and limestone, is formed by the consolidation of tiny particles, apparently eroded from older rocks, that have been transported by water and settled on the beds of rivers, lakes and seas. Sedimentary rocks may contain fossils.

The third type of rock, *Metamorphic*, is generally formed from sedimentary rock that has been by transformed by the action of heat and pressure. Slate, for example, is formed from shale, a sedimentary rock formed earlier from silt and clay particles.

A few minutes studying a geological survey report of an area such as Wales, for example, will demonstrate the incredible complexity of the formations that pioneers such as Murchison and Sedgwick struggled to explore, trace and map over wide areas - with some Cambrian strata being several miles thick, sometimes folded then corrugated, folded again, then overlaid in places by coal measuring a couple of miles thick. Such formations were traced over various parts of England and even Europe, being identified by their fossil content.

It is very hard to conceive that such massive folded metamorphic rock formations containing the fossils of extinct organisms could have been created by Noah's flood.

TWO KINDS OF EARTH

It should be pointed out here that the Hebrew word rendered "earth" is used in two ways in the Genesis creation account – first, to refer to the complete earth, the globe and the sea waters covering it, and second, in later verses, to describe just the continents that were raised up to form the "earth" - the dry, habitable land. The part that was separated from the waters of the oceans that had been drained off, and which were then named "seas".

When the Bible says that God "created" the heavens and the earth in seven days, the word "earth" in that context evidently refers to the land mass that man later lived on, that had been drained and made habitable during creation week, not the whole planet, which had evidently been created possibly many millions of years earlier, in Genesis 1:1.

2.17

ROCKS & FOSSILS

The fossil record is crucially important to evolutionists because, as Darwin immediately realized, it is the one and only possible source of the information required to validate his theory according to the requirements of the scientific method.

THE ORIGIN OF SOME GEOLOGICAL TERMS

Any encyclopaedia or geology text book will show a diagram of the "Geological Column", the notional series of rock strata that supposedly span the history of the earth, from "Pre-Cambrian" times up to the present day.

The study of rock formations shows that by far the largest area of the dry land of the earth is made up of marine sediments, so that the present surface is not the original or "aboriginal" one. The sequence of fossils found in the layers of the column is supposed to illustrate a pattern of evolutionary development, and newly explored strata are fitted into the scheme and dated on the basis of their fossil content. The column has marine creatures at the bottom, extinct land creatures in the middle, and "modern" organisms on the top. The concept is apparently attributed to Charles Lyell, whom we met earlier.

From a G-Theory viewpoint, however, the vast bulk of the column relates to the pre-Adamic age (the *Paleozoic* and *Mesozoic eras*), the flora and fauna of which may have been catastrophically destroyed prior to the start of this present era (the *Cenozoic* era) – organisms, most of which, were clearly not the evolutionary ancestors of those with which we are familiar today.

Many of the rock formations that make up the column, identified by particular fossils they contained, were originally named after the locations in which early geologists found them – the term Cambrian, for example, coming from the Roman name of Wales, and Devonian strata (the Age of Fishes and Ferns - including armored fish) having first been recognized in Devon. The Cretaceous strata, however, as illustrated by the white cliffs of Dover and composed mostly of micro shell fossils, were so named, because of their composition, from the Latin for "chalk" in this case. Note however these terms have taken on chronological significance, so that rocks that contain no chalk at all may well be labelled Cretaceous because of their position relative to other already identified formations.

BIOSTRATIGRAPHY

The Silurian strata (named after an ancient Welsh tribe) were identified by Sir Roderick Impey Murchison in 1835 and traced through various parts of Wales and England on the basis of the fossils they contained, links sometimes also being made on the basis of banding patterns in the sediments. This technique, called "biostratigraphy" was apparently taught to Murchison by engineer and canal builder William "Strata" Smith, who had used ammonite fossils to correlate Mesozoic outcrops and excavations in various locations in his work in canal building. Although not interested in publishing his ideas himself, Smith was happy to explain them to other members of the Geological Society of London.

A CAMBRIDGE PROFESSOR

In 1831 at the suggestion of William Buckland, Adam Sedgwick, an Anglican minister, traveled to Wales, where he conducted research into the mass of rocks known as 'greywacke'. I believe it was Sedgwick who said, when he became a Cambridge professor: "Hitherto I have never turned a stone; henceforth I will leave no stone un-turned."

In the early 1830s, Sedgwick and Murchison worked together on the rocks of Wales, which were very difficult to study on due to extensive folding and faulting. A dispute arose, however, when Sedgwick's upper "Cambrian" system overlapped with the lower part of Murchison's "Silurian." Sedgwick had defined his "Cambrian" using physical characters of the rocks, and had not relied much on fossils, which could be found almost everywhere anyway.

Murchison, on the other hand, who had used fossils extensively in defining the Silurian, claimed at first that the upper Cambrian, and then the entire Cambrian, were really parts of his Silurian. The resulting quarrel between the two men left them never speaking to each other again.

Incidentally, during the summer of his work in Wales which was to lead to that dispute, Sedgwick made a fateful choice of field assistant, a young Cambridge graduate named Charles Darwin.

ENTER JOHN PHILLIPS

John Phillips, nephew of William "Strata" Smith, became keenly interested as a boy in his uncle's work and rose from humble beginnings to become a professor of geology at Oxford University. A man of insight and vision, Phillips suggested that rock formations should be identifiable top and bottom by their fossil content on a world-wide basis. As Sedgwick and Murchison argued about details of individual formations, as mentioned above, Phillips realized that all the periods they had identified and traced around the world could and should be grouped, on the basis of their three distinctive sets of fossils, into just three major Eras – hence the Paleozoic, the Mesozoic and the Caino - or Cenozoic.

KEEP IT SIMPLE, STUPID!

G-Theory simplifies that scenario by reducing the three eras to just two - by suggesting that the fossils of the Paleozoic and Mesozoic may simply show the full set of marine and land organisms of the Pre-Adamic age, with those of the Cenozoic relating to the organisms created in the Genesis account.

In other words, those pre-Adamic flora and fauna may have lived contemporaneously rather than sequentially, and may have been buried and destroyed by one massive catastrophe rather than several - resulting in their remains somehow being sorted and buried and distributed as fossils through the various rock formations of the Paleozoic and Mesozoic eras, basically with marine organisms at the bottom and land organisms above. Due to Darwin's dominance, however, data is always interpreted to suit the evolutionary model.

PHANTOM EXTINCTIONS

Although with the revival of catastrophism, geologist now believe there have been more than a dozen massive extinctions, G-Theory suggests that most of them may be mythical, such as the supposedly greatest-of-all between the Paleozoic and Mesozoic eras, the so-called End-of-Permian extinction.

Since evolution requires a gradual development of organisms from the marine forms of the Paleozoic to the land forms of the Mesozoic, rather than a magical jump, Darwin's great unifying force suggests that a whole slew of transitional fossil forms should exist to bridge the imagined gap between those two eras. Since they do not exist and never did, paleontologists assume that there must have been a massive worldwide extinction of life followed, somehow, by a miraculous revival. Not so. Again, data is arranged to fit the Darwin model.

A MEGA EXPLOSION

As noted earlier, a second implication of G-Theory seems to be that rather than evolving gradually in some kind of sequence, all those Paleozoic and Mesozoic organisms, not just those of the Cambrian formations, were created at the same moment in time. During the time period that followed, no doubt those organisms mutated and varied within their Pre-Adamic "kinds" as with the Genesis kinds that came later. This simplifying suggestion would obviate the need for the many mass extinctions required by the punctuated equilibrium theory which seeks to explain why organisms supposedly appear, thrive, then abruptly disappear with no evidence of evolution having taken place.

CREATIONIST EXPLANATION OF STRATA FORMATION

Young-earth creationists, who claim that most strata were formed by Noah's Flood, explain the fossil record by pointing out that currents of moving water can sift and sort flora and fauna on the basis of their density – so that in a massive swirling and subsiding deluge the denser organisms such as shell fish would be deposited first and so appear in the lower strata, and would already be under water anyway. The gases produced inside rotting dead bodies of larger creatures could also explain why their remains might be more buoyant for a time and so end up. in so-called younger, overlying strata.

A KEY FACT

Regardless of these complexities, the key fact to remember with regard to the geological column is that geologists all agree that the very earliest strata are the Cambrian and the Pre-Cambrian that underlie them. Evolution therefore requires that the fossils found in these strata should be of the very simplest, crude prototype organisms. However, as Darwin realized, and as we have discussed, the Cambrian organisms, such as Trilobites, that abounded there were massively complex. How can that simple fact be explained?

HOW FOSSILS FORM

The remains of most dead plants and animals simply perish due to the diligent work of teams of scavenging organisms. Fly maggots, for example, will do their job of burrowing and opening up the flesh of a dead body for the entry of other organisms and oxygen, a complex and thorough operation. As a result, most plants and animals usually never leave a fossil trace behind when they die, or if they do, just the hard parts such as shell and bone. A dead cat buried in the garden, would probably disappear without trace after ten years, which explains why the Church of England permits a burial plot to be re-used after 25 years.

As a result, the fossil record is, even now, relatively meagre – and since the organisms most likely to be fossilized are sea creatures with solid shells, a seriously distorted picture of the flora and fauna of any particular time is presented, compounded numerically by the fact that some marine organisms, such as the Trilobites, apparently grew and discarded several shells during their lifetime. The burial and fossilisation of organisms on the sea bed is favoured by the accumulation of sediments which fall continuously like fine snow,

For land organism to be fossilized, some kind of catastrophe or accident is probably required in order to bury and preserve their remains. Little wonder that 99% of the fossil record consists of marine organisms, with coal beds being the prime source of plant fossils.

Notice that although the fossil record is still comparatively meagre, as Darwin claimed, the overwhelmingly vast majority of the fossils found should be those of "missing links", imperfect and failed transitional forms. But they are not.

WHOLE BODY FOSSILS
The hundreds of woolly mammoth remains found in the frozen wastes of Siberia are interesting example of a whole-body fossils, which are not really fossils at all, but organism that perished in circumstances that actually preserved their flesh and bone and protected them from the assiduous attentions of the scavengers, maggots and bacteria that would normally consume them – events such as floods, mud slides and volcanic ash and scalding water, and at La Brea in Los Angeles by becoming trapped in tar pits.

Bizarrely, some creatures were killed so quickly that their final postures were also preserved – for example, a fish swallowing a smaller one, a marine creature giving birth, and even, one source claims, a mating mammoth with its long male member still in a state of erection. A small Siberian mammoth was found with the grass and buttercups, remnants of its last meal, still in its mouth.

Most fossils are actually mineralized copies of the organism's structure, sometimes both external and internal – created by a process of petrifaction in which organic tissues are replaced by elements such as calcium and magnesium. Usually, the finer the sediment that bury an organism, the finer the detail of the resulting fossil, which is why the flying reptile Archaeopteryx is known to have had feathered wings.

ANOMALOUS FOSSILS

Sometimes the "index fossils" used to "date" rock strata are found in the "wrong" strata, perhaps accompanied by fossils that are supposedly much older or younger on the notional evolutionary chart of descent. These are classed as being "anomalous", in order to preserve the evolutionary model.

A Google search using the key words "anomalous fossils" will throw up all manner of discoveries that fly in the face of orthodoxy, such as iron axe heads encased in rock supposedly hundreds of millions of years old, and artefacts constructed from alloys only quite recently invented

POLYSTRATE FOSSILS

Another casually dismissed problem is that of "polystrate" fossils mentioned earlier, such as petrified tree trunks that pierce several coal seams and the rock strata sandwiched between them, each of which apparently took millions of years to form by repeated ingressions and regressions of the sea.

Polystrate fossils are common in coal beds and were recognized as a "mystery" by geologists over a hundred years ago. The orthodox explanation is that a tree took root in a marsh, then died and stood there without rotting for hundreds of years and actually assisted the formation of further coal seams by helping entangle floating mats of vegetation around it when the area was flooded again.

As already mentioned, uniformitarianism does allow for relatively rapid acting local floods and changes to occur and for the formation of several seams of coal to take place in just a few hundred years, rather than millions.

A study of web sites devoted to such paleontological problems soon confirms the sheer complexity and the speculative nature of the subject. However, polystrate fossils do suggest sudden massive destruction rather than a whole series.

PRE-FLOOD CREATURES

Some extinct creatures, such as the woolly mammoth and the sabre-toothed tiger, were evidently variants on still-extant "kinds" of animals and probably lived in the pre-Flood world that lasted from Adam to Noah. In reading about strange and exotic creatures from the past, it should be borne in mind that mutation to giant forms has always been a possibility, as is even demonstrated today by dwarf and tall pea and bean plants and even dogs. According to the

Genesis account, the Flood did not make any land creature extinct because specimens of each were taken on the ark.

2.18

DINOSAURS AND DRAGONS

Any debate of the merits of evolution and creation will almost certainly involve some discussion of dinosaurs – with some creationists claiming that fossil footprints have been found, proving that man and dinosaur once lived side by side on earth.

Generally speaking, however, dinosaurs appear to belong to the Mesozoic era, part of the Pre-Adamic world, as already discussed. As reptiles, the gigantic size they attained may, at least in part, be attributed to their sheer longevity and continuous growth, which in turn may have been a consequence of the absence of cosmic radiation at the earth's surface prior to the Flood, as we shall discuss later. Perhaps as a result of the movie "Jurassic Park", a vast amount of information regarding dinosaurs is now available in most public libraries as well as on the internet.

TERRIBLE LIZARDS
The large dinosaurs may also have been genetically giant forms of lizards, and it was their similarities with modern-day forms that led William Owen to coin the name dinosaur – "terrible lizard", although he did note that their physiology was somewhat different.

We read in Genesis that there was a race of giant people on the Earth in the age before the Flood – just as today there are giant turtles and giant varieties of certain plants today. However, scientists still continue to speculate, on the basis of scant remains, as to whether dinosaurs were warm or cold blooded, if they made sounds, and even if they were feathered and possibly brightly colored.

Young Earth creationists, who have to fit the age of reptiles into the period between Adam and Noah, always point to two strange creatures that were clearly extant in the days of Job as possibly being dinosaurs. Although often identified in Bible reference books as elephants or hippopotami or crocodiles, they were clearly more than that.

SILLY CREATURES

In humbling Job, God begins by describing some of the amazing animals he has created, including some seemingly silly creatures that make a nonsense of evolution. The wild donkey, for example, chose to live on the arid salt flats where food was hard to obtain. Why? The ostrich lays her eggs on the ground, God points out, and leaves them covered with sand where they can easily be accidentally crushed. As the account also points out, the horse even happily exposes itself to danger and possible death by rushing boldly into battle at the sound of the trumpet. How did such unfit creatures ever evolve and survive?

BEHEMOTH

Next God draws attention to Behemoth, "the Beast", of which he comments, "I made with you". In other words, at the same time man was created, indicating that this particular creature was a separate creation from the dinosaurs of the pre-Adamic age.

The account then describes Behemoth as a herbivore living amongst the reeds in the marshes, and as having his strength in his loins, with powerful muscles in his belly. His tail was as stout as a cedar, which is a very large tree, and he is described as ranking first among the works of God, possibly by virtue of size. Another clue to his stature is the description of his bones as being like tubes of brass, and his limbs as rods of iron.

The description would seem to fit very well with a dinosaur, but if so, what happened to it? Perhaps the clue lies in the phrase "yet his Maker can approach him with his sword", implying perhaps that God chose, for some reason, to render Behemoth extinct – perhaps anticipating the advent of guns and bombs which nothing composed of flesh and blood can possibly resist.

Although Behemoth appears to have been a great monster, the impression given by the account is that he was quite a rare sight, and certainly did not rampage the countryside in herds like the dinosaurs, whose numbers are attested to by the mass burial graves and large number of eggs that have been discovered in various locations.

LEVIATHAN

A second monster brought to Job's attention was Leviathan, a "coiling serpent", that was apparently a fierce, probably a four-legged sea serpent of the type depicted in ancient seascapes. Elsewhere, Leviathan is described as a crooked and piercing serpent, possibly having an armored snout that was able to penetrate the hull of wooden ships.

Leviathan is also described in the book of Job as having powerful jaws and a frightening array of teeth. His back had a row of shields or plates that were tightly jointed together, and his underside bore an array of jagged scales that left a trail in the mud has he emerged from the water. His chest was apparently as hard as millstone, quite impervious to swords, spears, harpoons or arrows.

In Jewish belief, we are told, Behemoth was the unconquerable monster of the land, and Leviathan was monster of the waters of the sea.

FIRE-BREATHING DRAGONS?
As with medieval dragons, which, we are told, figured in serious books on zoology until the Middle Ages, the account in Job seems to be saying that Leviathan could belch fire and smoke. Although such claims would be quickly discounted as myth by most modern readers, a few moments' thought suggests that such a thing might be quite possible - given the fact that the flammable gas methane is generated in the digestive tract of animals, and could conceivably be exhaled through the mouth or nose from a storage bladder, and catalytically ignited.

Even a cow produces enough methane in a week to fill a barrage balloon, so how much would a large dinosaur produce? According to Michael Benton, one of a hundred theories of dinosaur extinction is that they polluted the atmosphere and suffocated themselves!

Finally, we read that nothing on Earth was Leviathan's equal, possibly referring to its ferociousness. Although a four-legged serpent, or dragon, it could apparently rear up to a great height and glare down on any who dared approach.

Again, I think the implication of the account is that Leviathan was a rare sight, but there is no indication of its extinction. Might its kind still lurk in the depths of the oceans, or even Loch Ness?

2.19
RADIOMETRIC DATING

Claims by early Victorian geologists such as James Hutton that some of the Earth's rock strata were formed millions of years ago have been supported in recent times by the use of radio-isotope dating methods, the results of which, in most cases, accord well with G-Theory.

GEOLOGICAL CLOCKS

Radioactive materials found in the earth act as natural geological clocks that were somehow "wound up" when the unstable nuclei of their atoms were created, possibly multiple millions of years ago - clocks that are slowly running down as those nuclei disintegrate in a random fashion, emitting radiation, such as alpha particles which can be detected with Geiger counters.

The half-lives of radioactive elements, the time required for half the nuclei existing at any given time to emit radiation and transmute themselves into different elements or isotopes, which may also be radioactive, can vary from multiple millions of years, in the case of Uranium, for example, down to a few minutes, or even fractions of a second for the highly unstable man-made isotopes created by neutron bombardment inside a nuclear reactor.

A useful metaphor here would be to compare the decay of a radioactive substance to water running out of the plug hole of a bath, with the water's half-life being the time for half of it to escape, and then for half of that remaining to escape, and so on. Since the pressure pushing water out of the plug hole reduces as the level falls, the escape rate is proportional to the amount remaining. A graph of water level against time, at least for a bath with vertical sides, would therefore resemble that showing how the activity of a radioactive material varies with time. In this simple model, different radioactive isotopes could be represented by different liquids that flow out at different rates depending on their viscosity and density.

At the present time, orthodox physics teaching is that radioactive half-lives are invariant, totally unaffected by physical conditions such as extremes of temperature or even the most corrosive chemical attack, which only affects the electron shells in the outer part of atoms, and not their nuclei.

The fact that elements with half-lives measuring millions of years still exist in the ground, strongly suggest that the Earth is at least several times older than that – unless, as some creationists would contend, God actually created the Earth in an "already old" state, with its radio-active uranium already partially decayed into stable Lead – by analogy, they would argue, with the fact that Adam and Eve were also created "old", as adults rather than babies.

Another fact that Young Earth creationists have to explain away is that the light currently arriving from distant stars has taken multiple millions of years to make its journey in some cases - and so must have set out long before Adam was even created, unless of course the speed of light has changed dramatically or that God created not only the stars but also, at the same time, streams of light waves already extending from space to the earth's surface.

THE AGE OF THE EARTH
One early non-radiometric attempt to estimate the age of the Earth was to compare the amounts of salty minerals being transported by river waters into the oceans each year with the total amount already accumulated there. The age came out in the hundreds of millions of years, but again creationists were quick to point out that God may have made the seas salty to begin with, and that Noah's Flood would have added greatly to the mineral content anyway.

Radiometric methods are susceptible to fundamental problems, assumptions and simplifications that are metaphorically similar to this, but harder for the non-scientist to understand.

As already mentioned, G-Theory has no argument with the vast ages that radiometric methods attribute to the oldest rocks, the Paleozoic and Mesozoic strata, which it assigns to a pre-Adamic age. If there is disagreement, it concerns dates assigned to some more recent rocks, Cenozoic strata. Incidentally, it is important to understand that the radiometric techniques do not date the Cenozoic rock strata themselves, which consist of sediments, but igneous intrusions made into them since their formation - lava flows that accompany them in various locations.

Clearly, an intrusion of volcanic magma into already existing sedimentary strata should be younger than those strata. Conversely, the sedimentary formations must be older than the dates assigned to the solidified magma by the Potassium-Argon technique.

POTASSIUM-ARGON DATING

The well-established but unreliable potassium-argon technique depends on the radio-active decay of the isotope Potassium-40 (symbol, K-40) with a half-life of 1.3 billion years – the time required for half of the original K-40 atoms in a sample to turn into Calcium-40 and Argon-40 atoms. Argon-40 exists as a chemically unreactive gas which remains trapped in cold, solid rock but can be boiled off from a test sample in the lab by intense heat, and the amount measured using a mass spectrometer.

The key to dating igneous rocks by this process is the simplifying assumptions that when lava erupts from the ground, all the gaseous Argon that had previously accumulated over millions of years and had been trapped under ground, supposedly boils off into the atmosphere – thereby resetting the radioactive clock to zero. The gradual build-up of Argon in the solidified lava then starts over again from that moment in time, so that when a geologist appears on the scene many years later and chips off a sample for dating purposes, his careful measurements of the relative amounts of Potassium and Argon should enable him to work out the time elapsed since the eruption took place.

Naturally, any old Argon that failed to boil off during the eruption, or any that diffused in from concentrations in magma deeper down, or later from the air, could make the sample appear very much older than it really was. As a result, the potential for serious error is immense.

Incidentally, it has been said that using a radio-isotope with such a long half-life for dating strata as young as 6,000 years is a bit like using a clock with only an hour hand to time a 100 metre sprint. Nevertheless, the technique usually generates dates of millions of years for Cenozoic samples, which is what most scientists want to see and so find "acceptable".

ARGON-ARGON DATING – THE HOLY GRAIL

To overcome the problems of Potassium-Argon dating, the Argon40-Argon39 method has been devised. Although less reliable in younger rocks (such as the Mesozoic, which have had less time to accumulate measurable amounts of Argon 40), when it was used to date the historically verified destruction of Pompei by the eruption of Mount Vesuvius in 79 AD the result was only seven years off. The method is now called the "holy grail" of radiometric dating, being applicable to igneous rocks from a few thousand up to millions of years old. Up-to-date information is available on-line at the University of Berkeley "Geochronology Center".

This extremely sophisticated technique involves first of all exposing the test sample to neutron bombardment in a nuclear reactor to convert the solid Potassium to gaseous Argon 39, then heating it step-wise to higher and higher temperatures in an oven or laser beam to enable comparison of the amounts of Argon 39 and Argon 40 "boiled off " at each step, and so obtain an age measurement. Although Dr. Roger Wiens, a professional scientist working at Los Alamos, confirms the validity of the physics involved in a paper entitled "Radiometric Dating - A Christian Perspective", there are clearly many complications.

The web site of the New Mexico Board of Geology and Mineral Reserves, for example, discusses a number of difficulties - in particular that the Ar-Ar method is not absolute and so cannot measure ages directly, but has to first be calibrated using a sample of known age. That other sample will usually have been dated by the questionable Potassium-Argon method.

Although G-Theory has no argument with the dates assigned to Paleozoic and Mesozoic strata, it does suggest that a very critical look needs to be taken at the way these techniques are applied to Cenozoic strata. One implication of G-Theory is that if any Cenozoic strata were formed by Noah's Flood, and contain evidence of human habitation, they should not be older than some six thousand years.

CAN PHYSICS GO WRONG?
The expert opinion of Dr. Wiens not withstanding, the absolute assertions of Science have so often later proved to be wrong – and mistakes can of course occur in the application of even an accurate technique to complex, confusing and poorly understood geological situation. Consequently, when Science does conflict with an accurate reading of the Bible, we may well be justified in adopting the attitude of the great Albert Einstein, who, when once informed that an experimental result disagreed with his beautiful theory of relativity, famously retorted "Well, then, the experiment is wrong!" - as later proved to be the case! It may be significant, as we shall see, that the fundamental assumption of radiometric dating, i.e. the assertion that the half-lives of radioactive materials are invariable, is now being seriously questioned. Scientists want their results to comply with the orthodox predictions of evolution anyway, and so tend to

reject "wrong" results as being "anomalous".

THE ELEMENTARY DAWKINS DEFENCE

Incidentally, since radioactive decay involves probability, some might be tempted to resolve any conflict between science and Genesis by adopting what might be termed the "Elementary Dawkins Defence".

Since radio-active decay is a random process, to arrive at an accurate half-life value for a given isotope, scientists have to take the average of repeated measurements over periods of time – just as a large number of coins would have to be tossed before the numbers of heads and tails obtained were exactly equal, in line with the 50-50% head-or-tail probability for each throw.

It is, in fact, physically and mathematically possible for a given sample of Potassium-40 to decay into Argon very much faster than expected – with the result that the rock stratum containing it will appear far older than it really is – just as tossing a coin a dozen times could end up with all heads or all tails. We might ask if the same thing could then happen in dating two rock strata . . . or 10, or 1000 . . . or, purely by chance of course, in all the igneous rock strata that have ever been tested?

Clearly, no reasonable person would accept such an absurd possibility, yet that is precisely the calibre of arguments Richard Dawkins offers in support of evolution – namely, that every single plant and animal in the world resulted from the fortuitous accumulation of zillions and zillions of mutations, DNA copying errors and random re-arrangements of atoms and molecules! No wonder many mathematicians are outraged by the infantile assumptions of Darwinism.

CARBON-14 DATING

Although the Argon-Argon technique is suitable for dating igneous rocks and, by implication, sedimentary strata into which magma may have intruded, it would be nice to have a method for dating organic remains directly.

Just such a technique was invented in the 1940s by Willard F. Libby, making use of the relatively short-lived radio-active isotope Carbon-14 (C-14) which is being continuously generated in the atmosphere by the action of cosmic radiation from space. The technique is useful to paleontologists for two reasons: first because C-14 has a half-life of only 5570 years, and second because the C-14 in the air is absorbed in the process of photosynthesis and becomes part of the tissues of all plants, and then in turn the animals that consume those plants as food. When a plant, such as a tree, or an animal dies, no more C-14 is assimilated, and that already present starts to decay with a half-life of 5570 years – thereby providing a measurable time-dependent variable.

DATING ORGANIC REMAINS
Scientists using the technique assume that if a piece of wood, for example, is found by careful measurement to contain half as much C-14 as the wood of a living tree, then it must have come from a tree that died or was cut down approximately 5570 years ago – and one with a quarter as much, over 11,000 years ago. Such C-14 measurements have been used to date artefacts and plant, animal and human remains from Cenozoic strata as being many thousands of years old – far beyond the mere 6000 years indicated by Bible chronology. How might that anomaly be explained?

Although C-14 dating has been calibrated against artefacts of known age, the method makes the simplifying assumption that the intensity of cosmic radiation and also the structure of the Earth's atmosphere have always been the same as now. However, if the cosmic intensity were lower before Noah's Flood, for example, wooden artefacts from that age would appear to be vastly older than they really were because they would have contained much less C-14 to begin with.

MEANINGLESS RESULTS
Attempts to calibrate Carbon-14 dating based on counting tree rings in cores bored from California's ancient Bristle-cone Pines, such as the famous Methuselah tree, which may well have survived Noah's Flood, are also unreliable because a tree can form more than one growth ring in a year, depending on the seasonal conditions—thereby making it look much older than it really is. Several other calibration methods involve similar assumptions. It would seem, therefore, that the results obtained by carbon dating for materials from before the Flood are quite unreliable.

STOP PRESS: HALF-LIFE HERESY
By one of those odd coincidences, as I edit this material, my attention has been drawn to an article in the New Scientist magazine entitled "Half-life Heresy" which discusses recent findings by Claus Rolfs at the Ruhr University in Germany that challenges the fundamental assumption that the half-lives of radioactive materials are invariable - and suggesting that, given the right conditions, they may be dramatically reduced, possibly from thousands of years to mere hundreds.

Rolfs commented: "When I was studying physics, my teachers said nuclear properties are independent of the environment - you can put nuclei in the oven or the freezer, or any chemical environment, and the nuclear properties will stay the same. *That is not true any more.*" N.B. Not true anymore!

"New Scientist" commented: "If Rolfs is right, it could have profound implications not just for nuclear waste management, but also for understanding the Earth's interior and *measuring the age of the universe.*" N.B. Profound implications!

Rolfs' discovery, we are told, sheds light on a long-standing puzzle, namely the fact that there is more heat being generated in the earth's core as a result of the decay of uranium and thorium than physicists can account for. Rolfs theorizes that the high temperature of molten metals in the earth's core is speeding up the supposed invariable rate of decay of these radio-isotopes – and speeding up the radiometric clock too.

This news, which does of course have serious implications for the much vaunted reliability of the radiometric techniques used to estimate the age of the earth, will be welcomed by Young-Earth creationists who maintain the earth to be only six to ten thousand years old. As we have discussed however, G-Theory has no problem with a very old earth, although it does challenge any claim that man has existed on earth for much more than the six thousand years suggested by Bible chronology.

2.20

THE CURSE OF EVOLUTION

For most people, the Evolution-Creation controversy may seem totally irrelevant to the practicalities of daily life, a mere philosophical or religious disagreement. Sadly, nothing could be further from the truth.

Thanks to Charles Darwin, human beings and all other organisms are now regarded by science and industry, not as the creative handiwork of divine genius, but as the unplanned outcomes of evolution - as marvellous yet nevertheless accidental accumulations of complex chemicals. If everything was created by accident, however, then where did moral values come from – and why does anything matter at all? No wonder even devout evolutionists are bothered by Darwin's materialistic and meaningless philosophy.

THE NATURAL ORDER OF THINGS

As a result, there is no longer a divinely ordained "natural order of things" – so that even the food we eat is now regarded as mere chemical "stuff" rather than a miraculous creation - stuff that "food technologists" have been allowed to "process" and "refine", often removing important natural constituents, such as bran and wheat germ in the case of flour, and introducing instead all manner of exotic man-made chemicals.

As a result, our children are being fed cocktails of very suspicious chemicals, the long-term effects of which on their health have never been fully investigated, effects which can only be compounded by the irresponsible pollution of our air, our water and our environment by thousands of other substances whose overall effects are too complex, subtle and possibly synergistic for science to understand or even begin to seriously investigate. But not to worry, says science, because just as man has supposedly evolved a tolerance and even an appetite for the complex chemicals we call food, so he will, given enough time, adapt to the thousands of synthetic additives the food industry has more recently introduced.

CROOKED COW SHEDS

Of course, when enough damage has been done, we do sometimes learn from our mistakes - but too often as one toxic substance is banned, others, whose long-term lethal effects are not yet known, are waiting in the production pipe-line to replace it, ready to ensure an uninterrupted flow of profits to the coffers of fat corporations that now influence and even dominate governments.

As Perucca and Pouradier catalogue in their revealing book "The Rubbish on Our Plates", when growth hormones were finally banned, their place was taken in the "crooked cow sheds" of the farming industry by the anabolic steroids beloved of dishonest body builders. Such substances go undetected by veterinary testing at the abattoir if discontinued a few days earlier.

According to the same source, there are numerous other unpublicised chemicals with similar properties that have yet to be fingered and forbidden. According to reports in "Que Choisir?" magazine, the French "Which?", and the newspaper "Le Figaro", as many as 50 per cent of French cattle could be affected by this illegal business – all part of an international meat racket run by ruthless gangs.

Spot checks on cattle breeders in Belgium and other places have on occasion resulted in gang retaliation, with, in one case, a vet's car being run off the road and actually machine gunned. As a result, police escorts for vets are now routine in some places.

THE OBESITY EPIDEMIC

Chemical additives in our food and even our water, rather than simple over-eating, may well be cause of much obesity – a possibility recently demonstrated in experiments with mice.

The classic book "Folk Medicine", which extols the virtues of cider-apple vinegar, also stresses the value of iodine from kelp tablets in maintaining a healthy thyroid gland, the body's "weight thermostat" – pointing out that the addition of the more chemically active fluorine to our water supplies can drive its chemical cousin, the essential iodine, out of our bodies, causing the thyroid to malfunction, thereby making it harder to control our weight.

DARWIN'S GUILT

How tragic the consequences have been, and how massive the guilt that lies at the door of Charles Darwin and others who know better – consequences that include, for example, the birth each year of thousands of children with "malformed genitalia" that makes then neither truly male or female. Add to that curse the suffering of multiple millions of people afflicted with cancers, asthma, allergies, heart disease, fungal infections and other man-made miseries such as autism, the latter a sad condition which looks suspiciously like yet another symptom of befuddled body biochemistry.

GENDER BENDING

How shocking too a "Daily Telegraph" report that "gender-bending" chemicals have now been identified in a whole range of products used around the home, including air fresheners, scented candles, mobile phone casings, and even the plastic used to make babies' feeding bottles! Are the people who do this bonkers, or just plain evil?

As the article explains, researchers now strongly suspect these "endocrine disrupters" of feminizing fish, producing malformed male reproductive organs in humans, and causing breast cancer in women. Little wonder a spokesman for the World Wildlife Fund was said to be "outraged". Sadly, however, the spokesperson of Cancer Research UK was quoted as saying: "It has not been proven conclusively". So, no worries, then. He ain't bovvered.

A SILENT PANDEMIC DESTROYING OUR CHILDREN

Another report by American and Danish researchers, published in the "Lancet" medical journal, speaks of a "silent pandemic" of brain-damaged children suffering from conditions such as cerebral palsy, autism, mental retardation and attention deficit which are attributed to the widespread and virtually unregulated use of some 202 toxic industrial chemicals.

According to the report, as many as one in six children is thought to have some kind of developmental disability, usually involving the nervous system. How astonishing it is that the mighty European Union has 100,000 chemical registered for use in various ways – less than half of which have been subjected to even token laboratory testing for their effect on adults, children and human foetuses. No wonder that even back in the 1960s, one baby in fourteen had a visible birth defect.

WOULD YOU ADAM AND EVE IT?

The naïve attitude of the food and farming industry towards nutritional matters is reminiscent of the foolishness of Adam and Eve in eating the fruit of the "Tree of the Knowledge of Good and Evil", in the Garden of Eden, even after being sternly warned by God to not even touch it, let alone eat it.

Urged on by the devil, in the way the modern corporation is urged on by profits at all costs, Eve and then Adam soon decided that since the forbidden fruit looked good and was then found to taste good when they tried it, then it must indeed be good – and that fuddy-duddy God had made a mistake, and was imposing unnecessary restrictions on their freedoms.

Unfortunately, although its deadly effect was delayed for some time like the subtle action of many toxic chemicals on the human body, the juicy and enjoyable forbidden fruit ended up killing them, and also disrupting their DNA in such a fashion that death became the sinister legacy bequeathed by them to every human being ever since.

Just as Adam and Eve in their ignorance felt confident to cope with the complexities of life on earth without God's niggling interference, so our scientists feel fully confident that their elementary understanding of nature's incredible complexity qualifies them to interfere with our food and the biochemistry of our bodies. In both cases the outcome has been untold suffering and death.

WE AIN'T BOVVERED!
Yet still the idiocy continues, as the authors of the report just cited are accused by other scientists of "gross over-statement" – with Professor Nigel Brown of London University, for example, describing the report as "verging on scare mongering" – adding however, that "It is possible that there is a problem".

With so many people sick and dying that we have to build ever-bigger hospitals to contain them all, the good professor thinks that it is just possible there might conceivably be a problem. He ain't bovvered, chuck, he ain't bovvered!

GM CROPS
How tragic too, that supposedly intelligent scientists, with their inadequate and incomplete understanding of cellular matters and influenced by the short-term economic outlook of their paymasters, now apply the same simplistic Adam-and-Eve logic to the use of GM crops - saying in effect: "If it looks good and tastes good and needs less pesticide so that it saves money, then it must be good!" Are these the same individuals, I wonder, who have been using human sperm to fertilize hamster eggs?

THE LETHAL LEGACY
How incredible also is the stupidity of scientists who seem to see cure as more important than prevention - so that drugs and surgery are often touted as the keys to health, rather than sound nutrition and exercise. How ironic that

Science, having already blighted so many lives so badly by the debasement of our food, now plans to banish the disease they themselves have created by the use of ever more powerful drugs and new techniques of "genetic engineering".

Even now for example, in a TV interview, we were assured by a glib "health expert" wheeled out by the BBC that the answer to arthritis does not lie in proper nutrition, but in more stem cell research. In just a few years, we are assured, arthritis will be cured by a simple injection.

BE VERY AFRAID

Should we not be afraid, indeed terrified, of feeding our children the hazardous chemicals labelled on every package of what now passes for food - as if the admission of their presence and their mere listing in print will somehow prevent their assimilation, or that their arcane nomenclature implies that scientists actually understand what they are doing to us. Is there actually any single item in the supermarket that is really fit for human consumption, even a plastic bottle of water?

Complementing the addition of harmful chemicals into out food is the depletion of the natural nutritional content of many crops even as they grow in the fields, long before they even reach the factory. According to some research reports many hybrid cereals, for example, which have been developed in order to maximise yield, do so at the expense of greatly reduced protein and mineral content – and then only with the application of liberal amounts of artificial fertilizer and pesticide.

In order to enjoy the economic benefits of these crops, the seed has to be sold to farmers in the form of F1 hybrids, so that farmers around the world are now required to purchase new seed each year rather than saving their own.

PERFECT TEETH

Ironically, even the teeth we use to eat our processed foods are suffering as a result of their consumption.

Why is it that the dental health of so many western nations is so appalling – when a century or more ago people in isolated communities, such as the Eskimos of Alaska, were found by researchers to have near-perfect teeth – to the extent that even women who had mothered twenty or more children still had perfect dental health?

Perhaps a clue to the source of the dental problems of so-called "advanced" nations was provided by the same research, which found, by way of sharp contrast, that Eskimo groups which had come in contact with "civilization" and had begun to eat the refined foods on sale at the trading posts, soon developed the same dental problems we now take for granted.

These and other startling findings were reported by American dentist Weston Price in his book "Nutrition and Physical Degeneration". As Price points out, since calcium which is vital for our teeth is also the stuff from which bones are made, a depleted diet also has the effect of shrinking the whole skeletal structure – and even the acoustical cavities of the head, with the result, he claims, that fewer men now have the capacity to sing bass.

CLOGGED ARTERIES

A Time-Life publication at the time of the Korean war, described how post mortems on soldiers killed in the conflict revealed that although the arteries of Korean and Chinese young men were clear and healthy, those of the Americans were already clogging up and narrowing down, warning signs of serious heart disease to come – the only possible causative factor for the dramatic differences between the two groups being their daily diets, the one consisting of natural foods such as brown rice and vegetables, the other of refined food from a factory.

WHITE STUFF

A recent book, "Bread Matters" by Andrew Whitley, reveals that the "white stuff" that passes for bread in British supermarkets is not only made with hybrid wheat having a greatly reduced content of essential minerals such as magnesium and zinc compared to that grown fifty years ago, but is legally allowed to be marketed with no mention being made on the label of a whole range of enzymes used in its manufacture. Additives are employed to lengthen shelf life, keep the bread softer longer, enhance crust flavour and color, pump up the volume, improve crumb structure, and make flour easier to machine.

All this is in addition to, and sometimes as yet more technically advanced replacement for, other chemicals such as emulsifiers, bleaches, reducing agents and preservatives. Some of these enzymes, Whitley points out, are obtained from the pancreas of pigs, and some from hair and feathers, a reality unacceptable to many people once they become aware of it.

Add to that the use of massive amounts of yeast in a desperate attempt to reduce production time – plus, in white bread, the removal of the wheat germ, a vital source of vitamin E, and bran, a natural source of fibre. All this in the interest of increased profits, obtained at the expense of human health.

No wonder, as Whitley points out, more and more people find themselves allergic to, and made ill by this "stuff".

Incidentally, analysis of white flour compared to whole wheat shows losses of more than 50% for over a dozen important nutrients – such as Calcium 60%, Magnesium 84%, Phosphorous 71%, Copper 68%, Zinc 78%, Potassium 77%, Niacin 81% - and that after the depletion already mentioned due to the use of the modern hybrid wheat used to make the flour in the first place.

STOP WINING!

When a friend of mine was advised by his doctor several years ago not to drink Australian or American wine, it struck me that wine is just about the only item in the supermarket that does not display a list of contents on the label. The doctor's advice may be explained by a recent UK Channel 4 TV program which revealed that many wines are full of artificial additives - and that although European Union regulations allow 50 ingredients, only alcohol and sulfites have to be listed on the label. In one European country, the authorities confiscated millions of liters of "Frankenstein wine" which contained hydrochloric acid and fertilizer along with many other things! Good health!

CANNIBAL COWS

All this refinement of our food is sanctioned because the "natural order of things" has been lost sight of by Scientists - that erudite band of highly educated but sadly unwise individuals who, until very recently, saw no nutritional problem or danger in feeding cattle the ground-up remains of other cattle from the slaughterhouse. The bones and offal of which were regarded as useful and exceedingly cheap sources of protein.

I remember a court case in America some thirty years ago, regarding the controversial claims of a breakfast cereal – when "expert" witnesses had to admit that, chemically speaking, science could not distinguish between the nutritional value of the cereal and the box in which it was packaged.

How unethical too, as reported to me personally by a long-term employee of one of the UK's biggest cattle feed manufacturers, that the very day the use of ground-up bones was banned in Britain because of "mad cow disease", the surplus stock of body parts was immediately shipped to Germany for processing there instead.

Following up on findings such as these, Dr. Matthias Rath, one-time colleague of Nobel Prize winner Linus Pauling, found that the restoration of essential vitamins and minerals to the typical western diet, even in the form of good quality vitamin and mineral pills, can in many cases reverse and even cure degenerative diseases such as cancer and heart disease without recourse to powerful drugs and surgery. Such is the amazing but limited healing power of the body that evolution simply cannot explain.

In his fascinating book entitled "Why Animals Don't Get Heart Attacks but People Do", Rath explains, as an example, the importance of adequate vitamin C in coping with the toxins in our food and preventing the build-up of arterial plaque – stressing also the importance of cell nutrition in avoiding cancer and numerous degenerative diseases that have reached plague-like proportions in the western world. It now seems as if the big drug cartels want to restrict the sale of cheap vitamins and food supplements because they would rather have us get sick and rely on expensive drugs instead.

Like it or not, evolution has touched, and continues to touch, your life and the lives of those you love in extremely serious ways.

PART 3

A CLOSER LOOK AT
THE GENESIS ACCOUNT OF CREATION

3.1

QUESTIONS & ANSWERS

History, it is often said, repeats itself. In earlier centuries, for example, when the newly developed telescope made it possible for Galileo to observe the visible planets more closely, he saw that although they appear as stars to the naked eye they are in reality solid objects, like the moon, not being self-luminous at all, but simply reflecting the light of the sun, with a pattern of changing phases that could only be explained if they and the Earth were actually revolving around the sun - the revolutionary new Heliocentric (i.e. sun-centred) theory.

The leading bishops of the time, we are told, were so disturbed by this revolutionary new theory that they even refused to peer through Galileo's telescope to view reality for themselves.

SCIENTIFIC DISREPUTE
Unfortunately, the powerful religious authorities had been insisting that sun and planets all revolved around the Earth - the Geocentric (i.e. earth-centred) theory, although the Bible actually made no such claim. No doubt they thought that this erroneous notion somehow glorified God - but their belief was simply wrong. In a similar fashion, young-earth creationists currently present to the world a quite misleading exposition of the Genesis account of creation – bringing the Bible into scientific disrepute once again by insisting that the earth is only a few thousand years old, a misconception that informed evolutionists regard as nonsense, as did early Christian geologists such as the Rev. William Buckland of Oxford University who was not an evolutionist.

TWISTING THE SCRIPTURES
Threatened by Galileo's ideas, the theologians of the day immediately began searching out Biblical statements supposedly supporting their untenable position - for example: "He set the Earth on its foundations; it can never be moved" (Psalm 104:5). This statement, in a poetic section extolling God's majesty and power simply means that he made the Earth and put it in place,

and nobody can take it away of destroy it. It clearly does not mean that the earth cannot rotate on its axis or revolve around the sun. Scriptures must not be twisted out of context.

The account of Joshua's famous "long day" was also quoted in support of the Geocentric theory - in particular the sentence that reads: "the sun stood still and the moon stopped till the nation avenged itself on its enemies" (Joshua 10:13). Some today would also take this statement as indisputable proof that the supposedly simple-minded and superstitious ancients believed that the sun revolved around the Earth, when in reality it must have been the earth that apparently stopped rotating, if that in fact is how God chose to work the miracle. If, however, they heard a NASA astronaut saying that "the sun rose" at such and such a time, they would find it perfectly acceptable, because they would know what he meant. Such is the complexity of our language.

The same astronaut might also complain on a winter's day that his feet were "getting cold", all the time knowing full well that they were actually losing heat, not gaining "cold". For some reason, however, many people, even devout creationists, insist on applying different rules of interpretation to the Bible than they do to the language of everyday life - seizing on even individual words and squeezing their meaning in a far more rigorous and inflexible manner than was ever intended.

COMMON SENSE
The Apostle Paul was well aware of such problems, as the following example illustrates. Speaking of the return of Jesus at the end of this age when he will rule all people and every nation, Paul quotes the Psalm that says: "For God has put everything under his feet" (Psalm 8:6). No doubt hair-slitting philosophers could take this use of the word "everything" to include God the Father himself, but that is clearly not the intent.

Perhaps because he had once been an erudite and technically minded Pharisee himself, and fully aware of such a possible misinterpretation, Paul immediately adds: "But when it says, All things are put in subjection under him, it is plain that he is excepted who puts all things under him" (1 Corinthians 15:27). In other words, God expects us to approach the Bible with intelligent scholarship, tempered with a common sense appreciation of the nature of language.

Another example of the use of the everyday, common-sense use of language in scripture is found in the description of the apostle Paul's visit to Athens, where it says: "All the Athenians spent their time doing nothing but talking and listening to the latest ideas" (Acts 17:21). No sensible person would suggest that this statement was to be taken in its literal extreme, but some people insist on applying different, hair-splitting rules to the scriptures, especially the Genesis account of creation.

GRANDIOSE CLAIMS

That said, however, if and when the might of modern science does come into conflict with a carefully considered and accurate interpretation of the word of God, where should we place our trust?

In "The Doctrine of DNA", leading biologist R.C. Lewontin warns against paying undue obeisance to Science. Although a confirmed evolutionist, he seems troubled, like colleague Rupert Sheldrake, by the grandiose claims of the "reductionists", such as Oxford professor Richard Dawkins, the biological zealots who confidently proclaim that all and everything in this universe can be, or soon will be, explained in terms of atoms and molecules and nothing else.

SCIENTIFIC CELEBRITIES

Lewontin is suspicious of the personal motives of such publicity seekers, saying: "These intellectuals are aware of the power they have to mould public consciousness, and they constantly seek ways in which they can publicize their ideas . . . to become a minor celebrity . . . It's all sex or money or genes . . . good press, good radio, good TV, and best selling books." And some of them do seem publish a lot of best-selling books.

SIMPLISTIC CERTAINTIES

As Lewontin points out, if all the uncertainties of a new theory are mentioned – qualified by reservations such as "perhaps", "possibly", "some people suspect", "we cannot be sure", "some people are coming to believe", etc., - then the message is no longer simple and dramatic enough to capture the public imagination.

Thus the simplistic scientific certainties make their way into school textbooks and popular magazines and the electronic media. At stake, he claims, are lucrative careers, honorary degrees, and *even Nobel Prizes!*

THE IMPORTANCE OF ASKING QUESTIONS

Such individuals, Lewontin says, are so completely devoted to their ideology that they "*do not ask themselves more complicated questions*" - such as, we might suggest, why the so-called "early" and "primitive" fossil life forms seem to suddenly appear in the most ancient of rock strata as incredibly complex organisms? The Trilobite, as we have seen, which is found in the Cambrian strata, appears suddenly in several forms, having complex eyes containing calcite lenses of a sophisticated design, and two sets of paired legs, one jointed set for walking on the sea bed, plus another set which scientists suspect served as flippers for swimming, gills for breathing, and also to agitate the surrounding water to locate morsels of food, then pass them along the body to the mouth. What incredible design!

The only answer evolutionists have is that they have now found some "primitive" (but still immensely complex) single-celled organisms, micro-fossils, in the very oldest of rocks, the Pre-Cambrian. The unvarnished truth, as we have seen, is that the facts of geology show Darwin's simplistic theory and the relentless claims of his modern disciples to be infantile nonsense, and in sheer denial of the facts.

ESSAYS AND REVIEWS

The success of "On the Origin of Species" by Charles Darwin emboldened three English clergymen to publish a book that even outsold Darwin's at the time. That book, "Essays and Reviews", which elevated textual criticism and downgraded the Bible to the level of myth and superstition, supposedly also exposed its "erroneous views of nature".

Sadly, since that time many Anglican clergy and their leaders have surrendered belief in the Bible as the literal word of God, and bowed the knee to the great Lord Darwin. As a result they are reduced, with condescending smiles, to mouthing platitudes, such as: "Oh dear no, the Bible is not a science textbook!" Or, "Darwin tells us how, but the Bible tells us why!" Or as one leading cleric put it recently, in my hearing, "The Bible is just a book".

Ah well, moving on from that difficulty. Having examined the errors and assumptions of evolutionists and creationists - and outlined G-Theory in its simplest form - let us now take a much closer look at the meticulously worded Genesis account of creation and find out what it really says and where it fits in with the G-Theory model. And just where those erudite scholars with their evolutionary agenda go wrong.

A BATTLE ON TWO FRONTS

In overview, the conflict between Evolutionists and Young-earth Creationists is fought from two deeply entrenched positions, in battles concerning - 1) the age of the Earth, and 2) the origin of living things. Paradoxically, both groups are good at exposing the other's key errors, whilst remaining blind to their own.

The material that follows will lead to three basic conclusions:

1) that the Earth and the rest of the universe may well be very old indeed, as Evolutionists correctly claim, but Young-earth Creationists deny – it having been created long before Adam and Eve and start of this present age.

2) that the "kinds" of plant and animal forms with which we are familiar did not arise as Evolutionists claim, by descent with modification from now-extinct pre-historic organisms, but were created by God at the time of Adam and Eve and continue to reproduce "after their kind", as Creationists correctly claim - so that roses and tulips and cats and dogs continue to produce roses and tulips and cats and dogs, and millions of fruit flies bred in laboratories continue to produce nothing but zillions more fruit flies.

3) It seems to follow that the exotic extinct creatures whose fossils are found in ancient rock strata pertain to Buckland's mysterious pre-Adamic creation and were not ancestral forms of existing kinds of organisms – and are actually irrelevant to the evolution-creation controversy.

With these matters in mind, let us take a much closer look at what the Genesis account of creation does actually say . . .

3.2

IN THE BEGINNING

GENESIS 1:1
In the beginning, God created heaven and earth.

'In the beginning', says Genesis, God created 'heaven and earth', or as some translations render it: 'the heavens and the earth' – apparently signifying everything, the whole universe, including the sun, moon and Earth.

Speaking of Jesus Christ, the actual executive creator of the universe (Ephesians 3:9), the apostle John says that: 'In the beginning was the Word (the Logos), and the Word was with God, and the Word was God. He was in the beginning with God; all things were made through him, and without him was not anything made that was made' (John 1:1-3).

'In the beginning' is simply a phrase that signifies the start of a particular activity or undertaking, indicating in the present context a period or moment in or even before time, possibly remote enough to contain the wildest dreams of geologists - and even cosmologists.

The precise details of how God originally created time itself and matter and energy, and out of them constructed the material universe, including our solar system and the Earth with its chemical elements, mineral deposits, earth, air and water, we leave to the speculations of science - as we now journey on, possibly millions or hundreds of millions of years, to reach verse two . . .

3.3

CHAOS

GENESIS 1:2
The earth was (became) shapeless and empty, and darkness was upon the face of the deep; and the Spirit of God brooded over the face of the waters.

As our journey through time brings us to the near edge of pre-history, we find the Earth in a state of chaos - it being: 1) shapeless, 2) empty of all life, 3) completely flooded, and 4) shrouded in darkness – with the Spirit of God "brooding", as some translations put it, over the face of the waters.

Perhaps it is significant that some translations, such as the scholarly masterpiece, the King James Version, offer the enlightening alternative translation that the earth "became" shapeless and empty, thereby implying that it may have been quite different when first created. The same Hebrew word recurs in the later phrase that says that Adam "became" a living soul when God breathed into him the breath of life.

Although the First Day of Creation Week has not yet even begun, our Earth already exists – and "was", as the Spirit of God came on the scene, "shapeless and empty". At this point, for some mysterious reason, the account of its chaotic condition suddenly becomes much more detailed . . . and even somewhat odd.

For example, the Earth is shapeless, apparently lacking the normal topography of hills, valleys and mountains. Why? Did God make it that way "in the beginning", or has the shape he originally gave it somehow been destroyed – and why do we need to be told these details, anyway?

The planet is also devoid of life - but isn't that just what we might expect if life hadn't yet been created? Is the account simply stating the obvious, or does God expect us to read more into it, especially in the light of modern scientific discoveries?

The Earth is apparently flooded, probably because it has lost its topography. Furthermore, as some translation put it, the Spirit of God was "brooding" on the surface of the waters, as if contemplating a terrible turn of events. Could it be that God's original creation has somehow been reduced to a state of chaos - and any prehistoric life-forms that inhabited it now wiped out?

Finally, on top of this, there is darkness on the face of the deep waters, any light created by the "heavens" somehow no longer reaching it. Possible causes of this darkness might be: 1) that the Earth is enveloped in very thick clouds of some kind, and/or that: 2) the sun is no longer shining, for some reason, or, 3) as some would claim, the sun has not yet been created. We might speculate that since the account mentions "waters", the conditions described did not or could not exist for very long or the earth would have been encased in ice.

Incidentally, in view of what was said earlier regarding the common-sense use of language in the Bible, does the word "empty" in this verse necessarily mean total absence of life of any kind - such as bacteria in the soil and under and in the oceans, organisms which in some cases can survive in extreme conditions? Such is the sophistication of language usage we often qualify adjectives with adverbs in order to stress a point, for example in phrases such as: completely full, absolutely sure, almost unique, totally empty.

THE K-T EXTINCTION?
Although the interpretation so far suggested for these first two verses of Genesis would be totally rejected by Young-earth creationists, it is interesting to compare it with the current findings and speculations of science.

Geologists, for example, and all the other 'ologists' that work with them are increasingly convinced that many of the bizarre life-forms whose fossil remains are found in the lower groups of rock strata of the Paleozoic (Ancient life) and Mesozoic (Middle life) eras were wiped out in a series of mysterious, mass extinctions – numbering at least fifteen, according to the research of Raup and Sepkoski. If all those creatures were wiped out, how could they be ancestors of modern organisms? Or did Darwin's tree of life somehow survive -- and if so, how?

The most recent and most keenly debated of those events is the K-T (Cretaceous-Tertiary) extinction, which apparently wiped out the Dinosaurs a mere 65 million years ago, thereby ending the terrifying Age of Reptiles.

METEORITE BOMBARDMENT?

The extinction mechanism currently most popular with American scientists, is massive meteorite impact, possibly involving one gigantic specimen some six to ten miles in diameter that may have struck and buried itself in Mexico's Yucatan Peninsula - resulting in destructive tidal waves on the one hand, and volcanic eruptions and fire-balls on the other that then burned up whole continents, suffocating all animal life, and blackening the atmosphere with sufficient ash, dust and smoke to totally exclude all sunlight and so destroy all vegetation, causing there to be "darkness on the face of the deep".

THE DEMISE OF THE DINOSAURS?

An article in the "Times" newspaper of London described how Indian scientists, who have also been investigating the demise of the dinosaurs, discovered thousands of perfectly preserved, mostly spherical eggs in some 50 hatcheries scattered over an area of 4,000 square miles. Apparently many villagers pray to these fossilized eggs which they venerate as being the testicles of the Hindu god Shiva, the deity of destruction, and protect them in wayside shrines decorated with flowers.

The mass destruction of these dinosaurs and the abandonment of the eggs, is attributed by the Indian scientists to a meteorite some 25 miles in diameter which apparently created a vast, but now covered, crater stretching, from Bombay to the Seychelles.

They estimate that the impact released far more energy than the world's entire stock of nuclear weapons - thereby melting rock with intense heat, spewing out multiple millions of tons of debris, burning up the oxygen of the atmosphere, and creating an incredibly powerful shock wave. Again, the envisioned outcome was a black dust cloud which encircled the whole earth and obliterated the sun for six months, thereby also suffocating animals and wiping out plant life on land and in the sea.

Take your pick -- Hollywood or Bollywood -- or both together!

Having just read the second verse of the Genesis account of Earth's early history, do these two scientific scenarios sound familiar?

CHAOS ACROSS THE SOLAR SYSTEM?

Although American scientists are hot on the trail of the one gigantic meteorite that they see as the main perpetrator, the pock-marked appearance of the

Moon's surface, as well as the photographs NASA gets back from its planetary explorers, all seem to corroborate a theory of mass destruction by multiple meteorite bombardment across the solar system, rather than just one – possibly with the asteroid belt being the remains of a now non-existent planet. How could the Earth have escaped unscathed – and if the meteorite theory is incorrect, and the earth really is only six thousand years old, just how and when in human history were moon and planets reduced to their present state? One young-earther suggested to me that it had something to do with Noah's Flood!

EXTINCT PREHISTORIC MONSTERS

The Mesozoic era of life, a time when the world was apparently populated and dominated by strange and repulsive monsters including six-foot scorpions, forty-foot dinosaur-crunching crocodiles, and a wide variety of other fierce and even flying reptilian creatures, ends at the K-T boundary, as already noted – a marker which, we are told, is associated world-wide with a two-centimeter thin layer of clay that is greatly enriched in Iridium, a chemical element which is common in meteorites but quite rare on Earth generally.

What followed on from the Mesozoic was the present Cenozoic (Recent-life) era and the Age of the Mammals and flowering plants - a more familiar and friendly world, populated for the most part by warm-blooded, furry and potentially cuddly creatures that we find much more to our liking than reptiles - a new world that is strangely similar to one whose creation we are about to find described in the next couple of chapters of Genesis.

CATASTROPHISM VERSUS GRADUALISM

As a result of his studies of fossil remains of obviously extinct organisms, the 19th century anatomist Georges Cuvier became a great believer in 'revolutions' or 'catastrophism' as the cause of those extinctions. However, when Darwin proposed his theory of evolution which required vast stretches of "deep time" to have any possible credibility, geologists such as Lyell rallied to his cause by rejecting Cuvier's ideas and opting instead for 'gradualism', as we discussed earlier - the claim that the earth's sedimentary rock strata had been deposited extremely slowly on the beds of the oceans at rates that would require millions of year per metre of thickness.

One obvious objection that Lyell et al brushed aside was the need for the continents to repeatedly yo-yo up and down over the ages, in order to cause the ingressions and regressions of the sea required to create all those sedimentary rock strata – and to explain the repeated transformations of crushed vegetation into massive beds of coal sometimes consisting of hundreds of layers, each separated from its neighbors by sediments. More recently, however, evolutionists feeling confident of having won the war against creationism have been emboldened to return once again to catastrophism and the ideas of mass extinctions mentioned above.

CATASTROPHISM REVIVED

Incidentally, the notion of catastrophism was revived in 1980 by a paper by physicist Luis Alvarez and his son entitled "Extraterrestrial cause for the Cretaceous-Tertiary extinction". The new theory arose from studies that found concentrations of iridium over 100 times normal all over the world at the so-called K-T boundary, hence the suspicion that the earth had been bombarded by massive meteorites, resulting in yet another mass extinction.

The physicist's conclusions prompted paleontologist Robert Bakker to comment: "The arrogance of these people is simply unbelievable. They know next to nothing about how real animals evolve, live and become extinct!" Clearly, whiter coats are called for.

THE MASS EXTINCTION OF PREHISTORIC LIFE?

Because so many mass extinctions have apparently occurred, scientists are beginning to wonder if they are in some way connected – one theory being that they were all caused by a comet that swept by the Earth every 40 million years or so, triggering tidal waves and earthquakes each time it passed by.

A more simple explanation might be that there was in fact one massive extinction, as inferred in the second verse of Genesis – and that all the organisms found in the Paleozoic and Mesozoic strata, rather than demonstrating some imagined emergence of increasingly complex life-forms out of the ocean slime and onto the land and into the air, simply represent the complete flora and fauna of a prehistoric world that once existed but was then destroyed, long before the six days of creation had even begun.

If that were so, then each formation in the geological column might simply represent a thin slice, so to speak, of the complete pre-Adamic ecological system, the mass of organisms having been transported, sifted and deposited according to variables such density.

We can return later to a discussion of why that "prehistoric" world might have existed and why it was destroyed - but meanwhile, let us voyage on through time to Day One of Creation Week . . .

3.4

DAY ONE – A SPECIAL LIGHT

GENESIS 1:3-5
And God said, Let there be light; and there was light. And God saw that the light was good; and God separated the light from the darkness. God called the light Day, and the darkness he called Night. And there was evening and there was morning, one day.

If the G-Theory hypothesis is correct, what we begin to read here on Day One is a description of how God set about correcting the four conditions of chaos that had befallen the original earth – starting with the removal of darkness by the creation of light, and the restoration of the diurnal cycle of night and day – reconstruction, rather than a totally new creation.

A GEOLOGICAL GAP
"The New International Commentary on the Old Testament" says: "In essence, this reconstruction suggests that verse one describes the *original creation*, which was flawless. Then *something catastrophic happened*, throwing God's perfect earth into turmoil and judgment so that it became without form and void. Subsequently, God started a second creation, so that verse 3 describes not creation but re-creation. *The length of this gap between the first and second creation is impossible to determine.*"

The scenario the commentator is describing is sometimes known as the "Gap Theory" - the "ruin-reconstruction" theory which was promoted in the early 1800s by Oxford University's first professor of geology, Rev. William Buckland who died three years before "The Origin of Species" was published. The theory is also described in Dr. Bullinger's "Companion Bible", and was popularized over a century ago by the "Scofield Reference Bible". Oddly, this simple interpretation of Genesis, which provides easy answers to evolutionist errors, is now sadly neglected.

As a Christian and a leading geologist, Buckland came to realize that the earth was in fact much older than the six thousand years popularly supposed, and soon saw that a careful reading of the Genesis account easily accommodated that fact.

It is interesting that the ruin-reconstruction reading of Genesis 1:1 can be traced back to the Early Christian Church Fathers as well as Jewish writers such as Simon Episcopius (1583-1643) who rendered the key phrase as: "the earth became waste and void". The "Targum of Onkelos", we are told, a literal translation of the Hebrew scriptures into the Aramaic language of the day for reading in the synagogues, rendered it: "And the earth was laid waste". None of these writers was looking for an answer to evolutionist critics, but simply for an accurate exposition of the Holy scriptures. The gap theory is by no means new, but appears unfortunately to have been all but forgotten.

LET THERE BE LIGHT!
The creation of light on this first day, with no named source, is not apparently referring to the creation of the sun, as we shall discuss in a moment. On this point, the Jewish "Socino Chumash" commentary says: "This was a special light which functioned only during the seven days of creation."

If this is correct, the implication seems to be that the sun was, at this time, no longer radiating energy - its nuclear fusion chain reactions possibly having been shut down for some reason. In other words, perhaps, the destruction that had taken place in the solar system was more extensive than suspected by scientists in their meteorite theories.

DAY AND NIGHT RESTORED?
Perhaps we might compare God's action here to that of an emergency rescue crew setting up temporary lighting in the buildings of a city wrecked by an earthquake, for example, in order to get the reconstruction work under way before the permanent electric supply is re-connected – and, in this case, to provide a new baseline for the counting of time.

Alternatively, if we continue to identify this scenario with that following the K-T extinction, we might infer that on Day One God also removed the dust and smoke particles from the air in order to allow the light he had now created to spread out across the hemispherical surface of the waters on that side of the Earth.

Having, thus, illuminated the scene, we read that God next separated or divided that light from the darkness – possibly implying that the Earth had also been stilled on its axis and needed to be set rotating again, in order to restore the sequence of day and night.

We now journey on through time to Day Two . . .

3.5

DAY TWO – WATERS ABOVE & WATERS BELOW

GENESIS 1:6-8

And God said, Let there be an expanse in the midst of the waters, and let it separate the waters from the waters. And God made the expanse and separated the waters which were under the expanse from the waters which were above the expanse.

And it was so. And God called the expanse heaven. And there was evening and there was morning, a second day.

Following the common pattern, the creation account for this second day begins by describing briefly what was to be accomplished - namely, the formation of two layers of water with an expanse between them. The word rendered "expanse" comes from a Hebrew root meaning to expand, stretch or spread out, or hammer out, in the sense of beating metal out into bowl. It is variously translated in the Bible as dome, vault or firmament.

THE THREE HEAVENS

God named the expanse he had created between the waters above and below "heaven", which is translated from a Hebrew word meaning "lofty" or raised up, a term that is used in three ways in the Bible, to denote – a) the atmosphere, then beyond that, b) outer space where sun and stars are located, and finally, c) what Paul called "the third heaven", the place of God's throne. Here, on the second day, the expanse simply refers to the atmosphere, or sky.

Incidentally, Young-earth creationists quote the words of Moses from the Ten Commandments as their "killer text" that the Old Earth theory is seriously unscriptural, and that there could not possibly have been a "heaven" in the sense of either atmosphere or cosmos before Creation Week - Quote: "For in six days the Lord made heaven and earth, the sea, and all that is in them, and rested the seventh day" (Exodus 20:11).

As noted, there are three heavens, and the one being referred to by Moses is the one whose creation we have just read about, the restored existing atmosphere, not outer space with all its stars and galaxies. In this regard, notice also that although God created heaven and Earth in the beginning, it was only the Earth that was later found to be in a state of chaos. As we shall see in a moment, the word "earth" also has more than one possible meaning, referring either to the whole globe, or just the continental masses surrounded by seas. Evidently, the second meaning is the one referred to by Moses, the globe itself having been created earlier.

WATER ABOVE AND WATER BELOW
To continue with the account, the expansion that took place somehow lifted part of the surface water, perhaps half of it, up above the space that became the atmosphere – still leaving behind sufficient water to cover the solid part of the Earth, as we shall see later.

The commentator Driver says that God: "separated the huge mass of primitive waters enveloping the earth into two parts, one being above the firmament, and the other below it." Although there is always a certain amount of water vapor spread throughout the atmosphere itself, taking part in the water cycle, these verses seem to imply something more than that.

Again, we might ask why we are being given these details. Surely it would be sufficient, as in verse 1, to simply be told that God created the Earth ready for man to inhabit it. Might it be that by telling us what had to be done to reconstruct or restore the Earth, God is actually giving us insights into its earlier destruction?

AN ODD DAY
It does seem somewhat odd that a major part of one whole day is devoted to the creation of an obviously important feature of the Earth that apparently no longer exists - namely the positioning of a mass of water above the atmosphere, a feature which may well have been very significant for any organisms existing prior to Adam and from his time up to the Flood of Noah, as we see in a moment.

Since scientific exploration indicates that no such vast store of water now exists in the upper atmosphere, it is interesting to speculate what happened to it, and with what consequences for living things.

If that water layer no longer exists, what happened to it, and when? Asked this question, most creationists, I suspect, would immediately suggest the massive rainfall that contributed to the Flood of Noah as a possible mechanism - when the "floodgates of the heavens were opened" and it rained continuously on the earth for forty days and forty nights. Since the rainfall of the normal water cycle simply returns the same previously vaporized water back to the Earth's surface, a global flood would seem to require something more than normal rainfall.

COSMIC RAYS

We now know that the earth and everything in it, is being continuously bombarded and shot through by cosmic rays from outer space.

Cosmic rays, which consist at the earth's surface of particles such as neutrons and mesons travelling at incredible speeds, were originally discovered by nuclear physicists because they were so extremely penetrating that Geiger counters were found to give sporadic and apparently "impossible" readings even when shielded from all known sources of nuclear radiation by very thick sheets of lead.

A BIOLOGICAL SHIELD?

Some writers have suggested that this continuous cosmic radiation must have some effect on the cellular activity and the DNA of all living things, possibly playing a part in the aging process.

The plausible implication is that in the absence of cosmic radiation, living things might live much longer, and so it is interesting to speculate that the layer of water that once existed above the atmosphere, above the "void", could have served as a biological shield for all living things on earth - in the same way that water is used to shield scientific personnel working around nuclear reactors. Although, as just stated, cosmic rays at ground level consist of virtually unstoppable particles such as mesons and neutrons, these are "secondary" cosmic rays, initially produced by the collision of "primary" cosmic rays - protons and alpha particles - with atoms in the upper atmosphere.

It seems quite possible, therefore, that the band of water molecules established on this second day of creation, especially the hydrogen nuclei, could slow down and scatter those primary cosmic radiation particles - as when snooker balls collide en mass - and so prevent the formation of damaging secondary radiation.

METHUSELAH

If this suggestion has any validity, then several other puzzling statements in Genesis may also begin to make sense, such as the incredible ages to which most people apparently lived in these early times. We are told, for example, that Adam in particular lived 930 years, and that Methuselah, the oldest of all, for 969 years. This could also explain why human life spans after the Flood of Noah, when the water layer above the atmosphere would seem to have been removed, soon declined to the familiar three scores years and ten later described as typical by David in the Psalms.

If this is the case, then it would seem reasonable to wonder if the life spans of animals living before the Flood were also extended in a similar manner. Might the same conditions also have prevailed on the pre-Adamic earth – and if so, with what implication for reptiles which are said to reach no set maximum size with age, but simply keep on growing until destroyed in some manner?

We now move on to Day Three . . .

3.6

DAY THREE – THE DRY LAND, THE SEA & PLANTS

GENESIS 1:9-10
And God said, Let the waters under the heavens be gathered together into one place, and let the dry land appear. And it was so. God called the dry land Earth, and the waters that were gathered together he called Seas. And God saw that it was good.

As we begin Day Three, the shapeless Earth is still flooded, despite the apparent removal to a position above the atmosphere of the vast amount of water that was to return later when the "floodgates of heaven" were opened during the time of Noah.

THE FLOODGATES OF HEAVEN AND THE FOUNTAINS OF THE DEEP
Incidentally, the term "floodgates of heaven" was simply a metaphor used to describe a complicated process in one simple phrase. Scholars whose thinking is unconsciously shaped by evolutionary ideas, take the use of such language as evidence of the ignorance of ancient peoples – overlooking the fact that the modern science relies heavily on metaphors to get a handle on complex concepts.

To expose the dry land mass, still more water needed to be removed, and one obvious possibility is that God drained if off by raising the Earth's continental surface and lowering the sea bed. If so, it is easy to imagine how the ensuing torrent could gouge out a structure such as the Grand Canyon.

If we press the parallel with the Deluge a bit further, some of the excess water may have been drained off into vast subterranean reservoirs, possibly the "fountains of the great deep" that were to burst open again later during Noah's Flood - a serious possibility, given our general ignorance of the interior of our planet, or even its atmosphere, as demonstrated by current discussions of climate change mechanisms.

PANGAEA

Returning to Genesis, notice also that the waters were gathered together into one place, which seems to suggest the creation of one vast continent completely surrounded by sea – identical, it would seem, to Alfred Wegener's "Pangaea" (Greek, meaning "once joined"), a super-continent that later broke into the sections that now constitute the Earth's continental masses and large islands.

TECTONIC PLATES

After scorning Wegener's wild ideas for several decades, science now believes that there was indeed a Pangaea that later cracked up into a dozen or so Tectonic Plates which have ever since been slowly drifting on the oozing convection currents of the underlying plastic Mantle. As any atlas shows, the coastlines of South America and West Africa look as if they should fit together, like pieces of a giant jigsaw puzzle, a fit that is even closer when the submerged continental shelves are matched up.

Incidentally, some writers claim that the sides of the Pacific ocean also match, suggesting that rather than one vast continent drifting apart, the whole earth must once have been much smaller and then expanded - as can be convincingly demonstrated in a computer simulation.

EARTH AND EARTH

Notice again that the dry land is here called "Earth" - so that, as in English, the equivalent Hebrew word can signify either the whole planet or simply the dry land portion of it, in contrast to the waters of the oceans. It is this Earth, the continental land mass restored or "created" on Day Three, that Moses was evidently referring to when he said, as we saw earlier, that "in six days, God made the *heaven* and the *Earth* and all that is in them in, and rested the seventh day" (Exodus 20:11).

Having established the dry land, which was bare of vegetation, God, quite appropriately, next completes Day Three's global landscaping project as described in the verses that follow . . .

GENESIS 1:11-13

And God said, Let the earth put forth vegetation, plants yielding seed, and fruit trees bearing fruit in which is their seed, each according to its kind, upon the earth. And it was so.

The earth brought forth vegetation, plants yielding seed according to their own kinds, and trees bearing fruit in which is their seed, each according to its kind.And God saw that it was good.And there was evening and there was morning, a third day.

Commentators generally agree that what these verses are describing is the creation of vegetation in general, and two kinds in particular. The first kind are flower-less plants, such as conifers, that produce the bare seeds such as can be shaken out of pine cones – and which are therefore or called "gymnosperms" (i.e. "naked seeds").

The second kind, logically, are flowering plants, such as apples and plums, and peas and beans, that produce fruit with the seeds encased inside them – and which are therefore called "angiosperms" (i.e. "encased seeds).

MAMMALS AND GYMNOSPERMS
It seems significant that angiosperms did not, according to the current literature, appear in the fossil record until the Upper Cretaceous strata at the end of the Mesozoic era, as did the large mammals. Both are characteristic of the new earth, a different world from the one that existed "in the beginning".

AFTER THEIR KIND
The second significant statement in these verses, that the plants were created "according to their kind", a phrase repeated in order to stress its importance – the limited variation it implies being the key principle at the heart of the evolution-creation debate. That stress is almost uncanny, as if God foresaw the madness that would emerge from the minds of the likes of Darwin and Wallace, and also William Charles Wells, who first proposed the theory of natural selection some forty five years before the publication of "The Origin of Species" but was, for some reason, ignored by the scientific world.

GENESIS KINDS OR SPECIES?
Unfortunately, when Swedish botanist Carl Linnaeus published his plant classification system, Species Plantarum, in 1753, and extended it to animals in Systema Naturae in 1558, he seems to have regarded the Genesis "kind" in a narrow and rigid way, equating it to the term "species", believing that the organisms existing in his day were exactly as created in Genesis.

Consequently, as Richard Leakey explains: "In Darwin's time a species was seen as a distinct group created by God" - and therefore thought to be rigidly invariable for all time. Consequently, as a result of Darwin's studies, the much misrepresented Genesis account of creation was again brought into scientific disrepute.

Although both evolutionists and creationists now accept that plants possess the potential for creative variation, with the express purpose of enabling them to adapt and survive in the wide variety of forms and environments, that variation is always "after their kind" - so that roses, for example, will always remain roses, no matter how exotic they become.

JUNK DNA - A GENETIC WARDROBE?
As suggested earlier, it seems that God has provided each kind of plant with a genetic "wardrobe" of possible variation – and possibly even a mechanism for generating an endless stream of new variations, but all "after" and within the basic bauplan of "their kind". Scientists have now discovered what may well prove to be that "wardrobe", the masses of so-called "redundant" or "junk" DNA found in all organisms .

In "The Selfish Gene", Richard Dawkins says that biologists are "racking their brains" trying to find out what useful purpose these "junk genes" might have. Gordon Rattray Taylor, in "The Great Evolution Mystery" explains that in most cells the amount of surplus DNA varies from 20 to 80% of the total. These gene copies, as he calls them, are mysteriously imperfect and are apparently unstable, constantly breaking down and being renewed.

As to their purpose, Taylor says: "The most daring hypothesis, however, is that this redundant DNA might compromise a store of mutant forms which the cell is waiting to try out". What an astonishing discovery - and fully in accord with the G-Theory. A tiny additional insight into the unimaginable creative genius of God.

On to Day Four . . .

3.7

DAY FOUR – THE SUN, THE MOON & STARS

GENESIS 1:14-19

And God said, Let there be lights [luminaries] in the expanse of the heavens to separate the day from the night; and let them be for signs and for seasons and for days and years, and let them be lights in the expanse of the heavens to give light upon the earth. And it was so.

And God made the two great lights, the greater light to rule the day, and the lesser light to rule the night; (he made) the stars also. And God set them in the expanse of the heavens to give light upon the earth, to rule of the day and over the night, and to separate the light from the darkness. And God saw that it was good. And there was evening and there was morning, a fourth day.

The logical progression of Creation continues on Day Four - as God restores the permanent source of light required for the plants created on the previous day to continue to live, as well as to provide the daily and seasonal variations that influence life on Earth.

We saw earlier how, as part of the chaotic destruction that apparently befell the solar system prior to the creation of man, the earth may have stopped rotating, and the sun stopped radiating light energy.

If this correct, then the moon likewise, although damaged in the catastrophe as still evident today from its cratered surface, would also have been in darkness because it is not self-luminous, but simply reflects the light from the sun by means of a special reflective coating of glassy beads, similar to those suspended in the white paint now used in the construction of road signs and lane markings.

A KEY FAULTY TRANSLATION

According to G-Theory, the stars, like the sun and moon, were already in existence prior to the fourth day, despite the faulty wording of a key phrase in the translation quoted here, as we shall see in a moment, that appears to suggest otherwise.

Critics of the Genesis read into these verses that the sun, moon and stars were made by God on this fourth day of creation week, but that is not what the inspired account actually says. We saw earlier how God created a special light on Day One and used it to separate day from night as he set the Earth rotating. Here, that day-counting function is being transferred or restored to two lights in the sky, a greater one to rule the day and a lesser one to rule the night, the sun and the moon.

PUZZLED COMMENTATORS

Up to this point, according to G-Theory, although the sun and moon were not producing light, they were already physically present, and did not need to be created, which is why the account speaks of "luminaries", rather than the physical bodies themselves - a fact that has greatly puzzled the commentators. Evidently what God did on this fourth day, was to restore or "create" their light emission, as if switching on light bulb in the case of the sun, which thereby provided the light to be reflected by the moon.

LUMINARIES

Commentator Victor Hamilton says of the account's author: "He uses the unusual expression 'the greater luminary' instead of the normal word for sun – 'semes' - of which he was undoubtedly aware. In the same way he opts for 'the lesser luminary' instead of the familiar 'yareah' for the 'moon'." Hamilton, like some other commentators, suggests that the words sun and moon have been deliberately left out because those heavenly bodies were worshipped by the ancient pagans. Scholars therefore describe this avoidance as being "anti-mythical" - rather than probing to find the real reason for such a careful choice of words.

The simple fact is that the Genesis account is meticulously worded, and the sun and moon are not mentioned here because they were not created here. What was created or restored here was their luminary potential - in other words, the nuclear fusion reaction of the sun was re-ignited by God on the fourth day, thereby creating two sources of illumination in the sky.

ORIGEN AND AUGUSTINE

Even early Christian commentators such as Origen and Augustine seem to have lost the plot at this point. Origen in particular asserting: "What man of intelligence, I ask, will consider that the first and second and the third day, in which there are said to be both morning and evening, existed *without the sun and moon and stars,* **while the first day was even without a heaven"**. Sadly, that erroneous assertion is still quoted to prove that Genesis is no more than myth and unscientific superstion.

BLINDED BY SCIENCE

Even modern scholars fail to find the truth of Genesis, despite their erudition, because they are blinded by their evolutionary misconceptions into thinking in advance that the creation account must be unreliable and unscientific before they even begin – assuming that because the account is several thousand years old, it was cobbled together by semi-literate peasants who naively thought, for example, that the sun and moon were floating about in the sky like a high-flying bird or a cloud.

Typical of the comments of such scholar are those of the "International Critical Commentary" which say: "The whole conception is as unscientific as it could be - a) in its geocentric standpoint, b) in making the distinction of day and night prior to the sun, c) in putting the creation of the vegetable world before that of the heavenly bodies." With friends like that, does the Bible need enemies?

THREE VITAL FUNCTIONS

Returning to the account, three functions are assigned to the two luminaries - a) to create the cycle of day and night, b) to provide a calendar framework - months and years, and c) to provide the light that sustains all life by the process of photosynthesis.

The word translated "seasons" does not refer to the normal four seasons of the year, which are caused by the tilt of the earth axis, but to festival times. The Hebrew calendar involved a year of 13 months, based much more closely than ours on the movement of the moon - a solar-lunar calendar. Months began with the new moon and people could get a good indication of the progress of the month simply by observing the current phase of the moon, a very practical arrangement, especially in an agrarian society and long before the advent of clocks, radio and TV.

ANOTHER MISLEADING MISTRANSLATION

In its job of ruling over the night, the moon is assisted by the stars. This simple fact, however, is obscured by a misleading mistranslation. The phrase rendered: "He made the stars also" should simply read: "the stars also", or: "with the stars".

There is no "made" involved - because the stars had of course been made much earlier, "in the beginning". What the account is saying here is simply that the stars were to assist the moon in its job of ruling over the night. The wording should therefore read: "*the lesser light to rule the night, with the stars,*" which offers a dramatically different meaning. In other words, what is being described here is not the physical creation of the stars or starlight, but simply their function. But what is that function?

THE ORIGIN OF THE ZODIAC

As the earth travels in its orbit the sun - at a speed exceeding 30,000 miles per hour - a person gazing out into the night sky sees different groups of stars overhead week by week, month by month. As a result, when the sun rises in the morning, it does so out of a changing starry backdrop, featuring a different constellation each month. This enabled people in ancient times, in addition to using the phases of the moon to fix the time of month, to also identify the particular month or time of the year by means of the constellations, as the earth progressed on its annual 13 month journey around the sun.

As we know, the constellations that form a sequential belt around the equatorial region of the sky were given animal names, which accounts for the name "Zodiac". Accordingly, without the aid of printed information or clocks, people were able to tell at what period of the year important events, such as the birth of a child, had occurred. Thus the account suggests that the Zodiac is not of pagan origin, but part of the creative plan of God.

THE COSMIC CLOCK

Returning to the account, having made the two luminaries, God then says that he "set" them in the firmament. It has been suggested that the word translated "set" can also mean "regulated" - as when we "set" a clock or watch. The significance may be that God here adjusted the orbital speed of the earth around the sun and of the moon around the earth, and possibly also the period of rotation of the earth on its axis, all of which would have implications for their calendar functions.

As regards the final function of the luminaries, we now know that light itself is essential to life on earth, enabling green plants to manufacture food by the process of photosynthesis – and that the biological clocks of those plants which control factors such as blooming are influenced by day length.

We now travel on with the Earth into Day Five . . .

3.8

DAY FIVE – FISH & BIRDS

GENESIS 1:20-23

And God said, Let the waters bring forth swarms of living creatures, and let birds fly above the earth across the firmament of the heavens. So God created great sea monsters and every living creature that moves, with which the waters swarm, according to their kinds, and every winged bird according to its kind.

And God saw that it was good. And God blessed them, saying, Be fruitful and multiply and fill the waters in the seas, and let birds multiply on the earth. And there was evening and there was morning, a fifth day.

Having, on the previous days, established the Earth as a suitable environment for life, by providing land, sea and water, air and daily and seasonal light patterns, God now begins to repopulate it, starting with creatures that swim and fly.

The first verse may be rendered: "Let the waters teem with living creatures." The English word "teem", from a root meaning "to give birth", implies large numbers, or swarms and shoals. The word translated as "creature" comes from the Hebrew word "nephesh", which is rendered "living soul" when it is later applied to man, apparently indicating an organism that breathes oxygen to live. Thus the waters and the seas were to be filled with air-breathing organisms, both great and small.

In other words, all the sardines or salmon or squid in the world did not somehow evolve from single common ancestors, but were mass produced by God, with all that implies for their genomes.

NESSIE?

The word rendered "monsters", or "whales" in the King James Version, comes from a Hebrew word meaning "to stretch out" and may refer to creatures such as eels, crocodiles, whales, and perhaps also the Loch Ness type of monster, if such exists. However, it can also simply mean "creature". Likewise, the word translated as "birds" can also mean more generally "flying creatures".

BE FRUITFUL AND MULTIPLY!

Notice that the fish and birds were created according to their "kind", as were the plants. However, by way of contrast, God commanded these organisms to "be fruitful and multiply" - apparently conferring on these male and female creatures the instinct/volition as well as the ability to reproduce, a process which is not automatic in the way it is with the plants where insects and the wind are the agencies.

DARWIN'S GENIUS AS A BIOLOGIST

As organisms reproduce according to their kinds, a certain amount of variation does obviously occur. The extent of the variation potential that God built into the Genesis kinds is well illustrated by Darwin's own meticulous investigations into pigeon breeding. He found, for example, that the number of tail feathers varied from the normal 12 or 14 up to 30 or 40. Some specimens had much elongated bodies, legs and wings. By dissection he studied variation in the number of vertebrae and ribs. He even studied the skin growth between the toes, the shape and size of eggs, disposition, manner of flight and even voice.

Yet despite all this, any mongrels produced by crossing any two breeds were still found to be fertile, one with another, showing them to belong, at least by the modern definition, to the same species.

DARWIN'S FINCHES

As a naturalist attached to H.M.S. Beagle on its famous five-year trip (1831 to 1836) to the Galapagos Islands, some 600 miles off the west coast of South America, Darwin assiduously observed and catalogued the habits of yet more birds – including the fourteen now-famous families that inhabited the different islands of the chain, and also the Cocas Islands to the north, families later identified by his ornithologist friend John Gould, after his return to England, as being finches.

SPECIES NOT IMMUTABLE

As a result of his marvellous field-work, Darwin began in 1837 to suspect that the accepted "species" of any organism were not permanent and immutable, as was the orthodox belief of experts of the time, such as Linnaeus. Was it even possible that not just finches and birds in general, but the entire mind-boggling myriad of Earth's life-forms could all have developed from a common primordial ancestor, by the continuous accumulation of tiny variations – given enough generations and given enough time, of course?

An exciting idea, he thought, but how could it possibly happen? The additional insight Darwin needed in order to properly formulate his theory was found the following year, 1838, when he read "An Essay on Population", by Thomas Malthus - leading him to comment later: "Here at last I had got a theory by which to work."

VARIATION AND ADAPTATION OCCURS

Although the groups of finches Darwin observed were very similar, they had adapted to different island habitats - some living on the ground, others in bushes and trees or in the forest. There were also differences in diet, some eating seeds, some insects, others buds and fruit - and he was amazed to observe that differences in beak shape between the groups fitted them for efficient gathering of those different sorts of food.

It seems uncanny, also, that one of the types of finch he studied was, according to Taylor, one of the most extraordinary birds in the world – being the only known tool-using bird, having the habit of holding a twig in its beak and using it to lever insects out of holes in tree bark!

Assuming, no doubt correctly, as G-Theory allows, that all 14 "species" had developed from one original species that had somehow made the 600 mile trip from the mainland, Darwin concluded that the different types had developed in the habitats in which their beaks made them most fit to survive in the endless battle with others bird for limited food resources, just as Malthus had described. However, were any of the birds actually unfit to thrive and survive in any of the habitats?

DARWIN'S CRUCIAL ERROR

Dominated by his desperate desire to negate the Genesis account of creation and trace all creatures back to a common ancestor, Darwin's crucial error at this juncture was to speculate far beyond the reliable range of the data he had collected – not only his observations of the limit-ed variation within the finch family, but also from those of horse breeders, as well as his own experiments with pigeons – and to assume as a result that limit-less, or infinite, variation was possible. Big mistake.

MICRO-EVOLUTION - YES!

In his book "The Great Evolution Mystery", evolutionist Gordon Rattray Taylor admits that although many biologists are happy to accept that limit-ed variation and natural selection might operate to create new species from existing ones – a process called "micro-evolution" - they find it very difficult to accept that it could ever bridge the vast chasms that lie between more diverse groupings of organisms, such as classes and phyla, in other words, between the Genesis kinds that God originally created - a very radical process that would require "macro-evolution".

MACRO-EVOLUTION - NO!

Taylor cites the massive differences that exist, for example, between an insect and a fish, and admits that even he cannot stretch his Darwinian faith that far. The real truth of the matter seems to lie, as usual, between the two extreme views, namely, that God created "kinds" of creatures with an built-in capacity for limited variation, for the purposes of adaptability, as on Darwin's islands – so that Micro-evolution is an observed fact of life, fully in line with the Genesis account, but Macro-evolution is a complete myth.

On to Day Six . . .

3.9

DAY SIX – CATTLE,
CREEPING THINGS & BEASTS

GENESIS 1:24-25

And God said: Let the earth bring forth living creatures according to their kinds: cattle and creeping things and beasts of the earth according to their kinds. And it was so.

And God made the beasts of the earth according to their kinds and the cattle according to their kinds, and everything that creeps upon the ground according to its kind. And God saw that it was good.

As we read the inspired account of the creation of the land animals on Day Six, notice again the repeated stress on the fact that God made them "according to their kinds" – able to vary and adapt to the environment, but not evolve into different kinds in the way Darwin envisioned.

VAGUE SPECULATION FROM DARWIN

The Genesis account identifies three groups of land creatures – a) cattle or livestock, b) small creatures that move or creep along the ground, and c) beasts of the earth or wild animals – all designed to reproduce after their kind.

Speculating about the supposed evolution of farm animals, such as sheep which are of course totally "unfit" to survive without human protection, and also commercial plants, which he imagined arose accidentally over many millions of generations from wild ancestors, Darwin says: "One of the most remarkable features in our domesticated races is that we see adaptation, *not for the animal's or plant's own good, but to man's use or fancy.*" Note that point well!

Then, in a comment reminiscent of Gould's "punctuated equilibrium" theory, which allows sudden, massive and inexplicably complex mutations, he adds: "Some variations useful to him have probably *arisen suddenly.*" Then, in yet another candid admission of ignorance, he adds: "The origin of most of our domestic animals will probably for ever remain vague."

MERE VARIABILITY!

In the "Origin of Species", Darwin actually describes the wonderful adaptive potential that God built into domesticated organisms and also its purpose, but again blindly draws a wrong conclusion, saying, Quote: "When we compare the dray-horse and the race-horse, the various breeds of sheep fitted either for cultivated land or mountain pasture, with the wool of one breed good for one purpose, and that of another for another purpose; when we compare the host of agricultural, culinary, and flower-garden races of plants, most useful to man at different seasons and for different purposes, or so beautiful in his eyes, we must look farther than mere variability." I think not Chas -- I think you really mean the infinite creative genius of God.

FRUIT FLIES AND MORE FRUIT FLIES

The simple truth is that, although God ordained constructive variation, creatures always reproduce "after their kind", as Genesis says. No wonder Gordon Rattray Taylor comments: "Though geneticists have been breeding fruit flies for sixty years or more in labs all round the world - flies which produce new generations every 11 days - they have never yet seen the emergence of a new species."

Biologist R.C. Lewontin points out in "The Doctrine of DNA", that Darwin actually took the brutal ideas of early nineteenth century economics and applied them to the natural world, which is of course equally brutal as we have discussed. Incidentally, Thomas Malthus, whose writings provided inspiration for Darwin's idea of natural selection by survival of the fittest, resulting in "descent with modification", was an English vicar who thought that the Poor Law of the time was far too generous, and would encourage shiftless members of society to breed more quickly and so lead to social unrest. Apparently the Poor Law interfered with the process of natural economic selection.

But never mind that, because the account of creation for Day Six continues . . .

3.10

DAY 6 – MAN

GENESIS 1:26-27
The God said: Let us make man in our image, after our likeness; and let them have dominion over the fish of the sea, and over the birds of the air, and over the cattle, and over all the earth, and over every creeping thing that creeps upon the earth.

So God created man in his own image, in the image of God he created him; male and female he created them.

A DIFFICULT QUESTION FOR DOCTOR DAWKINS

Beginning with the second of these two verses, we read that man did not descend from some ancestor, such as apes that had somehow supposedly earlier evolved into male and female forms, but was created by God. If Darwin thought that the human eye was complicated, I wonder what he thought about the sexual mechanisms of the male and female anatomy, if even he dared think about?

No less an evolutionary authority than Richard Dawkins admits, in "The Selfish Gene", that the existence of sex is "an extremely difficult question for the evolutionist to answer" and adds: "I am frankly going to evade it." How astonishing it is, that, like Darwin, Dawkins can admit such abysmal ignorance of what he claims to understand, yet still be applauded by gullible intellectuals. It's all a matter of faith, I suppose.

A TREE OR A FOREST?

In the plant world, Dawkins points out, plants such as the elm tree are able to propagate themselves by putting out runners or suckers under the ground that then spring up as new trees – the amazing process of asexual reproduction that is very common in the plant world, and is familiar to any gardener. Interestingly, an elm sucker remains joined to both parent and daughter trees, so that, in due time, it is possible to have an entire elm wood that is in reality one individual organism. How odd it is that the brilliant professor, like his mentor, perceived the glory of Creation so clearly, but not its Creator.

AFTER THE GOD KIND

Returning to the account, we read in the first verse that in contrast to the creatures which were created according to their various animal kinds, man was made according to the God kind - in his image and after his likeness. This truth, which is repeated over and over again in the Bible, even in the Lord's Prayer, is just too amazing for even most Bible commentators to accept, as they search instead for some kind of metaphorical or "spiritual" meaning to the phrase. The common sense interpretation of these verses is in fact verified later in Genesis, where we read that Adam, at the age of 130 years, became the father of a son "in his own likeness, after his image" (Genesis 5:3) who was named "Seth". A possible implication of this verse may be that his earlier sons, including Cain and Abel, were somewhat different in appearance and perhaps in skin color.

We see then that man was made like God in two ways - in his image, and after his likeness. The first word, "image", is a concrete word, referring to shape, and is also used to describe idols. In other words, man looks like God - although at this time our bodies are composed of flesh and blood, or "clay" (2 Corinthians 4:7), rather than spirit. That weakness will be corrected, the apostle Paul tells us, in the resurrection to take place at the return of Jesus Christ, when he will "transform our lowly bodies so that they will be like his glorious body" (Philippians 3:21) – a message Paul confirms elsewhere (1 Corinthians 15: 49-52).

PROGRESS—FORWARDS OR BACKWARDS?

Sadly, this incredible fact is clearly unwelcome to the erudite authors of the "International Critical Commentary", who say: "The Old Testament writers constantly attribute to Him bodily parts; and that they ever advanced to the conception of God as a formless spirit would be difficult to prove." In that quotation, perhaps the word "advanced" should be changed to "regressed".

The second word, "likeness", we are told, is an abstract word and seems to imply that man is like his Creator in important ways other than bodily shape. One way in which we clearly resemble God is in our intelligence and creativity - the ability to think, to analyze and understand, to use mathematics and language, to hypothesize and experiment, to imagine, and to conceive and achieve purposes.

Perhaps this is why, in the very next sentence, God gives man authority, or dominion, over this tiny corner of the universe - to rule over the animals and to subdue the earth, as we now read . . .

GENESIS 1:28
And God blessed them, and God said to them, Be fruitful and multiply, and fill the earth and subdue it; and have dominion over the fish of the sea and over the birds of the air and over every living thing that moves upon the earth.

Notice that in effect, man was commanded here to be creative, to use his God-like intelligence and creativity to subdue but also preserve the world and rule over it - to investigate, invent and build, to create beauty and excellence, to make life on this third planet from the sun a fun and fulfilling experience.

MAN NEEDS MEANING
How tragic, then, that by Darwin's time, the religious leaders who claimed to represent that God were encouraging intellectual stagnation - leading Gordon Rattray Taylor to comment: "If Darwin plunged us into a purposeless world of chance, it was because he was in reaction from a philosophical and theological position which not only ruled out scientific inquiry but denied man's freedom to modify his own future."

Mankind having been fed such distortions, economically oppressed and encouraged to remain ignorant by "religious" authorities, it is no wonder that Taylor also comments that many people opt for evolution because they "very much prefer to think that we live in a world which we, by our own efforts, can alter" - which is of course precisely what God wants man to do!

Troubled himself by the futility of evolution, Taylor concludes rather sadly that there is "something repellent" about the idea that the world we live in is totally meaningless.

MAN'S CREATIVE POWER
Man's ability to carry out God's creative command, at least in the fields of plant and animal breeding, is well described by Darwin himself in the following comment: "We cannot suppose that all the breeds were suddenly produced as perfect and as useful as we now see them. The key is man's power of accumulative selection: nature gives successive variations; man adds them up in certain directions useful to him."

He continues: "The great power of this principle of selection is not hypothetical. Several of our eminent breeders have, even within a lifetime, modified to a large extent their breeds of cattle and sheep. Breeders habitually speak of an animal's organization as something plastic, which they can model almost as they please." Darwin's wonderful observations simply confirm the scientific accuracy of Genesis.

MAN'S DESTINY

A hint of man's destiny and the purpose of his creative power is given by the apostle Paul when he tells Christians at Corinth that they will one day rule the angels (1 Corinthians 6:3), and even ultimately the whole universe (Hebrews 2:5-8, quoted from Psalm 8:4-6).

3.11

DAY 6 – EVERYTHING WAS VERY GOOD

The account for Day Six now concludes . . .

GENESIS 1: 29-31

And God said, Behold I have given you every plant yielding seed which is upon the face of all the earth, and every tree with seed in its fruit; you shall have them for food.

And to every beast of the earth and every bird of the air, and to everything that creeps on the earth, everything that has the breath of life, I have given every green plant for food.

And it was so. And God saw everything that he had made, and behold, it was very good. And there was evening and there was morning, a sixth day.

Having completed his work of creating animal and plant life, God observed that it was "very good".

A WORLD OF PEACE AND HARMONY

Thus the restored Earth became a pleasant and safe place to live, a world of beauty, peace and plenty. There was no evil, anxiety or fear, and no killing, because there were no carnivores seeking to destroy the lives of other creatures. The whole ecology was initially benign, not "red in tooth and claw" as it is now. There was no struggle for the survival of the fittest, with strong destroying the weak in a manner that repulsed Darwin and drove him to develop his deluded theory.

DARWIN'S HIDDEN AGENDA

Nature today, however, is violent and competitive and often repulsive, a fact that greatly bothered Darwin, who was apparently a kind-hearted and gentle person. Having at one time trained for the Christian ministry, he was troubled by the evil he saw in nature, and it pained him to think of a God of love creating such a violent world.

That thought was so unbearable to him that he began, in desperation I believe, to search for an alternative solution, one that would let God off the hook, so to speak, and ease his own troubled mind of the painful burden of resenting his Creator. Evolution, which laid off the blame for the violence and bloodshed onto mindless Natural Selection, was the answer he found - but as he makes clear at the end of "The Origin of Species", his motives were never atheistic.

HERBIVORES, NOT CARNIVORES

A further implication of these verses seems to be that human beings were originally vegetarians and fruitarians – herbivores, as were the animals. Commentators make the distinction that man was to eat cereal grains and fruit, and animals the foliage of plants, including grass. At that time, also, there were evidently no poisonous plants that could be eaten by mistake as there are now.

THERE'S A NEW WORLD COMING

The prophets Micah and Isaiah foretell the restitution of those idyllic conditions - a time when the wolf will live with the lamb, the leopard will lie down with the goat, and a little child will lead them. Then the lion will eat straw like the ox, the toddler will play near the hole of the cobra, and the young child put his hand into the viper's nest (Isaiah 11:6-8). At that time, as in Eden, no creature will do harm or destroy, says God, for the Earth will be full of the knowledge of the Lord, as the waters cover the sea. Neither shall men learn war any more (Micah 4:3).

Incidentally, Young-earth creationists seize on God's declaration that everything was "very good" to claim that everything could not have been good if the remains of evil and violent creatures lay buried beneath the ground as the Old Earth theory implies. The obvious point is that God's observation applied to the new age – and in any case, Satan himself was already in existence, with motives and a philosophy of life that was certainly anything but good, as they well know.

However, there may be an instructive parallel with the situation described by the prophet Malachi that yet another new earth will exist in the future when: "All the arrogant and every evildoer will be stubble; and that day that is coming will set them on fire . . . then you will trample down the wicked; they will be ashes under the soles of your feet on the day when I do these things" (Malachi 4:1,3).

3.12

THE GARDEN OF EDEN

Supplementary information regarding the Days of Creation is found in the second and third chapters of Genesis.

GENESIS 2:7

Then the Lord God formed man of dust from the ground, and breathed into his nostrils the breath of life; and man became a living being.

Here, the creation of man [Hebrew - adam, meaning "ruddy"] from the elements of the ground [Hebrew - adamah] is likened to the work of a potter. God then breathes into man the breath of life, and man becomes a living being, or "soul" as the King James Bible expresses it, just like the animals, breathing air and extracting the oxygen and combining it with carbon extracted from food to supply the energy required to move and the warmth to stay alive.

TWO ACTS OF CREATION

However, there is more to man than mere biological, chemical life, as already noted, and it is interesting that the Jewish Chumash says that the verb "form" in this verse is written in the Hebrew in such a way as to imply a double action, so that two separate but parallel acts of creation are being described.

THERE IS A SPIRIT IN MAN

In this regard it is significant that the word rendered "breath" can also mean "spirit", and in several other scriptures, as already noted, we are told that there is a spirit in man - a non-physical component. For example: "As long as my breath is in me and the spirit of God is in my nostrils; my lips will not speak falsehood" (Job 27:3-4), and: "It is the spirit in man, the breath of the Almighty, that makes him understand" (Job 32:8).

It seems therefore that the spirit, which imparts intellect, was given to Adam at the moment he started to breathe his first breath.

MORE THAN MERE ATOMS AND MOLECULES

At death, the physical body begins to decay and that spirit, is taken away - as we read in Ecclesiastes: "The dust returns to the earth as it was, and the spirit returns to God who gave it" (12:7).

It is interesting too that Solomon, who was as avid a student of nature, like Darwin, implies that there is also a spirit in animals. Comparing the death of man and animals, he says: "All are from the dust, and all turn to dust again. Who knows whether the spirit of man goes upwards and the spirit of the beast goes down to the earth?" (Ecclesiastes 3:20-21).

Evolutionists and even many creationists seem to share a common false assumption - believing that living organisms are nothing more than elaborate arrangements of atoms and molecules, and that life itself is no more than a chemical reaction that somehow creates consciousness, mind and emotion.

The account continues . . .

GENESIS 2: 8-9, 15-17

And the Lord God had planted a garden in Eden, in the east, and there he put the man whom he had formed. And out of the ground the Lord God made to grow every tree that is pleasant to the sight and good for food, the tree of life also in the midst of the garden, and the tree of the knowledge of good and evil . . .

. . . And the Lord commanded the man, saying, You may freely eat of every tree of the garden; but of the tree of the knowledge of good and evil you shall not eat, for in the day that you eat it you shall die.

Here Adam and Eve are warned not to eat the fruit of the "Tree of the Knowledge of Good and Evil", the consequence of so doing being death, or at least a sentence of death. As the rest of the account tells us, although they did eat the fruit, they did not immediately drop dead, but the sentence incurred that day was carried out later when they died almost a thousand years later – instead of living forever as the human body was then apparently capable of doing.

The implication of this incident seems to be that the mysterious ageing process that leads finally to death was somehow triggered by the act of eating and digesting the forbidden fruit. Such a suggestion, however, flies in the face of Francis Crick's "Central Dogma" of genetics which asserts that although genetic information can travel outwards from the DNA in the cell nucleus in order to direct the formation of proteins, information from the body cannot travel back into the nuclei of germ cells and modify the DNA pattern.

THE MYSTERY OF THE AGING PROCESS

Another implication of the account would seem to that Adam and Eve, as originally created, were biologically capable of living for ever. The cells of the human body have amazing self-replicating powers, apparently replacing themselves about ten times during a typical lifetime - but biologists are somewhat puzzled as to why the process finally breaks down instead of carrying on for ever. In fact, in a recent BBC radio discussion, a leading evolutionary biologist cited the aging process as one of the great mysteries - along with the "miracle", in his words, of cell structure.

In light of our earlier speculation, it would seem that the increased intensity of cosmic radiation following the Flood somehow accelerated that ageing process once triggered, thereby drastically reducing average human life-spans.

Catastrophic as the process triggered by the forbidden fruit was, it could apparently be reversed by eating the fruit of the "Tree of Life" - and it was to prevent this cure taking place that Adam and Eve were driven from the Garden of Eden, as we read in the last few verses of the third chapter.

3.13

THE FLOOD OF NOAH
Some Questions

Noah's Flood, sometimes known as the "Deluge", is a key issue in the Evolution-Creation debate because Young-earth creationists attribute to it the formation of most fossil-bearing rock strata – in defiance of much seemingly obvious geological evidence to the contrary, evidence that early Christian geologists actually accepted and had helped to accumulate. As already noted, G-Theory, as taught by William Buckland, attributes most of those strata to a much earlier age.

Evolutionists, on the other hand, like to imagine that the fossils of extinct organisms found in ancient rocks somehow support Darwin's claim that present day plants and animals are the result of multiple millions of years of "descent with modification" from primitive, ancestral organisms, as cleverly illustrated by the imaginary "tree of life". that has since been buried.

SOME FACTS OF GEOLOGY
One of the seemingly indisputable facts of geology is that most of the Earth's land surface, including even mount Everest, is covered by or consists of sedimentary rock, sometimes several miles thick – materials that were, by definition, deposited out of watery conditions of some kind.

Although modern Young-earth creationists teach that the vast bulk of sedimentary rock strata were formed quite rapidly in a matter of months by the waters of Noah's Flood, early geologists such as Lyell believed the exact opposite, claiming instead that each one of the hundreds of strata they investigated had been formed extremely slowly, possibly over many millions of years by the gentle accumulation of sediments on ancient sea beds – despite objections by anatomist Georges Cuvier that the extinct animal forms they discovered must have been wiped out by rapid, catastrophic events.

No doubt both gradualism and catastrophe could have taken their turns at shaping the earth's surface in the mysterious pre-Adamic age.

INCREDIBLE CHAOS

A second indisputable fact of geology is the incredible chaos and destruction evidenced in the Earth's sedimentary rock strata. As geologists struggle to make sense of the muddle, Darwin's theory of evolution is the simplistic organizing framework on which they continuously rely for guidance.

As a result, observations that seem to support the idea of a gradual development of life from simple to complex are welcomed – but those that deviate from the theory are rejected as anomalous, or explained away in some contrived fashion. Situations where groups of strata are in the wrong order, for example, or randomly arranged, or even upside down, are quietly ignored as being the exceptions that prove the rule.

No wonder Paul spoke even in his day of enemies of God who actually suppressed what they knew to be true (Romans 1:18). As with some esoteric mystery religion, it seems, the peasants are only supposed to hear what the priests want them to.

SOME QUESTIONS FOR YOUNG-EARTH CREATIONISTS

In the light of the above, what are we to make of Noah's Flood, and its possible impact on the geology of the Earth's surface? Could it, acting alone, as required by the Young-earth creationists, be responsible for situations such as those listed below?

A) There are many extreme angular unconformities where underlying strata have been turned vertical and eroded and even metamorphosed by volcanic action before additional strata were laid down on top, making a T-shaped formation.

B) Some strata are several miles thick, requiring sediments to have been deposited at a continuous rate of 15 meters per day to fit into the time frame of Noah's Flood.

C) Calculations suggest that the amount of organic matter stored up in coal beds is greater than the Earth could possibly have supported at any one time, even if densely forested all over. How could a single deluge create so much coal?

D) The Earth has massive salt deposits, normally created by the steady evaporation of sea water, which are separated by layers of soil. How could such formations have been laid down by Noah's Flood?

E) Sedimentary formations more than a mile thick exist in which the fossilized remains of dozen or more mature forests are piled up, one on top of another, some with evidence of forest fires. How could the Flood do that?

F.) If all the animals found in the rock strata were destroyed by the Flood, why did the fish and land animals that are familiar to our world manage to get buried in the uppermost strata, whilst equally mobile extinct forms apparently perished first and got buried lower down?

G) The fossil record shows many extinct land creatures, yet Noah's ark was used to preserve all kinds of animals from destruction. How, then were they made extinct?

EASY ANSWERS

Creationist web sites will carry answers to these and other technical objections raised by evolutionists -- how, for example, to explain away the simple fact that if the earth is only six thousand years old, why has the light from some stars and galaxies taken millions of years to reach us from the extremities of the universe -- or why, if they were formed by Noah's Flood, do the lowest rock strata not contain numerous human artifacts, dense and durable objects such as tools, building blocks and stone pillars?

Sometimes quite abstruse rebuttals are required, such as variations in supposed physical "constants" like nuclear decay rates or the speed of light. As a result, young earth creationism is often regarded as superstitious and anti-scientific.

I wonder if, like Darwin himself, some creationists could be driven, and their thinking distorted, by a hidden agenda -- namely the desire to deny evolution the "deep time" it demands in order to achieve the impossible. Ergo, the earth must be very young.

3.14

THE ARK

With such questions in mind, we can now return to the Genesis account of Noah's Flood which begins by explaining its purpose – and providing some brief insights into the sick state to which the ancient world had degenerated in the fifteen hundred years that elapsed from Adam to Noah:

GENESIS 6:5-7, 13
The Lord saw that the wickedness of man was great in the earth, and that every imagination of the thoughts of his heart was only evil continually. And the Lord was sorry that he had made man on the earth, and it grieved him to his heart.

So the Lord said, I will blot out man whom I have created from the face of the ground, man and beast and creeping things and birds of the air, for I am sorry that I have made them …

…And God said to Noah, I have determined to make an end of all flesh; for the earth is filled with violence through them; behold I will destroy them with the earth.

According to modern evolutionary myth, human society originated with grunting ape-like cave-dwellers who could barely speak, let alone read or write, backward peoples who then slowly progressed through the stone, bronze and iron ages. The reality may have been very different.

For example, the Genesis account shows that Adam and Eve had personal contact with God, as well as angelic beings who already possessed all the so-called "key inventions" of the ancient world—such as fire, the sword, the saddle, the stirrup, and the wheel, as well as musical instruments.

Consequently, I would imagine, for example, that when God assigned Adam the job of tending the Garden of Eden, he almost certainly also provided ready-made metal tools for the job. If so, then it is not surprising that the Genesis account tells us that Tubal-Cain, just a few generations on from Adam, "forged all kind of tools out of bronze and iron" (4:22).

No doubt the metal technology in which Adam's children became skilled was soon used to manufacture swords and spears and other instruments of warfare and cruelty as the pre-Flood world degenerated, in the following fifteen hundred years, into gross wickedness – dominated by violence and also perverted sex. No doubt, also, many disparate groups became isolated and degenerated into the stone-age, cave-dwelling culture that history books delight in depicting.

Fossilized human remains from what some archaeologists regard as pre-Flood strata show evidence of cannibalism - human bones and skulls opened up for the contents to be eaten - and Jewish traditions speak of mass incest. So foul and revolting did the world become by the time of Noah that God decided to intervene and destroy it. Which brings us to the Flood and the construction of the ark:

GENESIS 6:14-17
Make yourself an ark of cypress wood; make rooms in it and coat it with pitch inside and out. This is how you are to build it: The ark is to be 450 feet long, 75 feet wide and 45 feet high.

Make a roof for it and finish the ark to within 18 inches of the top. Put a door in the side of the ark and make lower, middle and upper decks.

I am going to bring floodwaters on the earth to destroy all life under the heavens, every creature that has the breath of life in it. Everything on earth will perish.

Influenced by their evolutionary outlook on history, critics insist that Noah could not possibly have built the ark with the technology available at the time – as with the construction of Stonehenge and the Great Pyramids, I suppose. Others suggest that wood was too weak for the job and would even have rotted away by time it was completed.

Notice, however, the detailed instructions – for example, to use a certain kind of wood and to preserve the timbers with pitch, both inside and out. Incidentally, the reference, prior to the Flood, to pitch or bitumen, a fossil product, offers interesting support for the Old Earth theory that most coal and oil deposits had already been formed much earlier.

Attempts have been made to work out the numbers of animals and even insects that Noah would have had to pack into the ark, how much space they would need and how much food and of what kinds. Such calculations necessarily involve assumptions about the breadth of the term "kind", as already mentioned.

The obvious implication of the account is that if dogs, for example, are a single kind, then only one breeding pair would have been taken on the ark, because they would contain the genetic potential to produce all the breeds of dogs with which we are now familiar.

It is interesting, also, as we shall read in a moment, that when the waters were receding later, after the Flood, Noah sent out a raven and then a dove. The fact that both sorts of bird were on the ark, the raven being unclean and the dove clean, suggest that they at least are different "kinds", which provides us with a small clue to the breadth of the term.

3.15

THE DELUGE

The account continues with a description of the flood itself

GENESIS 7: 11-12, 19, 21-22

On that day all the fountains of the great deep burst forth, and the windows of the heavens were opened. And rain fell on the earth forty days and forty nights....

...And the waters prevailed so mightily upon the earth that all the high mountains under the whole heaven were covered ...

...And all flesh died that moved upon the earth, birds, cattle, beasts, all swarming creatures that swarmed upon the earth, and every man; everything on the dry land in whose nostrils was the breath of life died.

Normal rain, acting alone, cannot create a universal flood, since the water that is precipitated in one place has to be evaporated elsewhere, as part of the hydrological cycle. However, the account tells us that two other sources were also involved – the "windows of heaven", about which we speculated earlier in the creation account, and also the "fountains of the great deep".

Although critics may scoff at the idea of water bursting from vast subterranean reservoirs, in the way lava erupts from a volcano, it is important to remember once again that our geological knowledge is quite limited – and incidentally, that lava is usually accompanied by steam. Indeed a recent National Geographic magazine article about the interior workings of the Earth pointed out that the conflict between opposing schools of thought on these matters is so fierce that some of our white-robed scientific saints are no longer on speaking terms.

As mentioned earlier, the word rendered here as "mountain" can equally well mean a modest hill, and the topography of the pre-Flood Earth may have been much smoother than now – consisting possibly of just one vast continent surrounded by sea. Although critics scoff at these verses, they happily accept the fact that even Mount Everest is apparently covered with or composed of marine sediments and has at some time or other been submersed – and that land levels can and do change with time.

Although the account suggests that the Flood was global, and water did remain on the Earth for about a year, the key question that concerns us here is: How great was its geological impact? Was the Deluge responsible for all or most sedimentary strata that geologists have studied, as Young-earth creationists insist? The following extract seems to provide an important clue:

GENESIS 8:11-12
He [Noah] sent forth the dove out of the ark; and the dove came back to him in the evening, and lo, in her mouth a freshly plucked olive leaf; so Noah knew that the water had subsided from the Earth. Then he waited another seven months, and sent forth the dove; and she did not return to him any more.

As already noted, the inspired account is meticulously worded – and we read here that the dove brought back a "freshly plucked" olive leaf. Noah and his family would have been very familiar with the olive tree and no doubt examined the leaf very carefully we see if it was dead or freshly plucked. The implication seems to be that despite the Flood, and the torrents of water that must have accompanied it as it rose and fell, especially on the valleys, trees in the mountainous locality where the ark cam to rest, were still in place and growing.

If this is so, it is hard to imagine that the remainder of the Earth' surface was violently ripped up and re-deposited to form sedimentary strata, some of which are several miles thick in places. In any case, G-Theory allocates most of the geological column to the pre-Adamic age.

A supporting point may be that the location of Eden is described in Genesis with reference to four rivers (Genesis 2:10-14), two of which, the Tigris and Euphrates, apparently survived the Flood and still exist, suggesting again that it did minimal damage. Young-earth creationists insist that all four rivers would have been erased by the Deluge - and that the present Tigris and Euphrates were simply named in their memory, in the way that settlers in America named cities after those in Europe.

Nevertheless, the familiar fossil content of some Cenozoic strata does suggest that they were somehow formed by Noah's Flood.

3.16

THE AFTERMATH

GENESIS 8:17-20

Then God said to Noah, Go forth from the ark, you and your wife, and your sons and your sons' wives with you. Bring forth with you every living thing that is with you, all flesh – birds and animals and every creeping thing that creeps on the Earth – that they may breed abundantly on the earth, and be fruitful and multiply upon the Earth.

And every beast, every creeping thing, and every bird, everything that moves upon the Earth, went forth by families out of the ark.

One atheistic critic argues that the Flood was an impossibility because there has simply not been enough time for the basic kinds of creatures released by Noah to mutate sufficiently to create the vast number of species that now exist, particularly in the case of insects. In this regard, perhaps the phrase: "that they may breed abundantly on the Earth" has some significance.

Somehow the creatures that Noah released from the ark were able to spread to the four corners of the Earth, such as Australia and South America as well as many smaller land masses that are today surrounded by water. This fact has obvious implications regarding the disposition of the continental land-masses at that time. Whether the migration process was facilitated by means of land bridges that have since subsided, for example, joining Alaska and Russia, or by the moving and splitting of continental land masses, we are not told. However, the Earth's surface is not static, and historical records still exist of Britain, for example, being joined to mainland Europe.

In this regard, it is interesting to read of a man named Peleg who lived several hundred years after the Flood, in the period when God was actively scattering the nations abroad "over the face of the earth" (Genesis 11:8). The name Peleg means "division", and we are told that he was so named because: "in his days the Earth was divided" (Genesis 10:25). Commentators point out that for the child to be named in advance of a momentous event suggests that his father, Eber, father of the Hebrews, was a prophet informed by God of what was to occur, in the same way Noah had been warned of the flood.

In a similar fashion, generations earlier his ancestor Enoch, another man of God, had named his son "Methuselah", which some take to mean "when he dies, then it will be sent", as an advance warning of the coming flood. Incidentally, the fact that Methuselah lived longer than any person before or since is taken as an indication of patience of God over hundreds of years as the world was repeatedly warned by preachers such as Noah (2 Peter 2:5) of the destruction that was come if the wickedness continued.

3.17

SOME CONCLUSIONS

The findings of geology and a careful reading of Genesis strongly suggest that the earth may be very much older than "creationists" currently believe, and that some kind of Pre-Adamic world or age almost certainly existed, a belief shared by early Christian geologists such as William Buckland.

That alien age, the history of which is written in the fossil record of the Paleozoic and Mesozoic strata, was apparently dominated by often-gigantic reptilian creatures engaged in a violent and a vicious struggle for the survival of the fittest – now-extinct organisms described by Victorian geologists as "Satan's creatures."

The evidence for the more familiar flora and fauna of the age that existed from Adam to Noah seems to be preserved in the Cenozoic strata.

The major point of contention between the G-Theory viewpoint being presented here and geology seems to lie in the area of radio-isotope dating as applied to the Cenozoic era, the latter part of which, if Bible scholars have done their chronology calculations correctly, apparently extends back no more than some six thousand years. Although rock dating techniques, as discussed earlier, are highly complicated and necessarily involve a number of simplifying assumptions, scientists insist that their results are reliable – and, consequently, that if Genesis disagrees it must be wrong, not them.

Although we can only speculate as to why, in God's plan, such a prehistoric world ever existed, it does seem significant that the way of life its ecology depicted was one characterized by fierce competition, violence, death and destruction – the exact opposite of the fluffy, cuddly, cooperative and kind world originally established for man in the Garden of Eden.

God is love, says the Bible, and, as Jesus preached, only those human beings who repent of selfish, predatory, arrogant and evil ways will be given eternal life – and entry to a restored new world, at the time when the meek will finally inherit the Earth, along with the peacemakers, the pure in heart, the gentle and compassionate.

Whereas in that fearful and violent earlier age only the fittest survived by dint of physical strength or speed and armor-plated bodies, God's way is precisely the opposite – a world or love, where every person will survive and thrive because every one will be actively seeking the good of every other, which is why Christ's teaching is summed in one simple sentence: "You shall love your neighbor as yourself".

Perhaps we should conclude by noting the deliberate parallel between the phrasing of the first few verses of Genesis and the philosophical gospel of John, in the New Testament, where we read: "In the beginning was the Word, and the Word was with God, and the Word was God. The same was in the beginning with God.

Through him all things were made; and without him nothing was made that was made. In him was life, and that life was the light of men. The light shines in the darkness, but the darkness understood it not" (John 1:1-5).

Is it reasonable to surmise, by way of analogy, that just as Jesus came to enlighten the darkened and wicked world that we read about in our ancient history books some two thousand years ago, so the Spirit of God - the Word, the same Jesus Christ - also came to the Earth some six thousand years ago to survey the pitiful darkened physical remains of the Pre-Adamic world – in order to begin the new, spiritual creation that is discussed in detail in the epistles of Paul (Ephesians 1:9-12).

Did angelic beings, who clearly existed prior to the creation of man (Job 38:7), live out some kind of Earthly existence, for some reason, possibly with some kind of humanoid body? Were they, like man, given a time of trial, and an opportunity to choose between right and wrong, good and evil? We can only speculate.

In conclusion, the simple truth of the evolution-creation debate is that, as described in Genesis, God created, along with Adam and Eve, a set of plants and animals, and other organisms in between that defy classification, which by reproducing "after their kind", over the several thousand years that have since elapsed, have resulted in the organisms currently populating our planet.

BIBLIOGRAPHY

Balcombe, J.
PLEASURABLE KINGDOM,
Macmillan 2006

Barnett , S.
THE SCIENCE OF LIFE,
Allen & Unwin 1998

Behe, M.
DARWIN'S BLACK BOX,
New York: Touchstone 1998

Cadbury, D.
THE DINOSAUR HUNTERS,
London: Fourth Estate 2001

Carroll, Sean B.
THE MAKING OF THE FITTEST
W.W.Norton & Co 2008

Coyne, Jerry A.
WHY EVOLUTION IS TRUE
Oxford University Press 2009

Darwin, C.
THE ORIGIN OF SPECIES

Darwin, C.
THE DESCENT OF MAN

Davidson, J.
NATURAL CREATION OR NATURAL SELECTION?,
Element Books 1992

de Vries, H.
SPECIES AND VARIETIES: THEIR ORIGIN BY MUTATION,
Chicago: Open Court, 1905
Dobzhansky, T.
GENETICS AND ORIGIN OF SPECIES,
Columbia University Press 1951

Fortey, R.
TRILOBITE,
Harper Collins 2000

Gee, H.
DEEP TIME,
London: Fourth Estate 2000

Henig, R.
A MONK AND TWO PEAS,
Weidenfeld & Nicolson 2000

Hough, D.
EVOLUTION, A CASE OF STATING THE OBVIOUS,
Berkeley Publishing 1997

Jarvis, D.
FOLK MEDICINE,
Pan Books 1961

Lewontin, R.
THE DOCTRINE OF DNA,
Penguin 1993

Numbers, Ronald L.
THE CREATIONISTS
University of California Press 1993

Perucca, F. and Pouradier, G.
THE RUBBISH ON OUR PLATES,
London: Prion 1996

Price, W.
NUTRITION AND PHYSICAL DEGENERATION,
Santa Monica, California: Price Pottenger Foundation, 1970.

Rath, N.
WHY ANIMALS DON'T GET HEART ATTACKS BUT PEOPLE DO,
Rath Foundation 2000

Rattray-Taylor, G.
THE GREAT EVOLUTION MYSTERY,
Secker & Warburg 1983

Roberts, M.
GENESIS AND GEOLOGY UNEARTHED,
The Churchman Oct 1998 vol 112 No3 pp.225-55

Rose, S.
THE CHEMISTRY OF LIFE,
Penguin 1979

Shreeve, J.
THE NEANDERTHAL ENIGMA,
New York, Morrow 1995

Sheppard, P.
NATURAL SELECTION AND HEREDITY,
Hutchinson 1958

Steele, E. Lindley, R. and Blanden, R.
LAMARCK'S SIGNATURE,
Perseus Books, 1998

Stringer, C. and Gamble C.
IN SEARCH OF THE NEANDERTHALS,
Thames and Hudson 1993

Whitcomb, J. and Morris, H.
THE GENESIS FLOOD
Baker Book House 1961

Whitley, A.
BREAD MATTERS,
London: Fourth Estate 2006

Zimmer, C.
PARASITE REX,
London: Free Press 2000

CPSIA information can be obtained at www.ICGtesting.com
Printed in the USA
BVOW011048060312

284553BV00012B/103/P